# Nation as Network

# Nation as Network

## DIASPORA, CYBERSPACE, AND CITIZENSHIP

### Victoria Bernal

The University of Chicago Press  CHICAGO & LONDON

VICTORIA BERNAL is associate professor of anthropology at the
University of California, Irvine, and author of *Cultivating Workers: Peasants
and Capitalism in a Sudanese Village*, coeditor of *Theorizing NGOs: States,
Feminisms, and Neoliberalism*, and editor of *Contemporary Cultures,
Global Connections: Anthropology for the 21st Century*.

The University of Chicago Press, Chicago 60637
The University of Chicago Press, Ltd., London
© 2014 by The University of Chicago
All rights reserved. Published 2014.
Printed in the United States of America

23  22  21  20  19  18  17  16  15  14      1  2  3  4  5

ISBN-13: 978-0-226-14478-8 (cloth)
ISBN-13: 978-0-226-14481-8 (paper)
ISBN-13: 978-0-226-14495-5 (e-book)
DOI: 10.7208/chicago/9780226144955.001.0001

Library of Congress Cataloging-in-Publication Data

Bernal, Victoria, author.
    Nation as network : diaspora, cyberspace, and citizenship / Victoria Bernal.
    pages cm
    Includes bibliographical references and index.
    ISBN 978-0-226-14478-8 (cloth : alk. paper)—ISBN 978-0-226-14481-8
(pbk. : alk. paper)—ISBN 978-0-226-14495-5 (e-book)   1. Eritreans—Political
activity.   2. Eritrea—Emigration and immigration.   3. Internet and activism.
4. Cyberspace—Social aspects.   5. Internet and immigrants.   I. Title.
    DT397.3.B475 2014
    305.892'89—dc23

                                                        2013050783

♾ This paper meets the requirements of ANSI/NISO Z39.48-1992
(Permanence of Paper).

# CONTENTS

ACKNOWLEDGMENTS

This project has spanned many years and benefitted from the formal and informal support and critique offered by various institutions and individuals. I cannot thank them each specifically here, but wish to express particular gratitude to those who had a lasting engagement with my research. Foremost among them is my husband, Tekle, who is the reason I first turned my attention from the site of my earlier research, the Sudan, to Eritrea. Since we first met at a talk on Eritrea (by Gerard Chailland, if I recall correctly) at the African Studies Program of Northwestern University in 1976, Tekle has made Eritrea a vital part of my life. I could never have completed this project without Tekle's enthusiasm and encouragement, as well as his contagious fascination with Eritrean politics. He is not responsible, however, for the arguments or mistakes set forth in this book. I thank my wonderful daughters, Olivia and Eve, for providing the best distractions from work anyone could wish for. In them and in Tekle, I am fortunate to have found such game and insightful travel companions for my research trips and for my life.

I would also like to thank my colleagues in the Anthropology Department at the University of California, Irvine (UCI), which has been my intellectual home throughout this project. Kris Peterson in Anthropology, Susan Coutin in Law, Criminology, and Society, and Laura Mitchell in History deserve special thanks for their steadfast interest in my work, as does the Faculty Group for African and Middle Eastern Studies at UCI whose phantomlike existence created exciting intellectual sparks at various moments. I appreciate the research and editorial assistance of my daughter Olivia Woldemikael, UCI undergraduates Varinea Romero and Renee Estoista, and the eleventh-hour readings of the final draft by Kathryn Ragsdale and Amanda Moore.

The research and writing of this project was made possible by the generous financial support of the American Philosophical Society, the University of California's Institute on Global Conflict and Cooperation, the Intel Foundation fund of the Anthropology Department, the Center for Global Peace and Conflict Studies, and the School of Social Sciences, Research and Travel fund at UCI. At the University of Chicago Press I am deeply grateful to David Brent for seeing value in this project from an early version of the manuscript and to Priya Nelson for her sane and kind responses to all of my anxious emails. My thanks also go to two anonymous reviewers who provided much-needed, valuable feedback.

Earlier versions of some of the material presented here appeared in two of my previous publications: parts of chapter 2 draw on my article in *American Ethnologist* (Bernal 2005), and some material in chapter 4 appeared in my *African Studies* (Bernal 2013b) article.

# Nations, Migration, and the World Wide Web of Politics

I would like to believe that Dehai is much more than acrimonious tit-for-tat self-defeating discourse. To me it signifies a movement whose energy is somehow translated for the good of Eritrea within and without.

Excerpt from December 12, 1996, post on www.dehai.org

Awate.com is what it is because of its writers and readers. In 2002, PFDJ [Eritrea's ruling party] began the year by telling us that the "chapter is closed" and we can all forget what happened in 2001. . . . Leave the governing to us; you just send your money and attend our meetings and do as you are told. Our writers had a completely different opinion. They were going to write, over and over if necessary, about the injustice that the Eritrean people are subjected to.

Excerpt from January 2, 2003, post onwww.awate.com

Asmarino is 9 years old, but it's mentality and way of thinking is like an adult, who is reasoning, thinks democratically and above all respects the human rights and gives all ppl the opportunity to express their opinions. I don't know what to do or where to express our opinions if we had no our Asmarino, since we have nobody who offers us this opportunity.

Excerpt from August 20, 2006, post on www.asmarino.com

The posts above come from websites established by Eritreans in diaspora to engage in national politics from outside the nation. This book examines Eritrean politics online to reveal the ways that new media and mobilities are transforming sovereignty and citizenship. A focus on diaspora and cyberspace reveals nations as dynamic forms that not only are increasingly difficult to map as bounded communities but also operate through networks in significant ways. There is a synergy between new communications technologies and migration that is changing politics. Relations of citizenship and sovereignty once rooted in national territory increasingly span borders, and the social contracts between citizens and states are being constructed and contested in new political contexts and spaces. There is a profound global shift underway as the mobility of people and the rise of internet communications in the twenty-first century alter the character of nations and the meanings of citizenship and sovereignty (Ong 1999; Al-Ali and Koser 2002; Appadurai 2003). New practices and ideals of citizenship are developing and forms of quasi-citizenship are emerging as industrialized nations grapple with noncitizens within their borders and less industrialized nations deal with diasporic populations that participate in their economies and politics from abroad (Balibar 2005; Glick-Schiller 2005; Coutin 2007). At the same time, the internet is allowing for the creation of an elastic political space that can serve to extend as well as to expose the limits of territorial sovereignty. The growing significance of diasporas coupled with the development of digital media have given rise to the nation as network.

In this book three strands of analysis—politics, media, and diaspora—are woven together to explore the nation as network. I develop the concept "infopolitics" to advance theories of sovereignty and understandings of the internet by foregrounding the management of information as a central aspect of politics. Infopolitics draws attention to the importance of relations of authorization and censorship that govern the ways knowledge is produced, accessed, and disseminated. The heart of this study is an ethnography of the vibrant Eritrean public sphere established on diaspora websites. My analysis of Eritrean politics online explores the significance of violence and conflict for the understanding of citizenship, the public sphere, and new media. Set in the context of Eritrea's turbulent history, the activities of the Eritrean diaspora online reveal the ways that sovereignty and citizenship are being reconfigured and reproduced by means of the internet.

In spring 2011 the Egyptian revolt, which some labeled a "Facebook Revolution," offered a new vision of the significance of the internet for political change. The way Egyptians used new media to circumvent and oppose a repressive regime is revealing. It shows, among other things, that many of our ideas and debates about the nature and potential of digital media are based in Western experience, and particularly, in Western middle-class consumer culture (Ginsburg 2008). Some of the most politically dynamic and innovative engagements with the internet are developed, however, by people in circumstances very different from those of quintessential Western computer users. In fact, by the time Egyptians and others throughout the Arab world drew the world's attention to their online organizing, Eritreans had been engaging in computer-mediated politics for well over a decade. In cyberspace, Eritreans in diaspora have developed a series of websites that continue to serve as an online public sphere where Eritreans around the world debate politics with each other, mobilize actions, and communicate their views to the Eritrean state and wider audiences. This study focuses on three key websites that have been central to this process—Dehai (www.dehai.org), Asmarino (www.asmarino .com), and Awate (www.awate.com).

The design and organization of these websites by their founders and web-managers, the ways they are used by posters, and the social texts, exchanges and activities they have generated offer insights into how political subjectivities are produced, policed, and transformed through the internet. Online Eritreans are engaged in articulating and revising the national narratives that bind Eritreans to each other and to the state as they take part in the construction of Eritrea as a nation and struggle over the dimensions and demands of sovereignty.

Eritrea is a small nation in the Horn of Africa that achieved nationhood in 1991. Eritrea's political culture and institutions, thus, have developed in the context of the growing significance of international migration and digital communications. Eritreans in many countries participate passionately in Eritrean politics, even though they hold citizenship in the countries where they live, work, and raise their children. While physically located outside of Eritrea, the diaspora is not outside Eritrean culture or politics. Moreover, they figure in the national imaginaries of Eritrea's leaders who have been actively cultivating the diaspora's involvement from abroad since before independence (Hepner and Conrad 2005). The resources Eritreans funnel to Eritrea from overseas are vital to the nation, contributing not only to national welfare but also to its resources for warfare (Bernal 2004, 2006; Fessehatzion 2005; Hepner 2009).

Through the web, the diaspora does much more than simply assuage their homesickness or vent their political passions. The websites are compelling for Eritreans in part because something is at stake—the shape and future of Eritrean national society. Online activities have off-line consequences. Eritrean posters shape public opinion, revise national history, mobilize demonstrators, amass funds for national projects, engage in protest, and exert influence and pressure on the government of Eritrea. We cannot understand these online activities simply as a feature of diaspora, but rather as part of the configuration of Eritrean nationhood. These innovative developments in Eritrean politics offer insights into the shifting meanings and experiences of citizenship and sovereignty in the contemporary context of migration, and elucidate the political significance of the internet.

Close readings of the impassioned, humorous, angry, and poetic posts of

Eritreans in diaspora reveal their struggle to understand the political conflicts that have shaped their lives, even as they strive to shape Eritrea's future. Posts illuminate the meanings of war, migration, and national belonging in people's lives and illustrate the ways that state power is being reconfigured and reproduced. Websites are sites of conflict that make dominant nationalist discourses and alternative perspectives visible and legible as ordinary people articulate to each other what things mean to them in their own words and collectively construct accounts and analyses of the nation. The websites serve as public, communal space in cyberspace that is a staging ground for ideas and practices that have no off-line counterpart, either inside or outside of Eritrea.

Many Americans have never heard of Eritrea. What Eritrea may lack in visibility to outsiders, however, it seems to make up for in the fervor with which it has been fought over by Eritreans and Ethiopians over the past fifty years, and by Italian colonizers before that (Jordan 1989; Iyob 1995; Doornbos et al. 1992; Negash and Tronvoll 2000). Indeed, I became interested in Eritrean politics on the internet during the 1998–2000 border war with Ethiopia when Eritreans in diaspora used websites to spread news and analysis, as well as to organize their support of the war effort. My attention was drawn to posts coming from Eritreans in many different countries like this one signed "Eritreans in Norway," detailing a meeting of Eritreans in Oslo where

> 250000 Kr ($33000 US) was collected immediately. And after hot and emotional debate it was agreed every working Eritrean over 18 should contribute 1000.00 US $. All other cities in Norway have also decided the same. Of course they [there] where [were] people who said they will give more. Some of them they said if necessary they will to go to Eritrea to defend our country. It was not just empty word. The Eritrean Information Centre is getting telephone call every minute by people asking how they can help. (Dehai post, June 10, 1998)

I was stunned by the vehemence with which some posters called for the deaths of Ethiopians and by the number of posters who signed off with slogans like "remember our martyrs." I was particularly intrigued by the diaspora's sense of participation in national politics. Posters were not writing as mere spectators to the events taking place in Eritrea. Rather, they understood themselves as deeply involved in the war and as obligated to act on behalf of their nation.

War and violence are significant experiences in the lives of Eritreans. Many posts relate to questions of life and death in which the past and future of individuals and the nation are deeply entangled, but there is also a lighter side of online politics. I was equally drawn to the wit, irony, and wordplay that posters use to convey their pithy and profound political insights (Bernal 2013b). The fact that many posters write in a kind of "accented" English gives an additional flavor to their posts. I have retained the unconventional spelling and grammar in the posts I quote to retain this distinct quality. As I read posts and followed debates, I grew to admire the courage and creativity of the Eritreans who devoted their energies to building this transnational public sphere and who expressed their political views with such intensity and humor. In this ethnography I seek to convey some of the profundity and playfulness of Eritrean online culture to readers, while pursuing an analysis that views the online public sphere in the context of Eritrean history and politics, as well as wider scholarly debates about nations and new media. To protect posters' identities, I omit their names. I identify posts by the date they appeared online, rather than according to the typical practice of reporting the date the researcher accessed them. The date that a post appeared connects it to a particular temporal context and/or to a sequence of events, whether to a series of posts or to unfolding events in Eritrea, whereas the date I accessed the post has no historical significance.

Like Eritreans, many populations of migrants and exiles are using the internet to connect with each other and with people and institutions of their homelands (Oiarzbal and Adoni 2010; Panagakos and Horst 2006; Gajjala and Gajjala 2008; Mannur 2003; Ndangam 2008; Ignacio 2005). This phenomenon is sometimes termed "digital diasporas" (Bernal 2005a; Diamandaki 2003; DeHart 2004; Brinkerhoff 2009). The online activities of diasporas are significant, moreover, because the rising influence of diasporas in the twenty-first century is a global trend (Knott and McLoughlin 2010; Clarke 2010; Diouf 2000). Diasporas, of course, have long existed and have been the subject of scholarship (Hall 1990; Clifford 1994; Gilroy 1993). But part of what motivates my study is a belief that contemporary migration and digital media are making a difference in what diaspora means for people and for nations (Piot 2010). Certainly contemporary diaspora populations experience relationships with their homelands that were not possible for the classical diasporas of Jews fleeing persecution and Africans taken overseas as slaves. But developments over the past two decades seem to indicate a disjuncture even with the experiences of more recent twentieth-century migrants and refugees. There is, moreover, a recent proliferation of groups identifying themselves as diasporas (Turner 2008; Ryang and Lie 2009). Diasporas can be seen as "margins of the state" in Das and Poole's terms, which afford us insight into "the ways in which the conceptual boundaries of the state are extended and remade" (2004, 20).

Diasporas are increasingly being recognized as important players by governments, policy makers, donors, and scholars (Page and Mercer 2012; Lyons 2012). The economic flows of remittances and investment, in particular, attract attention, and much of the interest of official bodies and international agencies is focused rather narrowly on development and the economic activities of diasporas (World Bank 2006; UN 2006). Far less attention has been directed toward what we might think of as the "political remittances" of diasporas and the ways geographic mobility and the internet are facilitating new forms of political agency and giving rise to new transnational public spheres where struggles over meanings, resources, and power are mobilized.

The significance of media and the dynamics of the internet comprise one major focus of my inquiry. Digital media has been seen as transforming, or potentially transforming, many aspects of economic, social, and political life (Castells 2001; Silver and Massanari 2006; Gershon 2010; Miller and Slater 2000; Coleman 2010). It has become clear that the internet has wide-ranging implications for the exercise and experience of political power. But, its potential effects are not the same everywhere. In this sense, the internet is not one thing; it is an array of diverse phenomena. Only through the study of online activities in specific communities and contexts will we come to understand what is truly distinctive about the internet and the ways it offers new political possibilities and fosters new subjectivities. Landzelius (2006a, 2) calls this method "grounding cyberspace." I take such an ethnographic approach here to reveal larger truths through a close examination of small details. From an anthropological perspective, I contend, the internet is not primarily a product of science and technology but rather a cultural medium where social texts and cultural artifacts are produced and circulated. Culturally, the internet is the most interesting of all digital media, moreover, because it is often used as a platform for collective social practices, public communication, and collaboration.

The websites created by Eritreans in diaspora are cultural products of Eritreans, not simply a technology they use. The interactivity of the internet means, moreover, that Eritreans are involved not simply as consumers of online content but also as creators of websites and producers of content. My analysis of websites, therefore, does not treat the internet simply as another research site or source of information but makes it an object of study, asking how and why Eritreans in diaspora have produced particular kinds of websites, online practices, and genres of posts and with what consequences. I consider why, beyond the relatively small number of webmanagers and prolific content-producers, many Eritreans have been drawn to these websites as devoted readers and posters year after year. I am particularly interested in the role of cyberspace in opening alternative spaces and channels of expression that challenge mainstream media, authoritarian governments, and practices of secrecy and censorship. Therefore, I ground the analysis of online activities in the context of the wars and violence that mark the unfolding story of Eritrean nationhood. This context includes three decades of brutal warfare fought on Eritrean soil during the struggle for independence from Ethiopia (1961–91); a devastating border war with Ethiopia (1998–2000); the increasing militarization and repression carried out on its citizens by the Eritrean state; and wrenching experiences of flight, displacement, and diaspora (Africa Watch 1991; Cliffe and Davidson 1998; Kibreab 2009a; Negash and Tronvoll 2000). My investigation considers how the online public sphere was established by Eritreans in diaspora and tracks the processes of its development and transformations over nearly two decades.

The second major focus of this study is political culture and the relations of citizenship and sovereignty. What binds people to their nation even when they live and work outside it? How does the state exert sovereignty in the de-territorialized spaces of diaspora and cyberspace? The Eritrean state has a distinct history and character, but many of the defining elements of Eritrean political culture—protracted war, militarization, censorship, repression, preoccupation with national security, and centralized, top-down command structures—are found elsewhere in Africa and around the globe. Therefore, an analysis of Eritrean politics speaks to larger questions of sovereignty, citizenship, and struggles for democracy in many contexts. To analyze Eritrean politics, I develop the concept of "sacrificial citizenship" to characterize the social contract between citizens and the state which is one in which citizenship is expressed through sacrificing for the nation. I explore ways in which war overflows the boundaries of the times and places of its occurrence. It does so materially, giving rise to refugees and diasporas, for example, but also culturally, giving rise to potent political narratives and symbols that define people's understandings of themselves and their places in the nation (Malkki 1995; Bernal 2013a). I connect the analysis of media and the analysis of political power through the concept of infopolitics, which foregrounds the management of information as a central aspect of power relations.

Diaspora and migration form the third strand of my analysis. Many diasporas and nations in the global south are developing new political practices and relationships that reflect and deepen the growing involvement of diasporas with their homelands. I argue that this "diasporic citizenship" signifies broader political changes. New forms of citizenship and sovereignty are emerging as a result of the rising global significance of diasporas as economic, cultural, and political actors across national borders. Transnational relationships link members of diasporas to each other, as well as to people and institutions back home. This does not mean that borders no longer matter. On the contrary, the locations of diasporas beyond the territorial borders of the state's authority give rise to particular challenges and potentials. Spaces of diaspora offer distinct opportunities for people to experiment with political expression and engage in dissent and other political activities that would not be safe in some homelands, such as Eritrea.

## INFOPOLITICS AND VIOLENCE

I contend that power, violence, and the politics of knowledge need to be placed at the center of analyses of the internet. I developed the concept of infopolitics to address the way that power is exercised and expressed through communication and through control over media, circulation, censorship, and authorization. Notions like "the information age," "information technologies," and "the digital divide" are misleading in their suggestion that the internet is foremost about access to "information" as if this were a preexisting, neutral, social good. Power relations are embedded in the circulation of knowledge and the management of information constitutes a central aspect of politics and a dimension of sovereignty. State power is constructed not only through control exercised over territory and people, but also through control over the production and communication of knowledge, information, narratives, and symbols. The exercise of infopolitical power by states is both more important and more difficult now that new media are decentralizing communication, opening up alternative avenues of knowledge production and distribution. Attending to infopolitics brings into focus aspects of media that have been undertheorized.

Anderson's (1991) influential conception of nations as imagined communities largely constructs nationalism in terms of a gentle process of belonging and mutual recognition mediated by newspapers and other national forms like the census and the museum, rather than in terms of the kinds of violent struggles over sovereignty, territory, and freedom of expression that have characterized Eritrea's formation as a nation. Michael Warner's (2002) important work on the nature of publics and public spheres also takes for granted the condition of freedom of expression without fear of violent reprisal. Discussions of the networked connectivity offered by the internet, likewise, often downplay or ignore altogether the role the internet might play in situations of violence or war (Castells 2001; Escobar 2000; Ess 2001; Wilson and Peterson 2002). It is only recently that a body of scholarship has emerged that explores questions of violence in relation to the internet (Axel 2004; Whitaker 2007; Turner 2008).

The transformative power of the internet is not that it allows access to information, but rather that it provides a public venue that allows ordinary people to question official discourse, to tell their own stories, to recontextualize existing knowledge and official narratives, and to create their own social networks for sharing ideas and analyzing information, rather than depending on mainstream media and official sources. This has wide-ranging political implications. As Eickelman and Anderson note (2003, 2), "The combination of new media and new contributors . . . feeds into new senses of a public space that is discursive, performative, and participative, and not confined to formal institutions recognized by state authorities."

While questions of access to information and to technology, sometimes framed as "the digital divide," have shaped much thinking about the significance of the internet, for Eritreans it was actually the limited access to the internet in Eritrea that heightened the political importance of the online public sphere at its outset. Access to the internet within Eritrea was largely confined to government elites through the 1990s, so the internet served Eritreans in diaspora, in part, as a special means of communicating their views to the Eritrean state. As the notion of infopolitics is meant to convey, moreover, the internet is not about communication per se any more than it is about information sui generis. What makes the internet a powerful and transformative medium is that ordinary people are able to use cyberspace as an arena in which they collectively struggle to narrate history, frame debates, and seek to form shared understandings beyond the control of political authorities or the commercial censorship of mass media. The fact that people can engage in these activities in a virtual space without the same risks of violence present in a physical space is particularly significant for many populations. The new perspectives that are generated in cyberspace reverberate beyond it and can serve as the basis for mobilization and action.

## NATIONS AS NETWORKS

If nations were once imagined communities as Anderson (1991) famously described them, in the current age of digital communications and migration it is more apt to think of nations as networks. No longer does the image of a nation as a bounded community imagined on a larger scale fit today's world where it is ever less clear what the boundaries of national territories enclose or exclude. National borders are porous, and relations once rooted in national territory—from family to livelihoods to political relationships—increasingly span borders, linking far-flung relatives and fellow nationals to each other and to other people and institutions in complex sociopolitical relationships. Digital media play a significant role by providing easy, cheap, and immediate means of communication across legal and institutional barriers as well as across geographical distances. Transformations of national politics and sovereignty are arising not only from the mobility of populations but also from new modes of communication.

Some of these cross-border relationships were brought into focus by scholarship on transnationalism (Basch, Schiller, and Blanc 1994; Portes, Guarnizo, and Landolt 1999). But attention tended to focus rather narrowly on the migrants who participate in more than one nation, rather than on the transformations of state power and the form of the nation. At the same time, attention to economic globalization and transnational cultural flows led some scholars to argue that the significance of nations was declining (Appadurai 1996; Hannerz 1996; Dahan and Sheffer 2001). In previous work, I drew on the case of Eritrea and its diaspora to argue that transnationalism does not necessarily work in opposition to nations but can support nations and strengthen nationalism (Bernal 2004). Today much evidence attests to the continued force of nation-states in the world, globalization and transnationalism notwithstanding. The relationships between states and citizens are hardly dissolving, but they are undergoing transformations, operating as networks that connect people and nations in new ways.

In thinking about the international mobility of individuals and populations, I find the concept of diaspora useful because it includes a wider range of political connections and loyalties than terms such as migrant or immigrant typically do. However, migrants, refugees, exiles, immigrants, and diasporas are not distinct populations; they are political forms that overlap and morph into one another. Scholarship on international migration focused on migrants' relations to states often does so through the narrow framework of a binary opposition between legal and illegal status. While legal status certainly has consequences in people's lives, the focus on citizenship as a legal status may obscure from view the growing range of intermediate or hybrid forms of national inclusion and belonging (Coutin 2007; Laguerre 2006; Glick-Schiller 2005). Furthermore, people's sense of belonging and political engagement may not correspond to their legal papers (Baker-Cristales 2008). Increasingly, diasporas are being enfranchised and included in various ways as nationals in their states of origins (Ong 1999; Itzigsohn 2012). We have not yet developed terminology to cover some of these relationships. In the case of Eritreans in diaspora and the Eritrean state, I use the term "diasporic citizenship" to reflect the fact that their membership in the nation is distinct from legal citizenship.

I argue that such relationships between states and diasporas are altering the meanings and practices of citizenship and sovereignty. Therefore, it is not simply the forms of diasporic citizenship that we need to understand, but the changing nature of relationships between people and states around the world. This comes into view more fully when we understand citizenship less as a legal status and more as a relationship of people to the state. As Sieder (2001, 203) writes:

> Citizenship is often conceived of as a fixed and nonnegotiable set of rights and obligations, such as those embodied in a written constitution. However, it is in fact best understood as a dynamic process rather than a static juridical construct. Both in terms of its legal attributes and its social content, citizenship is contested and constantly renegotiated and reinterpreted.

Diasporas are changing the ways states construct citizenship. One reason for this in the global south is the importance of remittances in national economies; vital human resources for the state lie outside its borders. In the case of Eritrea, the citizenship law established after independence defined citizenship through descent from an Eritrean father or mother rather than birthplace, so that Eritreans in diaspora and their children born abroad could be considered citizens. Elsewhere, particularly in the global north, changes in citizenship are designed to exclude certain populations. In Ireland, for example, citizenship was recently redefined around Irish heritage rather than place of birth to exclude the children of migrants from the global south, and from Africa in particular, born in Ireland (Moran 2012). Because so much migration is from the global south to wealthier countries of the global north, diasporas are produced through the combination of exclusionary practices on the part of northern nations toward certain migrants and inclusionary practices on the part of homelands in the global south. Coinciding with the growing significance of diasporas to their nations of origin, the rise of new communications technologies has made migrants' ongoing engagements with the societies they left behind increasingly immediate and continuous.

## NATIONS AND MEDIATION

While Benedict Anderson's conceptualization of nations as imagined communities has inspired my work and that of many other anthropologists, relatively few have pursued the focus on mediation in creating political community that Anderson's attention to print capitalism suggests. Scholars have found very useful the understanding that, at the level of the nation, community is imagined. But it is important to probe the processes through which the nation is imagined. The role of media is particularly interesting given the rapid transformations of communication technologies in the twenty-first century. In our hypermediated age, moreover, mediation is increasingly central to politics. What does it mean that political community and national belonging are mediated? If we attend to shifting forms of mediation, imagined communities are revealed from a different perspective. In the classic Andersonian scenario where the nation is conjured up through reading the newspaper, it is not so much that citizens imagine the nation, as that the nation is imagined *for them* and broadcast *to them*. If mediation is a core element of our experience of nations and nationalism, then that has important implications for the participation of diasporas and the extension of state power outside national boundaries. The internet makes it less important to be located inside national boundaries as long as one can consume and even produce national media. That is what Eritreans in diaspora are doing on the websites they have established to analyze, debate, and take part in national politics. Such activities entail multiple shifts in the Andersonian paradigm. The diaspora are producing national media from outside the nation, and they are imagining and publicly representing the nation in an interactive, collective, and participatory way through the internet. This process goes beyond the idea of "long-distance nationalism," because it is transforming the nation and the means by which nations and nationalism are sustained (Anderson 1992).

The position of the diaspora and of cyberspace as both inside and outside of the nation brings into focus the challenges faced by citizens and states in the present era of technology and mobility. Studies of migrants that see them simply as ethnics, refugees, undocumented populations, or exploited workers miss these complex processes. Eritreans in diaspora are to some degree quasi-citizens in their new homes where they often remain outsiders even if legal citizens, and quasi-citizens of Eritrea where they do not live and whose passport they do not hold, yet where they are recognized as nationals and where they see themselves and are seen as stakeholders. The diasporic citizen, therefore, is a key figure of global modernity; one that reveals the failures of postcolonial societies to provide peace, democracy, and welfare, and the failure of Western democracies to fully enfranchise populations marked as racially, religiously, or culturally different.

ERITREA, DIASPORIC CITIZENSHIP, AND CYBERSPACE

About the size of Kentucky, Eritrea lies along Africa's Red Sea coast, bordered by Ethiopia, Sudan, and Djibouti. Its population today is around five million. Historically, Eritrea came into being as a political entity when it was carved out of east Africa by the Italians who ruled it as their colony from 1886 until 1941. The British then administered it as a trusteeship until 1952 when Eritrea was federated to Ethiopia. Ethiopian Emperor Haile Selassie violated the terms of federation in 1962 by annexing Eritrea (Iyob 1995). Three decades of war fought on Eritrean soil followed (Cliffe and Davidson 1998; Connell 1993; Firebrace and Holland 1985). Eritrea's first major independence movement, the Eritrean Liberation Front (ELF) began armed struggle in 1961 (Habte Selassie 1989). The Eritrean People's Liberation Front (EPLF), which ultimately succeeded in winning independence for Eritrea, first emerged as a splinter group that broke away from the ELF in 1971. Emperor Haile Selassie was overthrown in 1974 and Ethiopia was ruled by a military council known as the Dergue. The brutality of the Dergue has been well-documented (Africa Watch 1991). Its leader, Colonel Mengistu Haile Mariam, eventually became prime minister. While fighting Ethiopia for independence, the two Eritrean liberation movements fought their own civil war in the 1970s in which ELF was defeated. The EPLF finally achieved victory over Ethiopian forces in 1991, aided in part by the breakup of the Soviet Union that had been providing military support to Mengistu. One of the EPLF's leaders, Isaias Afewerki assumed the presidency of Eritrea, and the liberation front transformed itself into a ruling party, calling itself the People's Front for Democracy and Justice (PFDJ) (Poole 2001).

The original Eritrean diaspora was a product of the three decades of war that drove Eritreans to flee their homes or stranded them abroad, as was the case for Eritrean students studying overseas who could not safely return. Hundreds of thousands of Eritreans were forced to make new lives for themselves in other lands under various circumstances. Half a million Eritreans became refugees in Sudan, some of whom eventually gained admittance to nations in the global north (Kibreab 1987). From their locations in North America, Europe, and the Middle East, Eritreans in diaspora played vital roles in supporting the nationalist struggle through public relations campaigns aimed at drawing international attention to their cause, as well as through their own donations and fund-raising campaigns to support the EPLF. The war ended in 1991, and, in preparation for a referendum on Eritrean independence, Eritreans in diaspora around the world, who had never held Eritrean citizenship since they were Ethiopian citizens when they left home and in many cases had become citizens of the countries where they now lived, were issued Eritrean national identity cards. These national IDs allowed Eritreans in diaspora to vote in the national referendum at polling places set up abroad for this purpose. Thus, at its very birth, the Eritrean nation encompassed this extraterritorial dimension of Eritreans politically included in the nation, despite their foreign residence and, in many cases, foreign citizenship. Eritrea gained international recognition as an independent state in 1993. The relative size of this diaspora is significant. At the time of Eritrea's independence, it is estimated that one million Eritreans were living outside the country, which amounted to roughly one of every three Eritreans at the time (United Nations 1994). As a point of comparison, the well-known Filipino diaspora accounts for only 10 percent of that nation's population (Ignacio 2005).

The new nation of Eritrea began with its infrastructure largely destroyed and its economy crippled by war. It remains one of the least developed countries in the world, with an estimated GDP per capita of $482, far below the $1,444 average for sub-Saharan Africa (www.data.worldbank.org, accessed March 27, 2013). In 1997, Eritrea stopped using the Ethiopian birr and introduced its own currency, the nakfa. Eritrea's predominantly rural population is engaged in agriculture and animal husbandry. The population is fairly evenly divided between Christians and Muslims, although Orthodox Christians have historically dominated Eritrea's political economy and continue to do so. Tigrinya and Tigre speakers are the dominant language groups and together make up four-fifths of the population. There is no official national language, but Tigrinya, Arabic, and English are used as official languages in practice. Eritrea's social landscape is broadly divided along the lines of highland Orthodox Christian farmers and lowland Muslim pastoralists and agropastoralists. There are nine official ethnic groups, most of which speak Semitic or Cushitic languages. One of the projects of the EPLF during the liberation struggle and subsequently of the Eritrean state has been to forge national culture out of diversity (Woldemikael 1993). The central thrust of this effort has been to promote loyalty to the nation above all, as well as to recognize diversity while attempting to vitiate its political base, so that ethnic and religious diversity might be converted into something as inconsequential as folkloric traditions.

Muslim Eritreans, whose cultural ties to the highland Christian elites of Ethiopia were weak, were among the first nationalists to take up armed struggle against Ethiopia, and the ELF drew considerable support from Muslim

Eritreans. The EPLF and the PFDJ regime it spawned, while also secular, are dominated by people from highland Christian backgrounds. The place of religion in Eritrea is fraught, in regard not only to the role of Islam and the full integration of Muslims but also in terms of Christian groups outside the Orthodox Church (Kifleyesus 2006). In 1998, only five years after Eritrea's formal recognition as a nation by the United Nations, and even as the country remained engaged in the tasks of reconstruction and nation-building, Eritrea entered a new war with Ethiopia. This war, which officially ended in 2000, was ostensibly caused by disagreement over the delineation of national borders, but may well have had deeper origins in rivalries between the Ethiopian and Eritrean regimes and the dissatisfaction of Ethiopians with having lost their access to the Red Sea (Jacquin-Berdal and Plaut 2004; Iyob 2000). The independence struggle of Eritrea was part of broader transformations in Ethiopia that ultimately had brought a new regime to power there led by Meles Zenawi. The ascent of Meles Zenawi in Ethiopia was based in the Tigrean People's Liberation Front (TPLF), a movement led by Ethiopian Tigre speakers that succeeded in breaking the long-established hold of the Amhara ethnic group on political authority in Ethiopia. During the war for Eritrea's independence, the TPLF was fostered by and allied with the EPLF. Tensions between the two new national leaders and former allies, President Isaias Afewerki and Prime Minister Meles Zenawi are believed by some to have been a contributing factor to the border conflict.

The border war exacted a great toll on Eritreans. In addition to the thousands of deaths and casualties of the conflict, the war displaced communities, disrupted agricultural production and foreign investment, and diverted public resources from services and development to the war effort. While the fighting took place in what for Ethiopia is a remote border region, because of Eritrea's small size and the short distance between the nation's capital and the Ethiopian border, this war was a national war for Eritreans. The war terrorized the entire population of Eritrea. People throughout the country feared for their lives and Eritreans everywhere feared for the survival of Eritrea as a sovereign nation. In the aftermath of the war, which appeared to have put so much at risk for so little, dissenting voices began to speak out against President Isaias's regime. Isaias responded by jailing journalists and critics, including members of his own government. Thus began a new era in Eritrean politics characterized by repression and widespread abuses of human rights (Tronvoll 2009; Human Rights Watch 2011). New waves of Eritreans began to leave the country and join the diaspora.

The relationship of Eritreans in diaspora to the Eritrean state continues to evolve, but its roots lie in the transnational relationships that were established during the war for independence from Ethiopia. Long before the internet, Eritreans in diaspora were geographically dispersed yet highly networked. Eritrean transnational politics, thus, are not a product of new communications technologies. The Eritrean diaspora helped sustain the nationalist movement within Eritrea, and after independence, the diaspora continued to contribute to the nation of Eritrea (Hepner and Conrad 2005; Fessehatzion 2005). Eritreans in diaspora and Eritrean nationalist movements were linked in what I think of as a nontechnological "world wide web" of Eritrean nationalism before the advent of the internet. Among other things, this network successfully circulated nationalist discourses, information, and resources transnationally (Al-Ali, Black, and Koser 2001; Conrad 2003; Hepner 2003; Bernal 2004). The historical development of that networked nationalism laid the groundwork for taking Eritrean politics online.

A vivid picture of the transnational organization of the EPLF was given in a series of long posts in April 1998 on Dehai, the first major Eritrean diaspora website (Bernal 2005b). The poster described this collective history from his own experience in Germany, asserting that "[t]he Eritrean network in Mannheim is a subset of a bigger network which covered areas where Eritreans resided—practically, the whole globe," adding that "[t]he Mannheim community can also give us a good picture of similar happenings in other parts of the world" (Dehai post, April 4, 1998). The poster explains that representatives of the EPLF organized networks of "cells" that fostered close local relationships among Eritreans but operated as part of a top-down, centralized political system ultimately under the leadership in Eritrea. He notes that "[d]iscipline was high and all meetings opened with *ZeKre Sematat* [remember the martyrs] and were concluded with *Awet Nhafash* [victory to the masses]." (Translations in brackets of transliterated Tigrinya phrases added.) Summing up the experience of the 1970s and 1980s, he writes:

> The community network acted as local, regional and *international informa-*
> *tion distribution system* for Eritreans. One can argue that this networking or
> mass mobilisation approach was one of the best features of the EPLF orga-
> nizational structure that materialised in amassing gross financial and moral
> support from its networked members and sympathizers. (Dehai post, April 9,
> 1998; emphasis added)

The transnational networks established by the EPLF helped produce the diaspora as a political force, organizing the diaspora's internal relations and connecting Eritreans in diaspora to each other through various organizations, as well as fostering loyalty and obedience to the leadership in Eritrea among Eritreans abroad.

Since independence the Eritrean state has deliberately and strategically maintained and developed links with Eritreans in diaspora. Before independence, no one inside or outside of Eritrea held Eritrean citizenship. Eritreanness developed in a transnational political field where the distinction between Eritreans within Eritrea and those located outside of it was not clear-cut in defining membership in the national community. What defined membership was not a legal identity or place of residence, but a subjectivity and the practices of political participation and commitment to the nationalist movement. Once statehood was achieved, Eritreans in diaspora were enfranchised by the Eritrean government in concrete ways that accorded them a form of diasporic citizenship.

Many Eritreans in diaspora were issued national identity cards to participate in the referendum when the EPLF went to great lengths to have the diaspora in many countries around the world vote. The new regime brought members of the diaspora into various posts within the government and also treated the diaspora as a constituency of sorts to be represented in various deliberations, such as the drafting of the Eritrean constitution. The national constitution (which is an inspirational and aspirational document, but not the law of the land, since it has never been fully implemented) defines Eritrean citizenship as based on descent from either parent rather than by place of birth. This projects a diasporic citizenry into the future of the nation. Eritreans in diaspora are also subject to taxation. They are expected to pay at a special tax rate of 2 percent of their net incomes. Though compliance has never been wholly enforceable, many Eritreans do pay something, and proof of such payment is often required of Eritreans who wish to transact legal or business matters in Eritrea, such as obtaining birth certificates, claiming inherited property, or buying land. The recognition of Eritreans in diaspora as nationals by the Eritrean state, even though they hold passports of other countries, is now well established.

The continuing importance of the diaspora for the state rests on a number of things. One is the large size of the diaspora relative to the resident population of Eritrea. The majority of the estimated one million Eritreans living outside the country did not repatriate to Eritrea when independence was won. It was clear that the war-torn new nation had no means of absorbing them and had few educational resources to offer their children. The educational opportunities for their children in Europe and North America were often mentioned to me by Eritreans as a reason for remaining in diaspora. In addition, families had been displaced and dispersed, and many communities had been destroyed so that some people had no close kin or community to return to in Eritrea. Another basis of the significance of the diaspora is its economic wealth relative to the poverty of Eritrea, which is a poor nation even by African standards. While Eritreans in the global north and the Middle East are largely working class, they have high incomes by Eritrean standards. The diaspora has contributed millions of dollars to Eritrea, not only in the form of remittances to family members but also through taxes paid to the Eritrean state, donations contributed to various nation-building and welfare-oriented projects, and, most significantly, funds sent to support Eritrea's war effort in the 1998–2000 border conflict with Ethiopia (Fessehatzion 2005).

Scholarship has established the basic outlines of Eritrea's national history; the same cannot be said for the history of Eritrea's diaspora. Despite some excellent research, particularly on Eritreans in the United States and Germany, comprehensive documentation of the Eritrean diaspora does not exist (Hepner 2009; Kibreab 2000; Al-Ali, Black, and Koser 2001; Conrad 2005; Anone 2011; Woldemikael 2005). As Koser notes: "There are no accurate data on the size of the Eritrean diaspora in Europe or North America" (2003, 112). Official records and statistics are scant because, before Eritrea's independence, its people were officially recorded as Ethiopians in the enumeration of refugees, asylum seekers, immigrants, foreign students, and so on. During the three decades of liberation struggle, the largest numbers of Eritreans who crossed international borders fled to neighboring Sudan where they settled in refugee camps under the auspices of the office of the UN High Commissioner for Refugees (UNHCR) or found ways to live and work unofficially in urban areas (Kibreab 1987, 1995). Eritreans already working or studying abroad remained overseas living in various circumstances when it became unsafe for them to return home.

As the war raged on for decades, Eritreans pursued various avenues to gain entry into, remain in, and achieve legal status in other countries. In many cases, this resulted in a series of international moves spread out over a number of years before a more permanent new home was established abroad, though, for many, "home" will always mean Eritrea. Sudan, in particular, was a first stop for many Eritreans who later were accepted as refugees in the United States, Canada, Germany, and elsewhere. Eritreans in diaspora often took on responsibilities for helping siblings and other relatives to settle abroad. Today the largest numbers of Eritreans living outside Africa are found in the United States and Germany (Conrad 2006a). Many are employed in service-sector jobs, such as hotel workers, parking-lot attendants, taxi drivers, and nursing-home staff (Woldemikael 1996; Matsuoka and Sorenson 2005). Some are overqualified for these jobs, including, most notably, a number of the most talented and prolific posters to the diaspora websites who work as parking lot attendants, night guards, and bus drivers.

Eritreans in diaspora tend not to participate as active citizens in the politics of their adoptive countries. They are de facto second-class citizens of their new nations, where they remain socially and politically marginalized and largely invisible to the wider public. There are now "Little Ethiopias" in Washington, DC, and Los Angeles, both of which include Eritreans among their clientele and as business owners, but nowhere is there a "Little Eritrea." Germany is host to the second-largest number of Eritreans in diaspora outside of Africa, yet when I mention this to Germans, they say they are unaware of the Eritrean presence. Eritreans in diaspora do engage, however, with broader national and international institutions in relation to Eritrean causes. In the United States, for example, they have conducted letter-writing campaigns to US representatives, demonstrated in front of the United Nations and in front of the White House, and carried out various activities on behalf of Eritrean causes. Eritreans in diaspora have thus acted on democratic freedoms, such as the right to public assembly and the right to make demands on their government representatives, but they have done so more as citizen-diplomats from Eritrea than as concerned Americans.

Eritreans in diaspora are passionate about their home country and its politics. Perhaps some of their fervor is related to the unfinished projects of nation-building and democracy even after Eritrean independence, as well as to the insecurity of Eritrea's existence as a nation given "the potential for rival forms of political legitimacy competing violently for dominance" in the Horn of Africa (Lyons 1996, 89). This potential was most clearly realized in the 1998–2000 border war with Ethiopia but did not end with it. As one observer commented, moreover, "the Eritrean boundaries of identity and borders of territory are still in the making, and what they will eventually embrace and contain remains to be seen" (Tronvoll 1999, 1037). Eritrean identity remains fraught both internally and internationally. Threats to Eritrea's unity and survival are perceived to lie both externally with Eritrea's regional neighbors and internally with the division between Christians and Muslims that underlay the conflict between the ELF and the EPLF and continues to be a source of tension. The traumas of Ethiopian repression, protracted war, and flight from home, combined with the isolation, discrimination, and disenfranchisement often experienced by Eritreans in the countries where they settled, have served to entrench their identification as Eritreans and have provided an impetus to maintain links to Eritrea and to fellow Eritreans across vast distances. Thus, even if the EPLF organized the diaspora for its own political and economic ends, and President Isaias's regime continues to foster such links for the same instrumental reasons, the rewards of participation for members of the diaspora are not only political but also deeply social and emotional. The enduring significance of Eritrean identity in the lives of diasporic Eritreans is shown in the efforts they make to sustain social and political networks across geographic distances and to build a sense of community with other Eritreans wherever they find themselves.

Eritrean activities online can be seen as part of a process of developing new forms of community, citizenship, and identity out of the experiences of war, displacement, and international migration. Through websites created by Eritreans in diaspora Eritreans realize some of the dimensions of citizenship that they experience neither in other countries where they are perpetual outsiders nor in Eritrea, despite the promises of national liberation and the references to "democracy" and "justice" in the name of the ruling party. The websites are spaces of experimentation where new kinds of political expression and action are developing that change the meaning and experience of the nation.

One of the most politically significant dimensions of Eritrean's engagement with the internet is that, in contrast to most of the organizational forms that have connected Eritreans in diaspora to each other and to national institutions, the websites were established independently rather than under the leadership in Eritrea. Dehai and other websites that followed, including Asmarino and Awate, were founded by ordinary Eritreans. As such, they represent something quite distinct in Eritrean political culture, which has remained highly centralized and top-down from the days of the EPLF to the current one-party state under President Isaias Afewerki. Although the internet did not create transnational Eritrean circuits of sociality, information, and resources, the launching of the first major Eritrean website, www.dehai.org, established a unique forum for expression that promoted the values of free and open debate and connected Eritreans around the globe to each other in a decentralized network.

From its early start in 1992 as a computer-mediated network before the World Wide Web had even been established, Dehai was designed to allow Eritreans to participate in nation-building in Eritrea from their remote locations in North America, Europe, and elsewhere. Dehai managed for years to capture the attention and energies of many Eritreans in diaspora. Dehai grew from the efforts of a few individuals to attract dedicated posters and followers, flourishing over the course of the 1990s as the preeminent internet link for Eritreans. While Dehai's popularity has waned since 2001, it played a crucial role in establishing Eritrean online culture. Its major successors, Asmarino and Awate, are offshoots of Dehai. The sense that posts on Eritrean websites are read not only by fellow Eritreans in diaspora but also by people in Eritrea, particularly Eritrea's leadership, gives the online public sphere a much deeper political significance and purpose beyond the sharing of news and analysis among members of the diaspora. Even today, however, with growing access to the internet in Eritrea, the main producers of online content continue to be Eritreans in diaspora.

In the early 1990s when Dehai began, Eritreans were coming together in the heady days of nationalist victory to contribute to nation-building. Later at the end of the nineties, Eritreans in diaspora rallied online and in other locales to insure Eritrea's survival in the face of the border war with Ethiopia. Since 2001, Eritreans have responded online to growing repression within Eritrea and the lack of free press and civil society inside Eritrea's national borders. The websites have come to serve as an offshore platform for civil society and a surrogate public sphere independent of the state, where a diversity of views, and particularly dissident views, can be expressed and accessed. Critics of the PFDJ and President Isaias remain profoundly committed to nationalist politics as they continue to post their views, seek to sway public opinion among Eritreans, and protest government actions. Eritrean nation-building is an ongoing project as the struggle for independence, ultimately, has been followed by a struggle for democracy. People in Eritrea have little political say in their government, opposition parties are not allowed to form, the media are state controlled, and independent civil society organizations are not permitted. Thus, what Eritreans in diaspora have created and continue to create on the internet has no counterpart on the ground.

## ETHNOGRAPHIC METHODS, DIASPORA, AND CYBERSPACE

In pursuing research on Eritrean politics, diaspora, and the internet, I faced a number of challenges as an ethnographer. To study cyberspace or diaspora calls for new kinds of methods. The challenges are both practical, such as how to conduct participant observation in cyberspace or among a scattered population, and theoretical, in that new conceptual tools are required to make sense of unprecedented social and political circumstances, as well as novel research sites. Diasporas are an unwieldy object of study; they have no specific location or fixed boundaries. The very notion of diaspora implies a population that is not defined by its actual location, but by the place its members left. Diasporas possess no territory; they exist, not by occupying space, but through transcending it. From that perspective, I consider cyberspace to be a key space where the Eritrean diaspora is located. Through their websites they are able to create Eritrean space online. As Setha Low (2000, 238) observes, public space is "a place where disagreements and conflicts over cultural and political objectives become concrete." Like Low's study of a plaza in Costa Rica and Haugerud's (1995) study of *baraza* (public political meetings) in Kenya, mine is a study of a particular public space and the public life and culture that take place there. However, I do not approach cyberspace as a virtual realm apart from other realities. To the contrary, in order to make sense of online activities I place them in the wider context of Eritrean political culture and institutions. This book then is not intended as the story of a diaspora, though to some extent it must tell that story, as much as it is the story of three websites, and, through those websites, perhaps, a story of Eritrea and Eritreans in diaspora as seen from cyberspace.

A focus on Eritrea and Eritreans in diaspora raises problems because few long-term ethnographic studies have been carried out among Eritreans, at home or abroad, and there are considerable gaps in knowledge. The ethnographic and social studies that could provide the groundwork and context for more focused research have not been carried out in Eritrea, primarily due to war. The 1998–2000 border war, incidentally, disrupted my own plans for a year of research in Eritrea, which already had been selected for funding by the Wenner-Gren Foundation and by Fulbright, but could not go forward because once war broke out, Americans were evacuated and Fulbright refused to release funds for research in Eritrea. Wars have not been the only obstacles to research in Eritrea. The Eritrean state has made research extremely difficult and, in some cases, impossible to conduct on Eritrean soil (see Hepner's [2009] account of fleeing the country).

Diasporas are an elusive research subject, particularly in the case of Eritreans who for decades prior to independence were included with Ethiopians in records of various kinds. Diasporas, moreover, are not singular, monolithic, or static. Successive waves of exiles, migrants, refugees, and asylum-seekers are produced out of different historical circumstances in Eritrea. Those who founded Dehai, Asmarino, and Awate, establishing the online public sphere and constructing Eritrean online culture, are members of the original core diaspora who fled Eritrea during the years of the independence struggle and eventually settled in the United States. Recent arrivals who fled the Eritrean

state, as well as children born or raised abroad from a young age are diversifying the diaspora and the understandings of what it means to be Eritrean.
Differences arise not only out of generation and age at arrival but also out
of distinct waves of refugees defined, in part, by the particular conditions or
events in Ethiopia and Eritrea that gave rise to their flight or expulsion from
home. Eritreans in diaspora are diverse in ethnicity, class, gender, region of
origin, and religious affiliations, among other things. Their experiences and
trajectories of flight, migration, and settlement abroad also vary temporally
and geographically.

The decades of nationalist mobilization, warfare, and dictatorship have
politicized knowledge about Eritrea and severely limited the access of independent researchers (Tronvoll 2009). Much of what is known about Eritrean
history, politics, and social conditions bears the influence of the EPLF's narratives, which have been further developed and elaborated in the national political culture promoted by the Eritrean state. Journalists, novelists, and scholars have contributed to nationalist myth-making with their inspiring heroic
accounts of the guerilla movement (Keneally 1990; Connell 1997; Pateman
1998; Wilson 1991). These accounts contribute to our knowledge but tell only
one version of the story, a version consistent with official EPLF and PFDJ narratives. Slowly and partially other accounts are emerging, not least on Eritrean
websites where the past is reinterpreted, new questions are raised, and secrets
and suppressed knowledge are sometimes revealed.

Cyberspace presents distinct research challenges. Studying a media space
is not the same as studying a physical space, and, as Abu-Lughod notes in her
research on television and nationalism in Egypt, in such open-ended and vast
domains of cultural production "it is difficult to know where to stop or where
to focus" (2001, 51). The rapid pace of technological and social innovation in
digital media present an additional problem since the object of study is evolv-
ing faster than our analyses can develop. I made a decision to focus on three
key websites, Dehai, Asmarino, and Awate, and to adopt a social history approach of deep and close analysis rather than to prioritize current events and
the latest developments as they unfold. Ethnography distinguishes itself from
journalism, for example, in part through its concern with finding the enduring
values and underlying understandings, the back story of culture that imbues
events and activities with meaning for people, rather than focusing on the
breaking news of the moment.

Multisited ethnography has emerged as a way to track a subject or object
of study across locations and boundaries (Marcus 1995). But for my study of
Eritrean cyberspace and politics, multisited ethnography seems a misnomer.

Rather than a multisited ethnography this is in some ways a no-sited ethnography, a de-territorialized or, perhaps, a viral ethnography. My research methods could be considered to be "viral methods" because I followed a process that involved connecting links in networks. The focus was not on particular communities or sites (other than websites), but rather on the links themselves and what flowed through them. I followed themes that emerged in discussions online into policies and practices of the Eritrean state, and deciphered the significance of certain posts through knowledge I gained in Eritrea and from Eritreans wherever I met them, whether from talking to a taxi driver in Gothemburg, Sweden, or to ex-guerilla fighters or university students in Asmara. I do not approach Eritrean websites as an "online community" so much as I explore the ambiguous boundaries and connections between online activities and wider circuits of Eritrean experiences, histories, and culture, as well as between national discourses, institutions, and events in Eritrea and actions and sentiments among Eritreans in diaspora. Indeed, one of the things that make Eritrean websites so interesting is their connection to networks of Eritrean politics beyond the internet. Rather than seeing cyberspace as a separate, virtual realm of human activity, I trace interconnections among online practices, virtual constructions of community, and other experiences of belonging, particularly experiences and understandings of citizenship, violence, and state power. I follow this set of themes across various temporal and spatial boundaries, while keeping the online public sphere as the nexus of my study.

My research began with a focus on Dehai.org and grew to include Awate.com and Asmarino.com once they emerged as major centers of political analysis and debate. Throughout the book, I refer to these as Dehai, Asmarino, and Awate as they are commonly called. These three websites compete with and complement each other and together they comprise the core of the transnational public sphere. There are now many Eritrea-related websites in existence, including Facebook groups and YouTube video sites, but I chose to focus on these three based on their long-standing record of political activity and my understanding of their significance for Eritreans in diaspora. I see these websites as "Eritrean" because they are explicitly created by and for Eritreans. Though not closed to others, the Eritrean identities of the majority of posters are clear, not only from their Eritrean names (which possibly could be faked), but even more from the content of their posts which reflect cultural perspectives, historical knowledge, and emotional engagement with Eritrean affairs that very few non-Eritreans possess.

My analysis of Eritrean politics online has developed out of a diverse array of sources including vast archives of Eritrean writings in cyberspace, as well as ethnographic research in Eritrea, and among Eritreans in diaspora. To date I have made three trips to Eritrea. In 2012 I expected to conduct additional research but was unsuccessful in my attempt to obtain an entry visa. I have compiled my own printed archives consisting of hundreds of pages of posts. These archives now have greater significance since Asmarino and Awate no longer keep their complete archives available online.

I first traveled to Eritrea in 1981 when it was still under Ethiopian rule and Asmara was very much an occupied city where a strong Ethiopian military presence was visible in the streets. I made two research trips after Eritrean independence, one in winter 1996 and another in summer 2001. There I spent time in Eritrean homes and talked with resident Eritreans, as well as with visiting and resettled diaspora Eritreans from a diverse range of countries and walks of life. In 2001 I also conducted participant observation in the recently opened cybercafes. At that time I also witnessed the flourishing (though as it turned out, short-lived) public sphere of independent newspapers. I was very fortunate to participate in the Eritrean Studies Association conference held in Asmara in 2001 where outspoken exchanges took place among diaspora intellectuals, Eritrean officials and party cadres, and members of the public. In 2001 I also traveled to the demilitarized zone along the border with Ethiopia, observing the bomb damage in Senafe, the makeshift tent hospital, encampments of displaced people, and farm land that lay uncultivable until the minesweepers could complete their job.

I came to this research from a lifelong interest in Africa. However, unlike my earlier research in Sudan where I spent two and half years, and the year of research I conducted in Tanzania, I am connected to Eritrea personally. Through marriage to my husband, Tekle, and through our children I am connected to Eritreans and Eritrea through family ties. Indeed, I have sometimes joked that I thought I was marrying an individual, but I ended up marrying a nation. These family relationships raise additional questions about research methods because where the boundaries between "the field" and so-called real life can be drawn is unclear. I have come to know much about Eritrea and about Eritrean life in diaspora over the years simply as a matter of course. As a result, it is not always possible to state with certainty how I know something or when or from whom or by what means I learned it. As all anthropologists know, we learn so many things simply by paying careful attention, listening, or expressing interest in other people's lives. My methods were not only viral but also serendipitous. At the core of all participant observation, however, is the faith that, if you hang around long enough, knowledge will come to you of its own accord.

As a participant observer of life in the Eritrean diaspora over the past three decades, I have visited Eritrean homes in the United States, Canada, Germany, England, Italy, the Sudan, and Ethiopia. I have also met with Eritreans who live in Saudi Arabia, Sweden, and the Netherlands when they were visiting the United States or Eritrea, and I have encountered Eritreans who resettled in Eritrea after living in diaspora. I am most familiar with the experiences of Eritreans in the United States. Eritreans in the United States are responsible for creating and maintaining Dehai, Asmarino, and Awate, and US-based Eritreans also contribute many of the posts. I have met and conversed with founders of all three websites.

From an ethnographic standpoint, it is important that, online, Eritreans are engaged in articulating their views and identifying the issues that are significant to them without any prompting from a researcher. Thus, "participant webservation" (Varisco 2002) is an unobtrusive method that paradoxically seems to offer access to natural exchanges and self-expression in the artificially constructed space of cyberspace. One feature of Eritrean websites that made them easily accessible to me is that most posts are in English, with some transliterated Tigrinya thrown in here and there. Until the development of software for Ge'ez script, which is used for writing Tigrinya, posters did not have the option of writing in Tigrinya. Websites today often include Tigrinya posts, but the dominant language in Eritrean cyberspace remains English. While I have studied Tigrinya off and on, without the experience of long-term immersion in Eritrea, I have never attained fluency.

In the course of this research I followed developments on Dehai, Asmarino, Awate and, to a lesser extent, other websites for well over a decade. To create a finite project in the face of continually breaking current events in Eritrean politics and the daily stream of new posts, I focus the core of my analysis on posts from around 1997 to 2007, with occasional inclusion of posts on either side of those boundaries. I also focus my attention on the main feature of the websites—the forum of originally composed posts—though each of the websites has other features, such as news reports recirculated from journalistic outlets, photos, and video from Eri-TV, the state-run television station. In addition to the webmanagers, I have interviewed writers and readers of these three websites. I chose to concentrate, however, on the operation of the online public sphere as a cultural and political phenomenon and to identify and analyze central themes, symbols, and discourses across many posts, rather than to focus on the individuals and personalities behind particular websites or particular posts. The amount of material posted in Eritrean cyberspace is huge and continually growing, so the problem posed is not one of gaining access to data but rather how to limit the scope of research.

The book is organized around a set of core themes—media and power, the significance of diaspora, and the legacies of violence—that bring Eritrean experience into dialogue with scholarly debates in anthropology and related disciplines, and that I believe speak to global shifts presently underway. In the course of my research I began to make my own intellectual tools as I went along, developing a number of concepts for defining and analyzing the core themes. I developed the concept of "infopolitics" to discuss the dynamics of politics and information I was observing. I chose "diasporic citizenship" to refer to the ambiguous political membership in the nation of people in diaspora. I developed the concept of "sacrificial citizenship" to describe the political culture of the Eritrean state with its boundless demands upon citizens, particularly its insistence on their willingness to die for the nation. The concepts of infopolitics, diasporic citizenship, and sacrificial citizenship elucidate the central themes of this study and are developed in relation to various kinds of data in the chapters that follow. My analysis of Eritrean diaspora websites, set in the context of Eritrea's turbulent recent history, reveals the ways that sovereignty and citizenship are being reconfigured and reproduced by means of the internet.

Chapter 1 argues that attending to infopolitics enriches our understanding of sovereignty. The chapter explores the social contract between the Eritrean state and its citizens that I describe as sacrificial citizenship, examining the ways this relationship is extended, negotiated, and reinterpreted in the transnational spaces of diaspora and cyberspace. I analyze the martyr as a key political symbol that has both shared and distinctive meanings for the state, citizens, and Eritreans in diaspora. Chapter 2 traces the construction of the online public sphere by Eritreans in diaspora through the 1990s, revealing it through textual analyses of individual posts, as well as through uncovering the written and unwritten rules governing practices of posting and debate. I argue that the diaspora used the internet to create Eritrean space online in ways that extended the nation and the sovereignty of the state into the diaspora and the virtual. Chapter 3 reveals how, since 2000, diaspora websites increasingly are used as an offshore platform where new political subjectivities can be developed, and perspectives on national politics independent of the state's national narratives are openly expressed, collectively developed, and circulated. Chapter 4 analyzes an unauthorized war memorial created on Awate using leaked government documents. I explore the politics of memorialization and argue that, through constructing a virtual memorial for the nation, members of the diaspora not only express their critique of the state but also seize power from the state. They do so through taking statelike actions they see the state as having failed to properly perform for its people. The final chapter, chapter 5, focuses on gender, politics, and the internet. This chapter examines online debates about allegations of military rapes to reveal the biopolitics of gender in the context of a militarized nation, and to analyze the tensions between notions of universal citizenship and gendered constructions of women as political subjects. I find that the internet lowers some barriers faced by women while reproducing others. The digital public sphere makes visible the mechanisms of silencing and patronizing that maintain politics as a domain of male authority where men assert themselves as citizens and as the public representatives of women. The conclusion considers how the ethnography and analysis presented here reveal the ways that nationhood, strategies of state power, and modes of political participation are being transformed in the context of the rise of digital media and the growing significance of diasporas.

# CHAPTER 1

# Infopolitics and Sacrificial Citizenship: Sovereignty in Spaces Beyond the Nation

How, in fact, can one continue to belong to a community in a context in which one is physically removed from it and in which one can no longer directly take part in the rituals that a sedentary life renders possible?

(MBEMBE 2005, 151)

[M]igrants have . . . emerged as the "bare life" of our times- the in between forms of life, uncoded substances without fixed belongings, unprotected by "their" states.

(HANSEN AND STEPPUTAT 2005, 35)

The powerful attraction of diaspora for postcolonial theorists was that, as transnational social formations, diasporas challenged the hegemony and boundedness of the nation-state and, indeed, of any pure imaginaries of nationhood.

(WERBNER 2005, 29–30)

Conventional notions of sovereignty are premised on the state's power over citizens or subjects in a bounded territory dominated by state authorities. Sovereignty is understood to include the relations of rule, the power of the state, the sources of its legitimacy, and the scope and limits of state control over its subjects. The flows of people and communications across political borders remake these relationships. The mutual engagement of the Eritrean diaspora and the Eritrean state cannot be analyzed solely from conventional notions of citizenship and sovereign power. The ways that relations of sovereignty and citizenship extend beyond national boundaries and operate outside of legal statuses begin to make sense only when we understand that politics is fundamentally cultural. Neither brute force nor the rational administration of law is what ties Eritreans in diaspora to the nation-state; the bond is a shared political culture. This chapter explores ideas about sovereignty, the contours of Eritrea's political culture, and the dynamic relationship of the diaspora and the state. Like cyberspace, the spaces of diaspora exist outside the authority of the Eritrean state. Yet, in ways I analyze here, neither of these spaces is outside the political culture of Eritrea or beyond the influence of the state. The concept of infopolitics is central to this analysis and complements recent theories of sovereignty that locate power in violence and control over bodies. The examination of Eritrean political culture, moreover, offers a counterpoint to the focus of so much recent scholarship on neoliberalism, a focus that obscures the realities of millions of people governed by or contending with illiberal regimes. While assumptions about the ubiquity of the neoliberal state are flawed, so too are labels like "authoritarian" state or "dictatorship," which fail to capture the cultural distinctiveness of different modes of sovereignty and the historical particularities of social orders and strategies of rule.

## BIOPOLITICS, NECROPOLITICS, AND INFOPOLITICS

Contemporary theories of power—Michel Foucault's biopolitics (1984), Achille Mbembe's necropolitcs (2003), and Giorgio Agamben's notion of "bare life" (1998)—share a focus on human bodies, life, and death. These theories provide insights into Eritrean political culture because war and sacrifice to the death are tightly bound up with constructions of Eritrean statehood and citizenship. Infopolitics builds on these insights by shedding light on the cultural and communicative aspects of sovereign power and the means by which power is exercised and contested, not only over bodies, but over minds.

The concept of biopolitics suggests that the exercise of modern state power is fundamentally a matter of life and death. Government entails managing the physical existence of subject populations and the conditions that affect human bodies (Foucault 1984). The concept of biopower has drawn attention to states' interests in public health, fertility, and sexuality (Greenhalgh and Winckler 2005; Petryna 2002). Mbembe has drawn attention to the operation of violence in constituting political formations and shaping political culture, through his notion of necropolitics, which he defines as the "subjugation of life to the power of death" (2003, 39). Necropolitics draws our attention to the operation of the state as a manager not only of life but also of death. The concept of necropower suggests a state that has the power of life and death over its citizen-subjects. Mbembe writes, "Among the dominant imaginaries of sovereignty in contemporary Africa is that which posits the fear of death and the will to survive as critical to any political practice" (2005, 154). The evocative notion of necropolitics brings to the fore the violence at the heart of state power, which is a politics of death (necropolitics) and a politics of life (biopolitics).

Agamben (1998) similarly considers life and death central to the workings of sovereignty. According to him, sovereign power creates the distinction between two kinds of human lives, the "life" of the citizen and the "bare life" of the person defined as outside the political community, this latter life symbolized by the figure Homo Sacer, one who can be killed with impunity. The work of Agamben and Mbembe is particularly relevant to the understanding of politics under authoritarian regimes because in their conception of politics, violence figures not as a breakdown in rational management or as a failure of democratic processes, but as the ultimate foundation of sovereign power.

Threats of violence certainly underlie state authority and can compel compliant behavior in many contexts. However, compliance under threat of force is a simple matter to explain. What is more interesting to try to understand is why people who are "free" and have established or begun new lives abroad, like Eritreans in diaspora, choose to participate in a relationship with a distant state. The concepts of biopower and necropolitics emphasize the power of the state, and the ways the state constructs and exercises its power over subject populations and territories. Eritreans in diaspora are outside national territory and beyond state authority. Moreover, they are active in maintaining their involvement in Eritrean national politics and in constructing and defending Eritrean sovereignty. Eritreans in diaspora are engaged in legitimizing and, increasingly, in challenging the legitimacy of the ruling one-party regime and President Isaias Afewerki. To understand these activities and the relationship of the diaspora and the state requires a conceptual shift.

Although the leading theories compel us to recognize power as a relation of life and death, the transmission of power through spaces beyond the nation reminds us that sovereignty must be exercised not only over bodies but also over minds. Alongside the necropolitical state is the infopolitical state, the state that manages information, censors, authorizes, disseminates, and communicates. Violence and communication are not opposites, however. Infopolitical regimes may distort, suppress, and censor through creating a climate of fear of violence. In her brilliant analysis of the Romanian state, Kligman (1998) dissects the intricacies of power exercised over and through information as a form of symbolic violence. When she observes that "self-censorship became a *natural* reflex" (Kligman 1998, 14, emphasis added), we see how infopolitics are literally embodied in political subjects. The Eritrean state exerts infopolitical power through overt censorship and by creating conditions for self-censorship as well as through the construction and deployment of potent national narratives and symbols. The communicative aspect of sovereign power takes on new dimensions in the context of the information technology revolution and the growing media saturation of our world.

## INFOPOLITICS AND THE INTERNET

If, as Coronil (2006) asserts, "state power lies in fixing meaning," then the possibility for that meaning to become unmoored from the state, to be circulated and recirculated, commented on, and reinterpreted independently by people in diaspora through cyberspace is a serious matter. As Sassen (2005, 82) points out, "Electronic space is, perhaps ironically, a far more concrete space for social struggles than that of the national political system. It becomes a place where nonformal political actors can be part of the political scene in a way that is much more difficult in national institutional channels."

The internet remakes our sense of place in a number of ways that are significant for states and sovereignty. Cyberspace is at once a deterritorializing force, a spatial illusion, and a reterritorializing force. Through the internet people connect across political borders in ways that make location seem invisible or irrelevant. The internet also allows for the production of virtual spaces. Websites offer a spatial illusion; we "visit" websites, and we take "virtual tours." This cyberspatiality is an important aspect of the websites created by Eritreans in diaspora. The first and longest running Eritrean diaspora website, Dehai (www.dehai.org), uses the tagline "Eritrea Online," on its home page, suggesting a version of the nation as a virtual community and implying that Eritrea can be accessed via the website. For many years a map of Eritrea appeared as part of the logo on Dehai's home page. On its membership sign-up page (most recently accessed 3–27–13), Dehai describes itself as "the Eritrean Community Online Network," which, like "Eritrea Online," blurs the distinction between Eritreans inside the nation and those outside it. Since Eritreans in diaspora have more access to the internet than their compatriots back home, and members of the diaspora are responsible for creating and maintaining Dehai and other Eritrean websites, as well as for producing most of the posts, this blurring of spatial distinctions works as a kind of illusion that bridges the diaspora's separation from Eritrea as well as concealing the dispersal of people within the diaspora from one another. In this sense, the websites they created reterritorialize the diaspora, locating them in Eritrea.

The speed of communications on the internet is significant for politics because it makes distant places seem as close and accessible as near ones and, moreover, eliminates the delays normally associated with distance. This technologically constructed proximity makes it possible for members of the diaspora to respond immediately and collectively to current events, national crises, and scandals in Eritrea. In this way they can directly participate in unfolding events by framing issues, shaping opinions, and mobilizing action.

If the Eritrean diaspora stands in a particular position in relation to the state because the state cannot control their lives and deaths, their position is especially distinct with regard to the state's infopolitics. The state cannot exercise its sovereignty over the bodies of Eritreans in diaspora, but it can reach their minds; therefore, infopolitics is particularly central to the dynamics of state-diaspora relations. The national leadership have sought to construct and perpetuate a distinctive Eritrean political culture, one that is defined by sacrificing for the nation. This ethos of sacrifice binds Eritreans in diaspora to the nation in powerful ways. At the same time, Eritreans in diaspora have freedoms of media consumption and production not accessible to Eritreans living in national territory. These conditions give rise to contradictions and radical possibilities.

## THE ETHOS OF SACRIFICIAL CITIZENSHIP

One of the most powerful symbols of Eritrean nationalism is that of the martyr who has given his life for the nation. Mbembe suggests that in colonial and postcolonial states, politics and problems of power have been particularly entwined with violence, war, and the authority to kill or to consign to death. He writes: "Imagining politics as a form of war, we must ask: What place is given to life, death, and the human body (in particular the wounded or slain body)? How are they inscribed in the order of power?" (Mbembe 2003, 12). Agamben's (1998) discussion of Homo Sacer similarly locates the political in the construction of the conditions under which life can be taken as a sacrifice or, conversely, simply killed without the death being accorded social value. These understandings of politics that place war and the sacrifice of lives at the center suggest that the elevation of the figure of the martyr by Eritrea's political authorities has deep significance. The martyr, I contend, not only is a key figure in the Eritrean national imaginary, but represents the essence of the social contract between Eritreans and the state in which the citizen's role is to serve the nation and sacrifice themselves for the survival and well-being of the nation. I call this "sacrificial citizenship."

Eritrean political culture was forged during thirty years of war for independence from Ethiopia. As Dorman observes, "the Eritrean struggle for self-determination . . . is constitutive of Eritrean identity and citizenship, as well

as of nationhood" (2003, 4, ellipses added). The Eritrean People's Liberation Front (EPLF) constructed a political culture within its own ranks and
worked to extend it beyond the guerilla fighters in its outreach to Eritreans
everywhere. A 2001 post that appeared on the website Awate (www.awate.
com) on Eritrea's Independence Day, reflecting on "the Armed Struggle Era"
represents that culture as follows: "Altruism became a national religion; self-
denial and self-sacrifice a way of life. Each wound, each terror, each death,
each birth was accepted as a down payment, an investment into the building
of a free Eritrea" (Awate post, May 24, 2001). The political education connected with the nationalist struggle permeated Eritreans' lives within Eritrea
and beyond it (Poole 2001; Woldemikael 1991). As Conrad (2006b, 69) found
among Eritreans in Germany:

> Until today, the question: "Where do you originally come from?" prompts
> diaspora Eritreans of all ages to embark on a lengthy (and always very similar)
> account of their country's history. Structure, vocabulary and vantage point of
> these narratives identify them unmistakably as products of the EPLF's nation-
> building efforts.

Every family, every home was affected by the decades of war fought on
Eritrean soil; therefore, ordinary Eritreans, even if they wielded little power,
came to feel that they had a stake in the political. The war is central to Eritrean
identity, as a national history and a collective experience that are distinctly
Eritrean. Perhaps, as Mbembe (2002, 267) suggests, "the state of war in contemporary Africa should in fact be conceived of as a general cultural experience that shapes identities, just as the family, the school, and other social institutions do." In the case of Eritrea, the Isaias regime has sought to unilaterally
define national political culture and Eritrean identity based on the struggle to
achieve national sovereignty. The image of the freedom fighter is a national
icon that appears on Eritrean currency, for example. Symbols of the war are
particularly evocative of and resonant with the profound losses suffered by
Eritreans during the long struggle.

Even more than the fighter, however, the martyr who died for the nation
has been made a core political symbol. Martyrs are an important part of Eritrean national mythology. As Matsuoka and Sorenson observe, "the dead became an inseparable element of national identity, an essential component of
an Eritrean structure of feeling (2001, 230). For Eritreans the term "martyr"
has a distinct meaning. "Martyr" was originally used by the EPLF to refer to
fighters who died in the liberation struggle. The PFDJ continued this usage

and expanded it to include others such as soldiers killed in the recent border war with Ethiopia. The EPLF was a secular, socialist organization and Eritrea is a secular state; therefore, their nationalist definition of "martyr" is distinct from the more common associations of the term in Islam and Christianity. However, since Eritrea's population is comprised of Christians and Muslims, the secular nationalist usage of "martyr" resonates with these sacred traditions. The meaning of "martyr" in Eritrea is explained in a post on Awate, dated January 16, 2005, by "The Awate Team" as follows:

> Various cultures give various names for those whom they want to honor for having paid the ultimate price for their nation. In the Eritrean context, the word is "martyr." The word has no religious or spiritual connotation: it is a hold-over from the Revolutionary War of Independence, and it applies to any Eritrean who died *while* in the service of the Revolutionary War or enlistment in with the Eritrean Defense Forces (EDF) or, in some cases, *after* a long service in the Revolutionary War or the EDF. In the Eritrean context, an individual does not have to die in the battlefront to earn the title of martyr.

The Eritrean state invokes the history of martyrs' sacrifices to legitimize itself and to demand unquestioning loyalty and sacrifice from Eritreans. It does so in part by situating itself as the achievement resulting from the huge sacrifices of human lives lost in the Eritrean nationalist struggle. This is not hard to do because the current leadership grew directly out of the EPLF. The state's construction of the martyr as an iconic national figure is reflected in the establishment of Martyr's Day as an official holiday celebrated every June 20th. Notably, it was on the first Martyr's Day celebration in 1991 in Asmara that Isaias Afewerki, then secretary general of the EPLF, introduced himself publicly to the civilian population, delivering the opening speech (Woldemikael 2008).

The ethos of sacrifice represented by martyrs was first established during the struggle for independence. This fight was not only an armed struggle on the ground against Ethiopian troops, but also a cultural revolution among Eritreans led by the EPLF. Constructing and communicating powerful narratives about Eritrean history and identity was a core activity of the EPLF. The Front waged infopolitical battle through the prolific production of nationalist media in the form of radio broadcasts, pamphlets, posters, videos, newsletters, staged performances of music and dance, slogans, and communiqués that were circulated locally and transnationally (Hagos 2002). The nationalist narratives and communiqués generated by the leadership in Eritrea had a strong impact on the diaspora, as McCoy observes: "After 1975, as the Eritreans fled in huge numbers into neighboring Sudan and to Europe and the United States, the information vacuum which confronted the Eritreans in the diaspora was filled by EPLF mass media" (1995, 37). The perspectives presented to the diaspora through EPLF media and informational meetings held in EPLF offices established abroad, moreover, were particularly powerful because world press coverage of the conflict was inconsistent and often lacked sophisticated analysis of the historical and political context (McCoy 1995). The EPLF was not only highly effective in communicating its version of Eritrean politics, it was also "relatively ruthless in dealing with dissidents" (Woldemikael 1991, 35).

Thirty years of war did not so much liberate Eritrea as create it. It did so through a transnational network that drew Eritreans around the globe into the struggle for independence in various capacities. Eritreans in North America held weekly study groups, some even slept on the floor rather than in beds in solidarity with the guerrilla fighters in "the field," or *meda*, as Eritreans refer to it in Tigrinya. Some others actually left the safety of North America and Europe to join the fighters. Eritreans in many countries maintained links with one another and with the liberation front that they supported emotionally, materially, and politically. Yearly meetings in Bologna, Italy, brought members of the diaspora together with EPLF representatives from Eritrea. Eritreans in diaspora demonstrated their nationalism in part through remittances, which were "an important source of external funding during the armed struggle" (Fessehatzion 2005, 169). Taxi drivers, parking-lot attendants, and others in low-paid service economy jobs (where much of the Eritrean population in diaspora is employed) contributed millions of dollars to the EPLF.

Over three decades, the EPLF successfully mobilized the population of Eritrea and Eritreans in diaspora, and at independence it became the ruling party of Eritrea's one-party state, the People's Front for Democracy and Justice. Since independence the Eritrean state has drawn on the culture of the EPLF to construct national political culture. The preamble to the Eritrean Constitution states: "We the people of Eritrea, united in a common struggle for our rights and common destiny, standing on the solid ground of unity and justice bequeathed by our martyrs and combatants." It goes on to assert that the "unity, equality, love for truth and justice, self-reliance and hard work, which we nurtured during our revolutionary struggle for independence and which helped us to triumph, must become the core of our national values." The constitution (which has moral authority if not legal standing, since it was widely publicized and ratified but never implemented) lays out the words of the oaths of office by which officials are to be sworn in to public service. The oaths are sworn, not in the name of any god, but rather "in the name of the

Eritrean martyrs." The Eritrean Constitution, thus, locates Eritreanness in the history of war and self-sacrifice for the nation.

President Isaias, in a speech he delivered on Eritrea's 16th Independence Day celebration May 24, 2007, outlined various plans for Eritrea, including modernizing Eritrean agriculture and achieving food security, then stated:

> How long will it take to implement, stage by stage, all the objectives listed above and to secure fulfillment of our needs? Inarguably, this cannot be achieved overnight. Nevertheless, *to shorten the time, redoubled efforts and sacrifice will always be necessary.* (emphasis added)

The president's speech focused on development and national security, while saying nothing about the constitution or democracy. Toward the end of his speech, President Isaias expressed thanks and congratulations "to all my compatriots at home and abroad," making it clear he was also addressing Eritreans in diaspora. Finally, he closed with: "Glory to our Martyrs who made our existence possible." President Isaias's assertion that the time needed to achieve certain national goals will be shortened by greater sacrifices, but that the need for sacrifice will never end, rather, it "will always be necessary," captures the ethos of sacrificial citizenship. The president's invocation of martyrs "who made our existence possible" adds a historical and spiritual dimension to the sacrifices he demands. Moreover, if Eritrea would not exist without martyrs, then by implication, to resist sacrificing is to threaten Eritrea's very existence as a nation. Isaias's inclusion of the diaspora ("compatriots abroad") makes clear they are not exempt from the call for sacrifice. The speech notably was accessible to Eritreans in diaspora since someone posted it on Dehai the same day it was delivered.

Like the EPLF out of which it grew, the PFDJ sees its role as leading society in order to transform it. In that sense, the PFDJ is best understood as a vanguard party which functions differently than does a political party within a democratic government. In its role as vanguard, the regime operates on the assumption that one of the responsibilities of the state is to tell people what to think. It does so through government-controlled media and domination of the public sphere in Eritrea. This infopolitics involves not only disseminating powerful narratives, but suppressing potential alternatives through censorship and secrecy. As a poster on Dehai put it:

> Information is also a privilege of the EPLF [PFDJ]. They decide what, how much and when we should be told about things that are directly affecting our

lives and future. . . . When we do get informed, it is usually last of all, after the state has already made its undebatable, irrevocable/unilateral decisions. (Dehai post, October 24, 1998, ellipses and material in brackets added)

In this political context, Eritrea's citizens are not constructed as the free, self-managing individuals imagined in neoliberal regimes (Ong 2006), but as masses that need to be mobilized by leaders (Muller 2006). In a widely publicized statement in May 2008, President Isaias asserted that Eritreans might not be ready for elections for another three or four decades (Wallechinsky 2009, 4–5). He reiterated this view the following year in an hour-long interview for Swedish television that quickly attracted global Eritrean attention on YouTube, stating bluntly, "We will not conduct elections any time soon. We have our ways of allowing participation" (YouTube video 2009; also see Bernal 2013b). An Amnesty International report notes, "The government has not allowed the development of an independent civil society outside the PFDJ. No independent NGOs have been allowed" (www .freeeritreanjournalists.org/background.html, accessed February 15, 2012). The Eritrean state seeks to dominate all aspects of Eritrean life. The state is a primary actor in the economy and many enterprises are owned by the PFDJ. There is no organized opposition within the country. There has been no free press since 2001.

Organizations that are allowed to exist, such as the National Union of Eritrean Women, may at times appear to represent civil society or operate as nongovernmental organizations (NGOs), but they grew directly out of EPLF mass organizations and remain closely linked to the state. The public sphere is mobilized and dominated by the government, and there is little scope or tolerance for independent perspectives. As one analyst notes: "decision-making powers are concentrated in a tiny core of political and military leaders . . . the regime is extremely closed, and almost no reliable uncensored information can be obtained" (Bundegaard 2004, 35–36, ellipses added). Another observes that

[t]he structure of government and party governance . . . gives a clear line of command from the President . . . all the way down to the smallest village. Accountability is one-directional, always to the upper level of command and not to the constituency supposed to be served . . . (Tronvoll 2009, 59, ellipses added)

The ethos of sacrificial citizenship is associated with the militarization of governance. This is especially evident in Eritrea's national service program.

National service began as an eighteen-month period of military training, service work, and socialization, required of all young men and women between the ages of eighteen and forty, but has turned into an open-ended period during which the state exercises direct control over youth and deploys them where it will (Kibreab 2009b; Muller 2008; Human Rights Watch 2009). The construction of sacrificial citizenship, while rooted in history, is projected into the present and the future where the nation's survival is seen as constantly under threat. Since independence, a series of external and internal threats to Eritrean nationhood, especially the 1998–2000 border war with Ethiopia, have reinforced the notion that, fundamentally, national leaders are military commanders and citizens are soldiers. The fact that national service has been interpreted by the leadership as conferring on them the right to keep citizens indefinitely, in paramilitary formations away from their homes and families, at the disposal of the state, enforces sacrificial citizenship on the nation's youth.

While many nations can call on citizens to defend their sovereignty, in the context of Eritrea, the obligation of citizens to die for the nation is not an abstract ideal. It is a material fact rooted in the devastation of three decades of war that brought Eritrea into being as an independent nation, the subsequent border war from 1998 to 2000, and the potential for future wars given the aggressiveness of Eritrea's leadership and the volatile politics of the Horn of Africa. In this context the state's elevation of the martyr as a symbol of nationalism reflects the implicit social contract between citizens and the state in which the state acts as if it owns the lives of Eritreans who are obligated to sacrifice for the nation. The state's claim on citizens' lives and on their deaths extends indefinitely into the future and is made tangible in the present by state violence against external enemies like Ethiopians and internal enemies like its critics.

The combination of an open-ended duration of compulsory national service, along with the lack of democratic freedoms, makes for a starkly one-sided relationship with the state. Citizens are disempowered from voicing their interests and making demands on the state but are required to serve national interests as unilaterally defined by the state. In this relationship, to demand something from the state is tantamount to disloyalty, because the state is supposedly serving the common good and ensuring Eritrea's survival as a nation. Thus, to demand something from the state, or even to resist sacrificing, is to undermine the state's ability to succeed and, therefore, by this logic, ultimately to threaten or betray Eritrea.

The ways state power is understood, exercised, and experienced by Eritreans, thus, is that the citizen must sacrifice for the nation, with death being the greatest sacrifice. This differs from Mbembe's notion of the necropoliti-

cal state deciding who is to live and who is to die, and from Agamben's notion of "bare life" as that of a subject stripped of membership in the political
community who therefore can be killed with impunity. The Eritrean state is
not engaged in creating an expendable subcategory within the nation whose
lives can be sacrificed, but, rather, with constructing a universal citizenship
predicated on sacrifice. Its underlying principle seems to be—in order for the
nation to live, the citizens must (be willing) to die. The nation (as embodied
in President Isaias and the PFDJ government) in this formulation represents
the greater good and the public interest, while the citizen, in contrast, is potentially self-interested and divisive, pursuing narrow loyalties, perhaps to an
ethnic or religious community, and therefore is suspect and possibly traitor-
ous. By this political logic, the citizen's commitment to the greater good of
the nation can never completely be sure until after he or she has died for the
nation. The martyr thus represents the ideal citizen.

There is an unboundedness in the state's demands on its citizens, which
extends to the diaspora. Eritrean sovereignty is rooted in relations of loyalty
and obedience, rather than the rule of law. People are imprisoned without
charges, and the constitution has not been implemented. In this political context, then, it is not a question of who falls inside the law and who falls outside
it, but rather who is seen as for or against the regime. The language of individual rights is not legitimated in this formulation; the focus is on society as
a whole, with the state presenting itself as the representative of the whole. As
Conrad (2005, 224) observes, the lack of distinction between Eritrean people,
the state, and the current regime has allowed "the current political leadership
to demand absolute loyalty on the basis of the assumption that nation (or people), state and government/party form an inseparable entity." The militaristic
orientation of the state draws legitimacy from the EPLF's past military success as well as from its own hyperpreparedness for war and perceived threats
to Eritrea's security. This works in turn to legitimate the top-down, centralized organization of command. There is a disturbing echo of what Kligman
(1998, 245) describes in Ceausescu's Romania:

> Under totalizing or authoritarian regimes such as these, the reach of the state is
> maximal, and the rights of persons as individuals are broadly denied. Instead,
> persons as members of the social body (the "people-as-one") *are considered
> properties of the nation-state to which they belong*. (emphasis added)

This kind of national belonging whereby people are treated as belonging to
the state is reflected in Eritrea's open-ended national service program. It is

also evidenced in conditions such as those described in a 2012 US government travel warning about Eritrea, which notes that "Eritrea has complicated citizenship laws and *does not recognize renunciation of Eritrean citizenship*" (http://travel.state.gov/trave/cis_patw/cis/cis_1111.html, accessed April 25, 2012, emphasis added). The same warning explains that people regarded as Eritrean citizens, even if they possess a US passport, may be drafted into national military service, arrested, and denied exit visas from Eritrea.

Seen in this context, the official rhetoric honoring martyrs can be read as concealing the underlying expendability of citizens' lives and the subordination of their lives to the nation. Although the religious overtones of the term "martyr" work to sacralize life, at least in death, and, therefore give state discourse about martyrs the appearance of attaching great meaning to life and to the loss of life, the celebration of martyrs in fact coexists easily with a necropolitical understanding of human life as expendable. There is an interchangability among citizen, soldier, and martyr. This underlying connection between citizens and soldiers and the special meaning attached to dying for the nation are not unique to Eritrea but present in all militaristic nations, with numerous parallels, for example, with the United States and Israel. But, the centrality of sacrifice in Eritrean political culture and the particular way in which it is elaborated by the Eritrean state are distinctive. Moreover, while martyrs are honored by the Eritrean state, it is not individual war heroes that are celebrated but, rather, the principle of loyalty to the death that is elevated above the lives of individuals. It is the sacrifice that is honored and not the person. From an infopolitical perspective, by calling the war dead national "martyrs," the Eritrean state acts to claim these deaths for itself.

It is significant that during the protracted struggle for independence the EPLF kept deaths secret. Woldemikael (2008, 274–75) argues that

> the widely acknowledged high morale of the EPLF fighters can be partially explained by the fact that the front controlled the flow of information about its casualties with strict secrecy, while it broadcast its achievements through its mass media and organized supporters both within and outside of Eritrea.

Families were not officially notified that their loved ones had been killed until several years after the end of the war when the government issued official martyr's certificates to families honoring each of the dead. Even so, mothers were instructed not to mourn their children because they had died for their country. This tight control over information and careful management of its form, content, and interpretation when released are hallmarks of the EPLF's and later the PFDJ's infopolitics. A similar shroud of secrecy around the lives lost was maintained by the government for several years after the border war, as will be discussed in chapter 4.

Sovereignty involves forms of state censorship and of state authorship, the management of information and media, the production of national narratives, the creation of potent symbols, and the defining of appropriate sentiments. The importance of exercising power over communication as a dimension of sovereignty and using communication strategically as a political tactic are particularly revealed in the Eritrean state's relation to the diaspora. This is so because the daily lives and practices of Eritreans in diaspora are not molded by the everyday presence of the Eritrean state that makes itself manifest in a myriad of ways to citizens in Eritrea (Bozzini 2011). In the absence of these quotidian interactions, it is largely in the realm of communication that the relationship between Eritreans overseas and the Eritrean government is fostered and maintained.

## YOUR MONEY OR YOUR LIFE: SACRIFICIAL CITIZENSHIP AND THE DIASPORA

The Eritrean state officially recognizes Eritreans in diaspora as Eritrean nationals, issuing them national identity cards and extending to them some of the rights and obligations of citizenship, as described in the introduction. These relations of diasporic citizenship partially include the diaspora in the nation as a category of insider/outsiders. In terms of the social contract between citizens and the state, Eritreans in diaspora also can be seen as an "offshore citizenry" in the sense that they are a vital economic resource for the Eritrean state outside its territory from which it can extract wealth. The diaspora are also in some sense "outsourced citizens" since the Eritrean state is under no obligation to provide them with services, welfare, or jobs. Those costs are outsourced, borne by the countries where Eritreans now live. In this respect, members of the diaspora are ideal citizens who consume no state resources but provide funds to the state. They are "outsourced citizens," whose welfare and security are maintained by other states, while they constitute an offshore resource for the Eritrean state. Extracting wealth from the diaspora, however, requires maintaining their sense of national belonging, and extending relations of sovereignty and citizenship into areas not demarcated by national territory or determined by legal identities.

The dual system in which Eritreans in diaspora use their foreign (non-Eritrean) citizenship for most purposes while using Eritrean national identity cards for Eritrea-related matters allows Eritreans in diaspora to simultaneously occupy multiple legal identities without creating legal problems, and without forcing individuals to choose between Eritrean national identity and citizenship in their country of residence. Eritrean national identity cards, for example, allow people to enter Eritrea as nationals who require no visa when they visit, even though their passports identify them as foreigners. National identity cards also serve to identify members of the diaspora as Eritrean nationals in conducting any Eritrean legal matters.

The transfer of funds from the diaspora to national leaders in Eritrea began during the fight for independence. When the 2 percent tax was introduced after independence, it was seen as representing a *reduced* obligation to Eritrea, compared to the demands for financial support that had been placed on the diaspora during the struggle. As a Dehai poster looking back on those days saw it: "The amount of contributions was reduced to the minimum and all opted for the 2% rehabilitation ('Mehwey') tax" (Dehai post, April 9, 1998). What started as a tax for Eritrea's postwar rehabilitation later became institutionalized simply as the diaspora tax. Many Eritreans apparently do pay something, though, not unlike taxpayers elsewhere, they reduce the amount owed by underestimating their incomes, for example. This has been easy to do since the state has essentially relied on an honor system. As Eritreans everywhere grow disenchanted with the Isaias regime, however, the Eritrean state has been seeking means to exact compliance. Recently, rumors circulated among the diaspora that Eritrean authorities in Canada were planning to ask for supporting documentation, such as Canadian tax returns. There are reports that this is already being done in some cases in Sweden. To date, however, enforcement measures remain variegated and piecemeal.

In addition to paying taxes as required by the state, Eritreans in diaspora have an established record of voluntary remittances to Eritrea. Not only do they send funds to support family members, but they also organize and contribute to various rehabilitation, relief, and development efforts. During the 1998–2000 border conflict with Ethiopia, moreover, the diaspora poured millions of dollars into government coffers to support the war. These wartime donations reportedly came to $400 million in 1999 and exceeded $600 million in 2000 (sources cited in Matsuoka and Sorenson 2001, 78). In 2002, Eritrea was the most remittance-dependent country in Africa, receiving around US$206 million from the diaspora which accounted for nearly one-third of the GDP (Fessehatzion 2005). More recent data are scarce; the *World Bank Migration and Remittances Factbook 2012* has none on Eritrea, for example (World Bank 2012). Other sources put remittances to Eritrea at $411 million or 37 percent of Eritrea's GDP, a rate far above the 5 percent average for the African continent as a whole (www.ifad.org, accessed March 30, 2013). The flow of money to Eritrea from the diaspora thus has been and continues to be quite significant.

The participation of Eritreans in diaspora in national projects, however, cannot be compelled in the same ways that the state controls citizens within its own territory. The regime makes considerable efforts to reach out to Eritreans in diaspora through offices established in many locations and through a steady flow of regular briefings, public relations campaigns, youth conferences, musical performances, and other events carried out overseas. Recognizing the importance of the internet to the diaspora, the PFDJ and the Ministry of Information each launched official websites, shaebia.org, in 2001 and shabait.com in 2003, to send the regime's message out and put its spin on national political developments. The names of these official websites reverberate with nationalist history, since *shaebia* (which is a transliteration of the Arabic word for "of the people" or "of the masses") is commonly used as a shorthand name for the EPLF. The PFDJ is likewise the "People's," Front, so the usage is current while calling up the heroic past.

Since the construction of sovereign power by the Eritrean state is one in which the bounds of state authority are not clearly defined, this allows the state to extend its sovereignty to the diaspora in ways that strict legal constructions of state power or citizenship would not permit. The fact that the diaspora are physically and geographically located outside of Eritrea, but are not outside of Eritrean political culture, is evident on Eritrean diaspora websites. Many posts reiterate EPLF/PFDJ national narratives about the struggle for independence, assert the importance of Eritrean sovereignty, and express the obligation of Eritreans in diaspora to sacrifice for the nation. It is not unusual for posters to invoke the sacrifices made by martyrs or to use sign offs, like "remember our martyrs" or "remember our martyred brothers and sisters." Such phrases are often written in transliterated Tigrinya, in contrast to the body of the post, which is in English. This perhaps reflects the formulaic and ritualistic quality of these phrases as EPLF and PFDJ refrains. This does not mean the sentiments are not heartfelt, however. Posters have lost siblings, parents, and other friends and relatives to the war which took many civilian lives as well as those of combatants. As a poster on June 4, 1997, on Dehai put it: "who hasn't lost someone . . . *swue* [martyred man], *sweti* [martyred woman], *swuat* [martyrs]. . . . In telling a story, it is a story of all of them, of us, and about us. . . . Their absence tells what it cost us to get here" (ellipses, italics, and translations in brackets added).

The martyr is both an abstract symbol of Eritrean nationalism and a lived experience of personal loss. Losses, moreover, did not end with independence since the border war took new lives. The martyr may work as a potent national symbol because of this multiscalar quality; it simultaneously represents an abstract ideal and a known loved one. All Eritreans are in some sense survivors of the wars that have cost so many lives, disrupted others, and dispersed families and communities. The symbol of the martyr resonates with the diaspora as with other Eritreans because of such losses. On June 20, which is Martyr's Day in Eritrea, someone posted a poem on Dehai "in loving memory of all our Martyrs" that went in part, as follows:

> My eyes search and seek in vain
> To make some sense of all this pain
> My heart and soul together pray
> To be with you so far away
> I curse that day, that battle day
> You left me here and went away
> To a far place, so quiet and brave
> While I wander this vast grave
> (Dehai post June 20, 2006)

The poem conveys something of the ways that national struggles have left all Eritreans as survivors with deep losses, who not only grieve for the dead but also may experience living as "wander[ing] a vast grave," while faced with the impossible task of making "sense of all this pain." The poem is, moreover, an example of how Eritreans in diaspora take part in national events such as Martyr's Day through the websites.

For Eritreans in diaspora, there is an added element involved in remembering and venerating martyrs, however, because at some point members of the diaspora fled to safety in order to survive, while other Eritreans, those who died and those who lived through the war, remained behind. Thus, as Conrad (2006b:124) found: "Eritreans in diaspora, who lived 'comfortably' abroad while others sacrificed their health and lives, grew up with a feeling of indebtedness to the EPLF and its 'martyrs.'"

However natural some form of survivor's guilt might be, it is also actively cultivated by the Eritrean state. While the state demands that people in Eritrea sacrifice by giving themselves and/or their children to the state in war and national service, the state calls on Eritreans in diaspora to give money. A flyer distributed widely in California in 2008 by the Eritrean Consulate in

Oakland offers a telling example of how the state promotes sacrificial citizenship among the diaspora. The bold headline of the flyer reads: "SPONSOR A MARTYR'S FAMILY" (the text of the flyer is written in English on one side of the sheet and in Tigrinya on the reverse). The martyrs to which it refers are those killed in the 1998–2000 border war. Underneath the headline are several bulleted lines of text that declare: "I commit myself to sponsor a martyr's family, I will support the family for a minimum of two years by sending them thirty (30) US dollars per month."

This call to help the families of martyrs plays on the survivor's guilt of Eritreans in diaspora. Reading between the lines reveals a substitution at work: money must take the place of lives. The underlying message is that others (martyrs) have given their lives for Eritrea, you (living in diaspora) should (at least) give money. This call for the diaspora to send money also brings into play the intermediate position occupied by the diaspora as people from the global south, and from one of its poorest regions, who are located in the global north and therefore relatively privileged with greater access to jobs and incomes. The contrast between conditions in Eritrea and life overseas is underlined by the flyer's statement that a family in Eritrea can be supported on $30 per month.

While Eritreans in the diaspora are called on to give money in lieu of giving their lives, there is also another substitution at work in this flyer. Instead of the government asking for direct contributions to strengthen the capacity of the Eritrean state to provide for development and welfare, martyrs' families are substituted as the recipients of the diaspora's financial support. The use of martyrs' families to request resources from the diaspora can be interpreted as a deft political strategy on the part of the Eritrean state to keep the diaspora's resources flowing into government coffers, even as the diaspora, like the Eritrean public generally, grow increasingly dissatisfied with the regime. The flyer's appeal thus involves a double substitution: giving your money as a substitute for giving your life for Eritrea, and giving your money to support martyrs' families, rather than to support the state.

The martyr's family is a powerful signifier, moreover, because it represents materially the connections between the nation's living and its dead. This is a form of biopolitics in which the martyr's membership in a surviving family serves to embody the link between individuals and the nation. This link connects the past (the war dead), the present (the surviving family members), and the future (the continued survival of Eritreans and Eritrea). The state's exhortation to "support a martyr's family" thus connects biological kinship to the symbolic kinship whereby a nation is understood as a people. The martyrs' family powerfully illustrates the idea of Eritrea as a nation constructed through relations of sacrifice. As Varzi (2006, 62) has written about Iran, martyrdom, in effect, creates blood relations, "a culture of survivors, bound by blood to the nation."

The long war for independence caused suffering, displacement, and loss of lives in ways that continue to shape Eritreans' lives and outlooks. The 1998–2000 border war, thus, echoed earlier traumas and inflamed old wounds, while inflicting new wounds and creating new victims of displacement of death. The flyer is an example of how the regime seeks to harness these shared tragedies for its own purposes. In the flyer, the principle of sacrificial citizenship is invoked by the state through the figure of the martyr, and the state's failure to provide for its citizens is recast into an obligation on the part of the diaspora to sacrifice by giving their money to support martyrs' families.

Such strategies on the part of the Eritrean state can only be effective to the extent that Eritreans in diaspora remain part of the political culture promoted by the PFDJ. The Eritrean state, therefore, clearly has an interest in maintaining the transnational political field that sustains diasporic citizenship and actively works to do so. The experience and meaning of diaspora for Eritreans cannot be understood apart from the power of the dominant national discourses and political symbols that serve to connect the diaspora to Eritrea. The next section examines how obligations to the nation are discussed in the online public sphere, revealing the ways that Eritreans in diaspora understand themselves as Eritrean subjects with obligations to the nation.

## DIASPORA WEBSITES AND SERVICE TO THE NATION

The internet did not create the transnational political field connecting the diaspora to the Eritrean state, but it ultimately transformed it, empowering the diaspora in new ways. The creation of Dehai (and, later, Asmarino, Awate, and other websites) facilitated the diaspora's participation in homeland politics and its self-constitution as a diasporic community. The development of an online public sphere, which is analyzed in detail in chapters 2 and 3, opened the possibility for Eritreans in diaspora not only to participate in the consumption and dissemination of national narratives but also to collectively construct and circulate alternative perspectives on Eritrean history, politics, and identity. The centralized, top-down infopolitics of the Eritrean state makes these online activities especially significant. Despite the potential freedom offered by the internet and by living outside Eritrea's borders, however, the degree to which posts reflect EPLF/PFDJ political culture is striking. This was particularly the case throughout the 1990s. As one Dehai poster critically observed in 1998:

> Over the years, I have discussed several issues with many supporters of EPLF/ PFDJ. In my opinion, the one characteristic that stands out with many of them is their intense, inflexible and often obsessive attachment to their organiza- tion. I have often wondered what the source of such mind set as that elevates a group (EPLF/PFDJ) to an almost divine nature. An example of that mind-set is evident [in a recent post that insists that the Eritrean government is] "IN THE OPINION OF THE OVERWHELMING MAJORITY, THE BEST GOVERNMENT, ELECTED OR OTHERWISE, IN THE WORLD TO- DAY!!!" (Dehai post, October 6, 1998, materials in brackets added)

The idea that Eritrea is unique and its government, though unelected, is "the best" is a view that President Isaias actively continues to promote. When asked to describe the political and economic system of Eritrea in a 2009 interview for Swedish television, he replied, "it's the best in the world." The interview presented President Isaias (and therefore, to some Eritreans, Eritrea) in a crit- ical light. An Eritrean posting on Dehai from the United Kingdom responded to the interview, defending Eritrea with a message that began:

> Eritrea was officially 18 years old on May 24, 2009 and her careful and diligent growth has attracted the world. In a volatile region, her upbringing was not easy and privileged to say the least. Eritrea had to suffer and work quadruple as much to set herself free from colonizers. In the last 50 years, she paid more than 85,000 Martyrs and tens of thousands were wounded to bring and pre- serve the hard fought freedom. (Dehai post, June 4, 2009)

The post ends with the following assertion: "Those who declared death on Eritrea have died and Eritrea is there and those who are declaring death on Eritrea will die and Eritrea will always be there. God Bless the Eritrean Mar- tyrs. Victory to the Mass." The imprint of PFDJ narratives that cast Eritrea as a nation in a constant struggle to the death for sovereignty, and whose contin- ued existence depends on martyrdom is clear.

In terms of sacrificial citizenship, many posts over the years indicate that the notion of a national duty on the part of the diaspora to help Eritrea comes not only from the state, but arises from within the diaspora. The diaspora's sense of obligation to the Eritrean state is revealed by a survey conducted on Dehai by one of its members at the end of the 1990s. The survey was completed in January 1998, several months before the sudden outbreak of a the border war with Ethiopia, and therefore offers a window on ideas about obligations to the state during peace time. According to the results posted on January 12, 1998, only 59 of 1,100 registered Dehai members at the time responded, or a little over 5 percent, so the results may not be representative, but the poll nonetheless offers food for thought. Dehai, like other discussion websites, has many members who rarely post (referred to on Dehai as "silent readers") and also has many readers who are not registered members (sometimes referred to as "lurkers" in internet research). Therefore, in terms of its reach and influence, Dchai in 1998 was much larger than any of these numbers suggest. The poll is revealing, moreover, not simply through the responses to it, but in the way the questions themselves were framed.

The survey included a multiple-choice question about paying the diaspora tax that asked respondents to choose a phrase to complete the following statement: "With respect to the 2% of net income tax requirement." The highest percentage of respondents (50 percent) chose the answer: "I meet my obligation primarily because it is my duty." The next highest percent (16 percent) chose an answer that read, "I don't meet my obligation primarily because I forgot." Another 14 percent of respondents chose: "I meet my obligation primarily because I require services of the government." (This refers to the fact mentioned earlier that Eritreans in diaspora seeking to conduct Eritrean legal matters are asked to show some evidence of having paid taxes.) Finally, a mere 9 percent selected the response: "I don't meet my obligation primarily because of my principle."

Several interesting things are revealed here. Whether their behavior lives up to their words, nearly two-thirds (64 percent) of respondents say they pay the 2 percent tax. Furthermore, the majority of them say they are motivated by "duty" alone. Looking at the survey with regard to the question of duty, it is significant that all the multiple-choice answers employ the wording "my obligation" in reference to the tax. Most telling is the absence of any option that says something to the effect that "I don't think I am obligated to pay taxes to the government of Eritrea because I am a citizen of another country and already pay taxes there." This could fall under the vague "because of my principle" answer, but even that answer is phrased to preclude a direct challenge to the "obligation" itself, and the "principle" involved could easily be construed to mean opposition to the Eritrean government, rather than simply opposition to the requirement that the diaspora pay for it. On the subject of taxes, a 2002 post on Dehai asserted:

> Every year we must pay this two percent. This should be our responsibility. . . . Government can not run without taxation. We all must pay this 2% at least. As mathematician I have calculated if every Eritrean pay this two percent. This money can help a lot. Displaced people for food and shelter and farming, education. (Dehai post, April 23, 2002, ellipses added)

The poster closed his message with the EPLF slogan "*Awet Nehafash*" [Victory to the Masses] along with "God Bless Eritrea." The displaced people he referred to are those affected by the border war.

The border war, which broke out in May 1998 and ended in December 2000, was perceived by Eritreans in diaspora as a grave crisis that threatened Eritrea's existence, and they felt compelled to take action to save it. Dehai was filled with reports of fund-raising as Eritreans in diaspora poured their money from abroad into Eritrea. Eritreans in different locations seemed to compete with one another as they boasted online about the amount of funds that Eritreans in their city or region were sending to defend Eritrea (Bernal 2004). A post from an Eritrean in Norway begins, "Are you aware of a fund raising campaign for the defence of our country is going on among all Eritreans in the diaspora" (Dehai post, June 15, 1998). The post goes on to give detailed information about funds raised at a meeting in Oslo and includes instructions about where to send money. A long post written later that summer stated:

> The entire Eritrean population is rallying behind its government; and we Eritreans in the diaspora, women, men, young and old, are shouldering the ambassadorial responsibilities of our country with excellence, pride, and dignity. Although no one should thank anyboud [anybody] for meeting the sacred national obligation, I still feel that we should be congratulated for our relentless dedication to our people and our homeland. (Dehai post, August 4, 1998)

The wartime activities of the diaspora are explored in greater depth in chapter 2.

As powerful as the social contract of sacrificial citizenship has been in its hold over Eritreans, including those in diaspora, it does not go unquestioned. Posts and activities like those described above demonstrate the sense of duty that Eritreans in diaspora feel, and show the degree to which the value of sacrificing for the nation that is promoted by the national leadership has permeated Eritrean political culture. Yet, there have always been some who expressed critical perspectives. Today, their numbers and outspokenness have grown. However, even at the height of nationalist fervor, when Eritrea's territorial integrity and sovereignty were threatened and many Eritreans in diaspora were rallying to support the war effort, some voices were raised in dissent. For example, on October 24, 1998, a poster wrote on Dehai:

> The only basis for EPLF/PFDJ/Shabias hold on power is that it evicted military occupants of our country and replaced them with itself. The government of Eritrea with its property and authority is possessed by the EPLF/PFDJ, which is the only "legal" party in Eritrea. The judicial system is under EPLF's control, they decide what is legal and illegal. (Dehai post, October 24, 1998)

The listing of multiple names "EPLF/PFDJ/Shabia" may be the author's way of suggesting that no matter what you call it, or however the leadership changes its name, it still amounts to the same thing, a guerilla front that took power after a military victory. This post speaks directly to the nexus of issues that scholarship on sovereignty has raised including the role of violence in underpinning sovereignty and what that means for questions of legitimacy and the rule of law. The critique expressed here is particularly severe since it likens the government of Eritrea to the brutal Ethiopian regime of Colonel Mengistu and the Dergue when it says, "evicted military occupants . . . and replaced them with itself."

The border war turned out to be a high point of solidarity among Eritreans inside and outside the nation. Once the war ended, dissent became more widespread and more outspoken. The rising tide of dissent in cyberspace led not only to outspoken posts on Dehai but also to a florescence of new websites that sought to establish themselves as rivals of Dehai, the most successful of these being Awate and Asmarino. As a post on Awate on May 1, 2003, by "Awate staff" put it, Dehai was seen as "Shaebia lite," meaning that the views expressed there tended toward uncritical support of the government. Awate and Asmarino attracted readers and posters to their websites because posts expressing outspoken criticism received a more welcome response than on Dehai.

While Dehai was explicitly created as an open forum, free from censorship, posters frequently questioned the loyalty and impugned the motives or identities of fellow posters seen as too critical. Comments like, "How much are the Ethiopians paying you to write that?" and "our martyrs didn't give their lives so that you could complain," reflect struggles over the parameters of what can be said in the public sphere. In response to the rise of online dissent, an editorial titled "Reaffirming our values" and signed "by staff" appeared on Dehai on April 19, 2005. It reads in part:

> if we are to build this country, which was brought about through huge sacrifice, . . . then we need to build upon, reaffirm and recreate as collective Eritrean culture those values that enabled us to accomplish incredible feats—values such as commitment, heroism, self-sacrifice, patriotism, and self-reliance. We also need to remain vigilant and relentlessly fight against those negative tendencies that are currently trying to frustrate these positive national values. (ellipsis added)

The post ends with "Victory to these superior Eritrean values!"

It is significant that, as in the phrase, "if *we* are to build *this country*," posters in diaspora often write as if they were located in Eritrea. This is one way in which cyberspace is not simply deterritorialized, but, through its disconnection with geography, allows for reterritorialization. Not coincidentally, the values trumpeted by Dehai staff are the familiar cornerstones of the political culture constructed by the EPLF and perpetuated by the Eritrean state that stress commitment to the nation and self-sacrifice, rather than human rights, democracy, or civil liberties.

Contestation over the meaning and value of sacrifice and service to the nation are revealed in contrasting responses to the death of Eritrea's foreign minister, Ali Seid. On August 29, 2005, the day after his death, a post on Dehai apparently written by Dehai's webmanagers announced that the "veteran fighter and Foreign Minister" had passed away and that the Government of Eritrea had declared three days of national mourning. The post went on to state, "The Eritrean Online Community Network, Dehai expresses deep sorrow on this sad occasion. Visitors: Please use the form below to pass your condolence messages to the family of Mr. Ali Seid back home in Eritrea." The form was set up with a blank message box in which to write, along with a link to click to send the message. This kind of post does not simply facilitate the diaspora's participation in national events, it promotes it and, furthermore, seeks to orchestrate its form and content.

A divergent perspective on the death of this former guerilla fighter and government official was expressed the following day in a post on Asmarino:

The task of government is to protect its people from poverty and conflicts, create jobs, providing health care and education. The government of Eritrea does the contrary it destroys every thing and creates conflicts/enemies.

By the way we were told that Eritrean mothers were uluating when they were told the death of their beloved sons and daughters because they died for their country. The death of foreign minister should be handled the same way. Lets ululate because he died while serving the nation. (Asmarino post, August 30, 2005)

This post uses irony to point out several contradictions, highlighting the contrast between the government's mourning of its own for three days, while telling parents not to mourn the loss of their children. It also questions what "serving the nation" really means, when the Eritrean government is not serving the people by providing development, peace, or public services. The post thus raises issues that challenge the implicit social contract of sacrificial citizenship that governs Eritreans' relationship to the state.

On Awate, a website known for its critical stance toward the government and its numerous Muslim posters, a poster goes even further, to directly question the state's demands on the diaspora. In a post that goes on for three-and-a-half, single-spaced pages the poster asserts: "The Eritrean people [are] living in 'banlieues' and [President] Isaias [is] squandering their hard earned currency arming rebels without a cause" (Awate post June 27, 2006; bracketed material added for clarity). This one line speaks volumes in calling up the racism, exclusion, and relative economic hardship experienced by hardworking Eritreans in diaspora who nonetheless send money to the Eritrean government, a government that some have come to see as pursuing militarization as an end in itself ("arming rebels without a cause"). The poster's use of the term *banlieu* invokes the ethnic and immigrant riots on the outskirts of Paris in 2005. It thus situates Eritreans as part of a larger African and North African diaspora, as well as part of a racialized, stigmatized population that faces hardship and exclusion in the global north. The term *banlieu* (which literally means suburb in French, but in many contexts is more aptly translated as "slum" or "ghetto") also signals the economic and social traumas associated with resettling abroad. Such images stand in stark contrast to how the diaspora feel they are seen in Eritrea, as living easy lives and enjoying access to abundant resources. Eritreans in diaspora often decry these stereotypes to one another and yet feel compelled to try to live up to them, at least in the eyes of their relatives back home. The poster's reference to Eritreans' "hard earned currency" is almost a play on words, combining the notion of hard currency (which Eritrea needs from abroad) and the hard work that Eritreans in diaspora perform to earn money. The poster is critiquing not only the state's prioritizing of militarization but also the specific role of the diaspora as a disenfranchised, exploited population being used as a source of financial resources by the Eritrean government.

A poster on Asmarino in 2012 advanced a bold critique in a very long post, the kind generally referred to as an article in Eritrean circles, that was titled "'Hadnetna' from Sahel to the Sinai." The title means: "'Our unity' from Sahel [the base region of the EPLF fighters] to the Sinai [the desert where in recent years Eritreans fleeing the country and trying to seek asylum in Israel are being kidnapped, raped, tortured and killed]." The poster asks in bold font, **"what kind of monster is this 'Eritrea' that it requires the kind of hadnet [unity] that demands endless sacrifice of its children, be it in death, slavery or rape, to sustain itself?"** (Asmarino post, December 1, 2012). The "slavery" he refers to is the national service program which is one of the factors behind the exodus of young people from Eritrea in recent years.

As these examples show, posters on Dehai, Awate, and Asmarino are drawing connections among issues of legitimacy, sovereignty, sacrifice, and violence. They are grappling with the state's prevailing narratives about these values, and their meaning for all Eritreans as well as for the relationship of the diaspora to the nation. At the most fundamental level, diaspora and the internet challenge the biopolitical basis of state power because subjects in diaspora and posters in cyberspace are outside the state's daily management of life (and death) and physically beyond the state's coercive grasp. The diaspora routinely reach the state in disembodied forms, through the money they send and through their internet posts. The state reaches the diaspora through a kind of diplomacy and soft power, rather than through the direct sovereign/citizen relations that operate in national territory under the government's command. Infopolitics are especially crucial in the state-diaspora relationship. As seen in this chapter, a shared political culture connects the diaspora to the state, and the lines of struggle over the limits of sovereignty and sacrifice are not clear-cut between the diaspora and the state, but rather crosscut a transnational field. The online public sphere created by Eritreans in diaspora offers an important arena of infopolitical struggle.

The next chapter explores the development and contours of the public sphere that Eritreans in diaspora created on the internet from its beginnings in the 1990s through 2000. I argue that, during this first decade, Eritreans used cyberspace to extend the nation and the state's sovereignty beyond its borders.

# CHAPTER 2

# Diasporic Citizenship and the Public Sphere: Creating National Space Online

Miles separate us, and many of us do not know each other personally, yet there is a string that keeps us bound to each other to make us one and the same. I believe, it is the greatest blessing we could have as one people. . . . Our hearts hum the same song when it comes to the love and passion, the desire and wishes that we nurture for Eritrea.

(Dehai post, December 16, 1996)

I hope and pray that everyone of us recognizes . . . the power of genuine and earnest participation, the responsibility to keep Eritrea a free nation; the obligation to pass on healthy legacy to our children and finally the individual and collective responsibility for how we handle the opportunity of a free Eritrea in its infancy.

(Dehai post, October 8, 1998)

Some members do not realize that DEHAI is an Eritrean bayto (bayto = town hall, forum). If a member wishes to be heard, he/she needs to respect the members of the bayto. They are both his/her audience and his/her judge and jury. Custom demands it and the law (the Charter) demands it.

(Dehai post, April 25, 2002)

The establishment of the online public sphere by Eritreans in diaspora is simultaneously a product of the location of the diaspora outside the Eritrean state and the intensity of their ongoing connection to it. Through Dehai and the websites that followed the diaspora created Eritrean space in cyberspace. In this chapter and the next one, I chart a historical shift in the diaspora's use of cyberspace from one that can be seen primarily as extending Eritrea's borders beyond national territory to one that uses cyberspace as a kind of off-shore platform from which the state can be openly challenged. Dehai (www.dehai.org) exemplifies the first kind of engagement, while Asmarino (www.asmarino.com) and Awate (awate.com) reflect the second strategy. At any given time, however, some posts can be found on any of these websites that reflect either of these strategies. I contend that the diaspora engage with the internet in ways that redefine what the nation is and where it is located, producing, as well as contesting, relations of sovereignty and citizenship.

Through the websites, Eritreans in various locations and from various backgrounds and walks of life from their origins in Eritrea to their circumstances abroad are brought into a common space of communication with each other that has no off-line counterpart. The websites are significant, moreover, as an initiative by ordinary people (rather than by an organization, officials, or government) to share knowledge and analyze national politics collectively. The websites, furthermore, allow a new form of communication from Eritreans to their national leaders. This second aspect of communication is the obvious one that scholars identify as political and on which much attention has focused. However, studies of publics and the public sphere (Calhoun 1992; Warner 2005; Boyer 2006) make clear that ordinary people discussing, producing analyses, and debating each other in informal settings constitutes a vital political activity.

## DISTANCE AND CONNECTION: MEDIATING DIASPORA THROUGH CYBERSPACE

Eritreans in diaspora feel empowered to speak for and about Eritrea and Eritrean affairs; they consider themselves and are considered by the government to be significant national actors. Websites devoted to Eritrean politics have captured the energies and attentions of many Eritreans in diaspora since the early 1990s. Indeed, the pull of the websites is so strong and the demands on an individual's time so great if they wish to keep abreast of the latest posts and, perhaps, respond to them, that some Eritreans liken it to an addiction. The Eritrean online public sphere is increasingly variegated and continues to develop, but the three websites I analyze, Dehai, Asmarino, and Awate, have been particularly central to Eritrean politics. All three were created by and are managed by Eritreans living in the United States and use English as the primary language.

The websites serve a transnational community with the majority of posts written by Eritreans living in North America and Europe, though messages also are posted from Australia, South Africa, Saudi Arabia, and from Eritrea, among other places. Posters' locations are often indicated by their email addresses (ending in .de for Germany and .ca for Canada, for example) and many posters choose to include their city in their signature lines. Posters generally use their real names. Thus, Eritreans who post are not for the most part seeking anonymity in cyberspace. (However, I made the choice not to quote posters by name to protect people's identities as is common in ethnographic research. This choice seems particularly warranted now that the Eritrean state has become so intolerant of dissent.)

Small groups created and manage the various websites, but their content is collectively contributed by various participants through their individual postings. The success of the websites in attracting posters and readers over the years rests on the continual flow of new content that is contributed by posters and sometimes by the website managers themselves. Some posters are dedicated and prolific writers who have been contributing a high volume of carefully crafted essays, spoofs, and commentary on a regular basis for years; others are occasional posters. While posters include students and professionals, some of the most prominent writers based in the United States are known to be taxi drivers and parking-lot attendants. Their invisibility on the American scene presents a sharp contrast to their stature as internet intellectuals and media personalities whose names are known throughout Eritrean communities because of the quality and abundance of their posts (Bernal 2005a).

The establishment of Dehai and the subsequent founding of other websites, most notably Asmarino and Awate, stand out as one of the most significant initiatives undertaken by Eritreans independently of the state. In fact, due to the Eritrean state's highly centralized orchestration of political expression and practice, and its suppression of independent media within Eritrea, the online public sphere created and sustained by the diaspora has no offline counterpart of free press or civil society within Eritrea. This infopolitical context has given diaspora websites a significance they might not otherwise have achieved. Through debates and dialogue among diverse interlocutors, the websites play a role in defining Eritrean identity, connecting the scattered diaspora, and contributing to the construction of Eritrea as a nation. By creating Dehai, Eritreans in diaspora constructed "national" space in cyberspace and established a transnational public sphere for Eritrean politics.

While theories of the internet have tended to emphasize its democratic role in making information widely available, Eritreans use the internet as much more than a means of gaining access to or circulating "information." Eritreans in diaspora are actively engaged in political participation, creating information as they produce and debate narratives about nationhood, citizenship, democracy, and relations of power and authority. Their posts seek not only to correctly analyze Eritrean politics but also to influence events in Eritrea.

Like the internet, diaspora engenders networked forms of community. There is a particular synergy between the internet's ability to form linkages among dispersed users and the relations of displacement and connection that constitute diasporas. Through cyberspace, Eritreans in diaspora transcend their displacement from Eritrea and their separation from each other to some degree. Diaspora is never simply a product of geographic distance from a homeland. Eritreans around the world were mobilized by the Eritrean People's Liberation Front (EPLF) during the struggle for independence and later by the state. For many Eritreans, diaspora also grows out of the cultural distance between the world they now inhabit and the world they came from, making their displacement or migration not an event but rather an ongoing process. This sense of national membership coupled with displacement and exile is expressed through a diasporic identity—that of an Eritrean located outside of "home." This is not to say that whether an Eritrean in diaspora lives in the United States, Germany, Canada, or the Middle East makes no difference. The particularities of social welfare systems, immigration laws and attitudes, understandings of "race" and religion, and other factors certainly affect daily life and the experience and intensity of displacement. Nonetheless, central to "diaspora" is an individual identity and a social imaginary that are distinct from location and also from nationality as defined by legal citizenship, for that matter. As a self-conscious diaspora, Eritreans see themselves as members of a dispersed community that, in effect, has no location other than Eritrea (where they are no longer located). The space of cyberspace has a similar amorphous and unbounded quality.

Spatiality is a distinctive feature of cyberspace as a medium. While thinking about the "internet" draws attention to connectivity in its social and digital forms, thinking about "cyberspace" draws attention to spatiality and the construction of space. We "go" online and "go to" or "visit" websites, and we speak of web "sites" rather than "sights," even though we are looking at visual data on a screen. We speak of "cybersquatting" and "lurking." We do not experience or conceptualize our engagement with broadcast media, whether print, radio, or film, in quite these ways. If websites are places, they are also no place or any place since their location is not territorial. Recently, people have started to talk about "the cloud" as if cyberspace exists above our heads, even though we know that computers, servers, and users are situated in specific locations on the ground. Diaspora involves similar acts of imagination, and through Dehai and their other websites, Eritreans in diaspora have created Eritrean space online.

Outside of Eritrea, members of the diaspora may live in societies that espouse freedom of expression, yet Eritreans find that their perspectives and concerns are completely absent from public forums and media outlets. Eritreans in diaspora, moreover, often are not recognized as a community or as individuals and are misrecognized as Ethiopians or other dark-skinned people. In diaspora, Eritreans, thus, experience a forced dissociation from their identities in their daily lives and are confronted on a continuing basis with forms of public invisibility produced through the ways that others misrecognize or fail to recognize them. In the United States, for example, most people seem never to have even heard of the country of Eritrea, and current events there are rarely covered in the news. Eritreans in this country experience a public sphere that in effect denies their existence. Not only that, but Eritreans face publics and media outlets that are ignorant of the wars, traumas, and ongoing political struggles that continue to affect Eritreans' lives so deeply. The significance of the websites Eritreans have created, therefore, stems not only from the tight control of the Eritrean state over public forums, political expression, and media in Eritrea, but also from the lack of media outlets outside Eritrea that give any importance to Eritrean affairs or perspectives. Diaspora websites offer a context where Eritrean concerns are paramount, attracting posters by providing outlets for publishing their opinions, poems, and analyses, as well as attracting readers who want to engage with Eritrean realities from Eritrean perspectives.

To say that the websites are Eritrean does not mean that others never go to them to read or post, but rather, that if and when they do, they are entering Eritrean space. There have been non-Eritrean members of Dehai, including myself. However, the overwhelming majority of posters to Dehai (and to Asmarino and Awate, as well) are Eritreans, as evidenced by their names, their writing style, their knowledge of Eritrean history and culture, and their self-identification as Eritreans. Outsiders are not excluded, but very few, if any, non-Eritreans are driven by the passionate concern that fuels the websites; therefore, through the process of self-selection, rather than gatekeeping, the websites' posters and readers are predominantly Eritrean. These websites offer a space where Eritreans can express and explore the Eritrean side of themselves; thus, perhaps what is posted overemphasizes that dimension of people's lives and identities and overrepresents political engagement because the less engaged either do not participate or participate less often. Maybe the websites are dominated by hyper-Eritreans, but, if the sentiments they post were so unrepresentative, the websites would not have been so successful in attracting attention and retaining a devoted audience. In any society, politically active citizens are in the minority, but they are the ones that make things happen, taking the lead in opinion formation and mobilizing the larger public.

The Eritrean character of the websites is their defining feature. The content of posts make clear that they are addressed to an Eritrean audience and posters generally do not provide the kinds of background material or explanations that outsiders would require. On Dehai, Asmarino, and Awate, shared memories, histories, understandings, and culture form the taken-for-granted context within which communication takes place. For example, a simple reference to "the field or *"meda"* [in transliterated Tigrinya] is all that is needed for a post to conjure up the life of guerilla fighters within the EPLF. As Rose M. Kadende-Kaiser notes for Burundinet, most messages "assume previous knowledge of Burundi: its culture, politics, social history, geography, and political leaders" (2000, 133). Not only is knowledge of Eritrean history and culture a prerequisite for fully understanding posts, but many of the most entertaining messages involve witty retorts or parodies of views expressed by other posters. In this way, and through their formal and informal posting guidelines and practices, the websites also create their own discursive context and online culture.

Posts include original essays, poetry, commentary, reports on current events, and the responses and debates these generate. Another common genre of posts is the media critique that takes issue with something reported in the Western press about Eritrea. Posts also announce Eritrea-related activities in diaspora and reminders about Eritrean holidays, historical anniversaries, and milestones.

It is not unusual for posters to include transliterated Tigrinya words or phrases in their English posts. These days some posts are written in Tigrinya using the Ge'ez script, which is the writing system for Tigrinya and related languages including Amharic. Unless you have downloaded the appropriate software, these posts appear as illegible rows of squares. English is the main language on all three websites, but Asmarino and Awate have separate links for posts and videos in Tigrinya and for those in Arabic. Discursively, socially, and visually (with the addition of Ge'ez script, and subsequent additions of photos and video), the websites constitute Eritrean space.

Eritreans living in diaspora were drawn to Dehai, in part, because it served as a surrogate homeland. Through Dehai, Eritreans in diaspora could connect to Eritrean national concerns, and thus were provided not only a means of political participation but also an emotional sense of connection to fellow

Eritreans and their homeland. A message posted on Dehai on April 4, 1998, describes the isolation felt by Eritreans in Germany:

> Soon after Eritreans settled down in their new society isolation dawned in their homes. Due to confrontations between Eritrean and German cultures, social mobility took bad turns and many Eritreans chose to stay out of the Germans' way. The German language became so "unlearnable" and Germans so un-approachable that life was simply passing many Eritreans by.

A humorous post titled "U know Ur Habesha when . . ." gives a sense of how Eritrean culture is carried on in family homes in the U. S., as well as conveying the feeling of outsiderness or disconnection that Eritreans experience. The post mentions common Eritrean mispronunciations of English words, distinct cultural practices, and offers telling examples, such as "ur house smells like shigurti (onions)," "u listen to the same tigrinya tape or CD every day for 6 mths. straight in ur home or car," "u have at least 1 relative living in America illegally . . . ur parents constantly tell u not to trust the americans, ur mom and dad tell u that back home everything perfect," and "no one can pronounce ur name right in school" (Dehai post, October 17, 2006; ellipses added). While *"habesha"* roughly translates as "Abyssinian" and is used in reference to highland Christian populations in Ethiopia and Eritrea, the poster used a screen name in his email address that leaves no doubt about his affiliation: "ethiopiankilla."

Dehai undoubtedly attracted Eritreans because of shared understandings, experiences, and the feeling of familiarity that can connect strangers to each other and make people feel at home. Yet Dehai accomplished much more than that. On Dehai, Eritreans established cyberspace as a significant sphere of Eritrean political activity and defined Eritrean online culture and practices. As one Dehai poster put it in 2002 when successful rival sites had arisen:

> Every kid, wet behind the ears, (nefaT) [clever or precocious] can post in any of the numerous alphabet zoo web sites in the internet without being challenged. I am sure you share with me that DEHAI is the mother of all Eritrean web sites and will continue to be the standard bearer for all Eritrean discussion forums if not all forums. (Dehai post, April 23, 2002)

For good measure, the poster also signed off with the EPLF slogan *"Awet nHafash"* (Victory to the Masses) before including his name and city of residence in California. Websites like Asmarino and Awate that grew to rival and eventually surpass Dehai in significance began as spinoffs. These websites and others that subsequently developed, thus, cannot be understood without reference to the social history and culture of Dehai.

## DEHAI AND THE WORLD WIDE WEB
## OF ERITREAN NATIONALISM

Eritreans' transnational online activities are built upon a network of relationships that I have come to think of as a world wide web of Eritrean nationalism that predates the internet. Beginning in the 1970s, Eritreans in diaspora, organized by the EPLF, played vital roles in the nationalist struggle through public relations campaigns, fund-raising, and other activities. The diaspora's participation in national politics thus precedes not only the internet but also Eritrean nationhood. The diaspora was produced by the three decades of war with Ethiopia that drove Eritreans to make new lives for themselves in other lands, but the diaspora also helped to produce Eritrea as a nation.

When Eritrea achieved nationhood in the early 1990s, the internet was beginning to get off the ground, and these two unrelated developments intersected and combined with the extensive transnational networks that already linked Eritreans in many countries. These conditions were particularly ripe with digital potential. Eritreans in diaspora were, in fact, early adopters of computer-mediated communications. In 1992, one year after the EPLF's military victory and one year before Eritrea's admission into the United Nations, a group of Eritreans living in the U. S. established Dehai which was the first computer-mediated network of Eritreans. (As a point of comparison, I did not set up my first email account until 1996, and only did so at the prompting of my university.) Dehai soon moved to the World Wide Web. Dehai's preeminence as *the* Eritrean website went largely unchallenged until the turn of the millennium.

Through the 1990s, Dehai worked in many ways to extend the nation beyond its territory. It was easy to do so because of the groundwork laid by the EPLF. During the nationalist struggle, the EPLF communicated with Eritrean organizational bases throughout the diaspora and developed various print media that circulated transnationally. Dehai thus built on an existing (trans) national community that was a series of interlinked networks, a nontechnological world wide web of Eritrean nationalist associations, social circles, and kinship relations. Dehai represented an important development, however— not simply because of its basis on new technologies, but because it was an initiative undertaken for Eritrea and Eritreans by ordinary Eritreans acting independently, not under the auspices of national leaders.

Dehai was initiated by Eritreans in the Washington, DC, area (which at the time was often jokingly referred to as "the capital of Eritrea" by Eritreans in the United States because of the concentration of Eritreans settled there). Dehai is a transliteration of the Tigrinya word that literally means "voice" but is also used to mean "news," and it also happens to be the name of one of the founders' sons. Most of the Dehai posts I quote come from Dehai's first decade when it alone essentially constituted the online public sphere for Eritreans. During that time, the website had a discussion forum called simply "Dehai," as well as a link for "Dehai-news" which was geared mainly for announcements and the reposting of news about Eritrea in the media. At last look in 2013, the website's home page opened to "Dehai-news" and the discussion list had been moved to a link called "Dehai-Discu." Dehai's webpages have remained largely true to its original message board appearance, but the website and its place in Eritrean politics have changed.

Dehai's origins were detailed by Ghidewon Asmerom, one of the founders in a paper presented at a conference of the Eritrean Studies Association held in Eritrea's capital city, Asmara in 2001 (Asmerom et al. 2001). There I listened as Ghidewon explained to a packed audience, which included Eritrean-based intellectuals, party officials, Eritrean diaspora scholars, and Eritreanists from other countries:

> At that time only hi-tech industry people were talking about the internet. But there was a list, socioculturalafrica. It was a thing where you post your message and debate. A lot of Ethiopians were posting messages against Eritrean independence. I posted replies and so did some other Eritreans.

Ghidewon said that in 1992 he was working with computers at AT&T in Virginia, and knew two Eritrean computer science students at the University of Maryland. He explained that they became so frustrated with the socioculturalafrica list that they said, "Forget those people. We shouldn't be discussing Eritrean independence with them," and they decided to create their "own list, an Eritrean list." Ghidewon continued,

> We wanted to make it a free and independent forum to discuss issues and we made it a closed list [members only] at that time because we didn't want to discuss with Ethiopians. But, even in the U.S., the people who had access to computers were very limited, so it was biased to techies, university Eri-

treans, and people in the IT industry. We set a board [of administrators] and developed guidelines. We invited social scientists, professors, and so on. Some [Eritreans] were reluctant to join, however, and one said, "You are creating a monster," because Dehai is a free forum and traditionally we don't have free forums. So they said, "It will be taken over by opposition." But, we wanted to prove them wrong and show that all kinds of views can be explored and discussed. (Asmerom et al. 2001, material in brackets added for clarity)

The "opposition" referred to above means any critics of the EPLF, perhaps particularly Eritreans who had been allied with the defeated rival nationalist front, the Eritrean Liberation Front (ELF).

From the founders' account, Dehai is a direct outgrowth of Eritrea's nationalist struggle and can be seen as extending the struggle to build Eritrean nationalism from within into cyberspace (remembering that the EPLF pursued a dual mission—fighting Ethiopians for the territory of Eritrea and mobilizing Eritreans, not only as guerillas but as nationalists, in order to transform Eritrean society). The founders of Dehai wanted to bring into being an Eritrean public sphere that would foster free and open debate, a "free forum" in Ghidewon's words, which, as he pointed out, was something unprecedented for Eritreans.

The Dehai charter (or "Dehai Charta" as it is titled) from 1995 states that Dehai's "mission" is to serve "as a free, unmoderated, and open communication medium among Eritreans and non-Eritrean friends of Eritrea for the purpose of discussing and exchanging information on Eritrean society, history, politics, economy, technology, culture, languages and current affairs" (www .dehai.org/aboutdehai/charter.html). The charter further defines the purpose of the website as follows: "The main objective is to provide a forum for interested Eritreans and non-Eritreans to engage in solving Eritrea's problems by sharing information, discussing issues, publicizing and participating in existing projects and proposing ideas for future projects." This rather technocratic formulation around "projects" conveys the intent of Eritreans in diaspora not simply to discuss but to actively participate in and contribute to nationbuilding. However, this statement understates the emotional engagement of posters and the obsession with political analyses and debates that has made Dehai such compelling reading for Eritreans (and for me).

It is significant that the core values enshrined in Dehai's charter are civility in the exchange of viewpoints and freedom of expression. Under the heading "Code of Conduct," the charter states, "Subscribers of Dehai SHALL NOT post articles that degrade or insult any subscriber, or group of subscribers' beliefs, creed, race, religion, gender, age, or national origin." The charter also includes a list of eight "Posting Guidelines." Several of the guidelines are specifically aimed at establishing social norms for appropriate communication on Dehai. The perceived need to do this on the part of Dehai's administrators reflects the novelty of this type of open public forum, as well as the unusual nature of internet communications where people previously unknown to each other and separated by distance can engage in highly emotional exchanges. Guideline 5 states that "postings should primarily address issues and not only critique or embarrass a subscriber or group of subscribers." Guideline 7 states:

> Subscribers should grant the benefit of doubt when attempting to figure out motivations—if any—behind postings. Before ex-pressing [*sic*] criticisms, subscribers are encouraged to explore privately e-mailed, diplomatic requests for clarifications. Such an approach should preempt misunderstandings, stop communication barriers from building up and provide respondents with an opportunity to explain their postings.

Through these guidelines, Eritreans were communicating about the ideals of the public sphere and how to conduct oneself there.

In its early forms, Dehai worked largely like a subscription list that members joined in order to receive and submit messages by email. Once it became a website, which in its early days was hosted on the server of Stanford University at http://diglib.stanford.edu/dehai through a contact there, Dehai could be accessed and read by anyone, but only members who registered and paid a twenty-dollar yearly fee (waived for members in Africa) could post and gain access to Dehai's archives. (In practice, some public access to the archives is available, however, from Dehai's archives link and from links to the archives that sometimes come up in internet searches related to Eritrea).

In creating Dehai, Eritreans in diaspora saw themselves as serving the nation as a whole. The online public sphere was never simply an offshoot of diaspora and a remedy for the nostalgia and isolation that often haunt them but, from the start, was rooted in a commitment to Eritrea. Posters express not only the desire to contribute to Eritrea, but a sense of national duty, a feeling in keeping with the culture of sacrificial citizenship. Notably, Eritreans did not establish websites in order to share information about surviving in diaspora, how to navigate refugee or asylum bureaucracies, how to find jobs, how to adjust to particular countries or cities of resettlement, or how to address any of the other pressing issues affecting their daily lives. Rather, they created an online forum so that they could more fully be part of the emerging nation and participate in constructing Eritrea as Eritreans from their remote locations in North America, Europe, and anywhere else in the world they found themselves. A poster who says he joined Dehai at its beginning in 1992, looking back on the early years of Dehai (in a post on Asmarino), explains: "Its mission was to help Eritrea and its people after decades long of devastation of war so that it would get on its feet economically. Most dehai-ers obviously supported the EPLF-led government. . . . The euphoria of independence endured for those formative years" (Asmarino post, August 20, 2005). Tellingly, he also points out that, in practice, supporting Eritrea was understood to mean supporting the government, with the consequence that "[t]he few souls that raised critical issues were politely dismissed for unnecessarily looking back into the troubled history of the armed struggle. They were labeled remnants of ELF and/or reactionaries" (Asmarino post, August 20, 2005).

A poem posted on Dehai communicates several ideas about the purpose of Dehai and the diaspora's relationship to Eritrea:

> Our posting is our profile,
> All Dehaier's credibility is on the line.
> Yes, respect is mutual & goes both ways,
> And also is the key in order to trade ideas . . .
> Can't we trade rudeness to politeness,
> Then Eritrea could benefit from our human resources.
> I think this generation has an obligation,
> To fulfill our martyrs dream & vision . . .
> Their sacrifice was not only, the land to be independent.
> If that was the case, why should I waste my time here,
> The ultimate goal was the people to be more freer.
> Lets speak our mind without hesitation.
> (Dehai post, December 15, 1996;<br>ellipses added to indicate omitted material)

The poem champions civility and freedom of expression, not only among interlocutors on Dehai, but as a component of Eritrean liberation ("not only, the land to be independent"). It also suggests that through Dehai Eritreans in diaspora have something valuable to contribute to the nation in the form of ideas ("Then Eritrea could benefit from our human resources."). The poem reflects the ethos of sacrificial citizenship when it states, "this generation has an obligation, to fulfill our martyrs dream & vision." The sense that posts serve a higher purpose, contribute to the nation, and honor the martyrs' sacrifice is echoed by another poster who wrote in response to the poem, "what we do here in dehai by way of such discussion, if nothing else, will serve the memory of our brothers and sisters, our friends and comrades [who fought and died for Eritrea], and we should never lose that defining memory" (Dehai post, December 15, 1996; material in brackets original).

Participation in Dehai was understood as participation in the nation. A post from an Eritrean in Sweden with the subject line "Dehai Vocabulary (Humor)" defines Dehaiers as: "A group of dispersed well-meaning Eritreans and others who discuss Eritrea and stuff. Some are more well-meaning than others" and defines the membership dues, as "A $20 version of the Eritrean 2% Income Tax" (Dehai post, May 5, 1998). As these posts indicate, free discussion, analysis, and the generation of ideas were understood as contributions to Eritrea. This makes clear that Dehai must be understood as an infopolitical project with greater meanings than simply keeping abreast of current events in Eritrea and being in contact with fellow Eritreans, for example.

A Dehai post on October 24, 1997, opens with a transliterated Tigrinya greeting, "*Selamat Eritrawian B'habera kemey a'Lo Sdetawi Nabra!*" which translates roughly as "Hello, Eritreans together, How is the diasporic life?" It then states,

> I would like to greet everybody politely and sincerely. I am sielent reader and observer of Dehai. I appreciate Dehai Administrators and all fellow Eritreans who contributed a positive, constractive, critical and somehow objective Ideas to the nation building of Eritrea.(odd spellings here and below are original)

The writer then goes on to praise by name some of Dehai's well-known posters and also to mildly criticize some of them, emphasizing the need for unity among Eritreans in nation-building despite their diversity. The post ends with the assertion that "Dehai is not a medium of false rumours and cheap propagandas. It is a constructive, communicative, progressive, critical and a SCHOOL to widen the Mind to learn new things which improve our knowladge in order to contribute to NATION BIULDING." Likening Dehai to a school might suggest the transmission of received knowledge, but the writer's adjectives, *constructive, communicative, progressive,* and *critical,* make clear that Dehai is understood as a site where knowledge is actively and collectively being produced, not simply being accessed or circulated.

Through much of the 1990s, as the exciting possibilities of the internet were developing, everything also seemed possible for Eritrea in the imaginable future opened up by the achievement of political independence and the end of thirty years of violence and uncertainty. For the diaspora, the apparent open-endedness of political transformation and nation-building that could begin in newly independent Eritrea offered a chance to contribute to the development of the nation, not simply through economic support, but through political participation. The people who created Dehai, some of whom, such as Ghidewon, have continued their efforts for two decades now, were seeking neither fame nor fortune nor political advancement. These webmanagers and the many posters who contributed content volunteered their time, energy, and skills. Until 2010, moreover, Dehai had no commercial content of any kind. The website ran on volunteer labor and membership dues helped to defray any other costs.

The fact that the founders of Dehai did not define the site as exclusively for Eritreans deserves attention. It may have roots in the fact that the nationalist movement sought and received recognition and political support from various sources, including Western journalists, members of progressive organizations, and scholars and writers who presented the EPLF in positive terms to international audiences. By 1992 there were thus established supporters of the Eritrean cause who were not Eritrean themselves. Furthermore, some of the posts on Dehai aim to correct Western media reports on Eritrean issues and set public records straight. There was the sense that outsiders interested in Eritrea might be part of the audience.

The choice to use English to discuss and debate Eritrean issues largely among Eritreans makes sense for several reasons, including the expectation that the audience would not be exclusively Eritrean. English generally dominated computing and the internet when Dehai was initiated, moreover (Keniston 2001). Other diasporas with strong bases in the United States like Haitians also use English online (Parham 2004; LaGuerre 2006). Posters' mastery of English grammar and spelling varies widely, and this accented English lends variety and gives a particular Eritrean flavor to the posts in a similar way that accented speech in spoken English might. At the conference in Asmara, Ghidewon made a point of assuring his audience that "Dehai is an antielitist list. A high-school student who doesn't know much English can write and no one would dare ridicule." To convey the distinctive qualities of posts I generally retain the original spelling and wording of those I quote as well as variations in the ways that posters transliterate Tigrinya words and names.

In Eritrea, language is a controversial issue because the population is nearly evenly divided between Muslims and Christians, and the most widespread language, Tigrinya, is associated with the highland Christian population that has historically dominated Eritrea's political economy. The choice to use

English online, therefore, may have been partly motivated by an effort to avoid a language choice that would be perceived as tainted by sectarianism. To this day, Eritrea has no official national language for this reason. Until software for typing the Ge'ez syllabary used to write Tigrinya first became available around 2000, Tigrinya was in any case not a viable option for use online.

There is a long-standing practice of using English at the national level in Eritrea since the EPLF generally produced slogans and pamphlets in three languages—Tigrinya, Arabic, and English—and these languages are all deemed acceptable for citizens to use in communicating with the government. President Isaias speaks all three languages fluently. English is used as the language of instruction in Eritrea beginning in secondary school. Thus, younger Eritreans in Eritrea can read diaspora websites and post in English if they wish. At the same time, technological advances have made it possible to post in Tigrinya, and Dehai, Asmarino, and Awate all now feature posts in Tigrinya, although English still dominates.

In a 2011 conversation, Ghidewon explained to me that Dehai had not yet taken advantage of the software for Tigrinya because "Eritrea has nine languages and we don't want to privilege Tigrinya or any other language." He also said that Dehai's technology remained very close to its early message board format on purpose so that the website could be more widely accessible to people dealing with limited bandwidth and outdated hardware and software (as might characterize readers and posters in Eritrea). It is interesting that both of these rationales are rooted in conditions in Eritrea, rather than in diaspora. For example, it would have been easy to justify the use of English on the basis of the large proportion of Eritreans based in North America and the children raised abroad whose knowledge of written Tigrinya or other Eritrean languages may be limited.

## INFOPOLITICS AND THE PUBLIC SPHERE

The desires of Eritreans in diaspora for freedom of expression that are expressed on and through the online public sphere are shaped by their experiences in Western democracies, as well as rooted in the hopes all Eritreans had for a democratic Eritrea after independence. Indeed the inclusion of "democracy" in the name of the ruling party (the People's Front for Democracy and Justice) speaks to this national aspiration. In a fundamental sense, Dehai and the websites that followed thrive on debate, and debate thrives online. This is not to say, however, that all sides are equally represented or even represented at all. Even if the websites are completely open in principle, in practice there are limits on what is acceptable to express, and on who reads the sites and who posts.

On the question of censorship by webmanagers, Ghidewon insists that Dehai's content is not censored: "Extreme *shaebia* [government] supporters will claim that we are anti-*shaebia*, and the critics say that Dehai is *shaebia*. But, basically, if the person has the guts, they are free [to say whatever they want]" (material in brackets added). To the audience gathered in Asmara in 2001, Ghidewon emphasized that "Dehai is not an organization or an association. . . . We are only the administrators. Dehai doesn't represent our views." He added that "in Dehai, if a person is a newbie, he or she can post a message and, without any interface, that message is distributed to Dehai members." In a 2011 conversation with me, Ghidewon reasserted his assurance that Dehai is completely uncensored, though this claim continues to be questioned by some Eritreans. In recent years, as dissent has grown and come to be expressed openly by posters on Awate and Asmarino, it remains muted on Dehai.

The degree of openness of the public sphere can be considered in terms of the diversity of views posted as well as the diversity among posters. As will be discussed in chapter 5, the Eritrean online public sphere is largely a male endeavor. However, this is hardly unique to Eritreans, but rather, representative of global patterns of universal citizenship that assume a male subject and women's exclusion from the public sphere (Fraser 1992; Pateman 1988). To depict the websites as dominated by elites, however, would be inaccurate. Some of the most prominent posters work in low-paid service jobs and are not members of any elite based in Eritrea or in the diaspora. Other posters could be considered elite through their education and professional employment in diaspora, but even many of these individuals arrived in their new countries with nothing and do not come from wealthy or prominent families. Some individuals have achieved celebrity through their posts, but these writers had no particular economic or social standing in Eritrean circles prior to their emergence as internet intellectuals or online media personalities. In fact, as I have explored in more detail elsewhere (Bernal 2005a), Dehai produced them and not the other way around. As Alireza Doostdar notes in relation to Iranian blogging:

> Just as the internet provides intellectuals with a much-less-restricted environment for publication and cultural-political actions, it also opens up possibilities for publication for nonintellectuals who have been excluded from this domain thus far. The absence of any kind of control means just about anything can (and does) get published. (2004, 658)

According to its founders and site managers, Dehai's "membership is diverse in age, profession, and viewpoint" (Asmerom et al. 2001).

Dehai helped to give the diaspora a voice (one meaning of *dehai* in Tigrinya is "voice"), and provided a transnational forum of communication across the diaspora and back to Eritrea proper. Even amidst the optimism of the 1990s when posters were overwhelmingly progovernment, some used the relative freedom offered by the online public sphere to criticize the state. Some of these criticisms focused on the infopolitics of the regime, in particular. For example, a call for greater transparency was expressed by this Dehai poster:

> There has been a deep-rooted culture of secrecy in the EPLF for decades. This may have kept the enemy and its collaborators guessing on the real intentions of the leaderships military strategy and administrative skills, thereby contributing in the victory of the Eritrean revolution against all odds. In these days however, I BELIEVE WE CAN AFFORD TO BE A LITTLE MORE TRANSPARENT IN THE FORMULATION AND EXECUTION OF OUR LEGAL SYSTEM. I believe such transparency will enable us to understand the rules of engagement that govern relationships between citizens and our government. Rules of engagement that are clearly set and that command the support of the majority of the Eritrean people can only help in STRENGTHEN OUR SENSE OF BELONGINGNESS TO ERITREA AND OUR SENSE OF OWNERSHIP (STAKE-HOLDERSHIP) IN THE GOVERNMENT OF ERITREA. (Dehai post, October 7, 1998, capitalization in original)

The poster's choice of words is significant with regard to the construction of Eritrea as a nation and the diaspora's membership in it. Throughout the post there is an inclusive use of "we." In saying, "'we' can . . . be a little more transparent" in the workings of "our legal system," moreover, the poster places himself among those whom he is addressing (rather than positioning himself as a critic or an outside observer). This language elides the distinction between the government and the people. The poster also elides the distinction between Eritreans in diaspora and actual Eritrean citizens when he writes of relations "between citizens and our government" and also when he refers to "the majority of the Eritrean people," since "people" is an all-encompassing term. When he writes of strengthening "our . . . belongingness to Eritrea" and "our sense of ownership . . . in the government," he seems to invoke the potential for the diaspora to become disconnected from the nation. Yet the "our" remains inclusive, since it refers back to "the Eritrean people" in the same sentence.

One of the defining features of posting on the internet is the ambiguity of the audience. For Eritreans in diaspora, this contributes to a sense that they are writing to people in Eritrea, and, especially through 1990s, to the government in particular. The post above is an example of this. It is not uncommon for posters on Dehai to address their posts explicitly to "Dehaiers" but also to write for a much wider Eritrean audience. Until 2000 when the first cybercafe opened in Asmara, moreover, government officials and high-ranking civil servants were the main people with internet access in Eritrea. The borderlessness of the cyberspatial public sphere, the fact that readers are anonymous and their locations unknown, along with the belief that Eritrea's leaders were reading posts and possibly even posting themselves under pseudonyms, all contributed to a sense of accessing Eritrea itself through the internet. From the inception of Dehai until today, posters to the online public sphere that now spans multiple websites are motivated in part by the belief that their words are read by those in power and are taken seriously, and that what is posted online can have real consequences, including influencing the government of Eritrea.

One example of this is the case of Eritrean journalist Ruth Simon who was working for Agence France-Presse when she was arrested in Eritrea in March 1998. Her arrest was hotly debated on Dehai, with some posters defending the government while others saw the arrest as a glaring injustice. Eventually, a poster took the lead in drafting a petition letter addressed to President Isaias that was circulated on Dehai asking for signatures. The petition begins with this statement: "Whereas we fully recognize your most distinguished and benevolent leadership that, along with the sacrifices of honorable ERITREAN martyrs and compatriots, brought about the independence of our country" (Dehai post, October 20, 1998, capitalization in original). It continues with other praise of Isaias and then segues to the following:

> And while we submit our unreserved support and loyalty to your leadership for providing guidance to the ERITREAN people to make continuing efforts and sacrifices to rebuild and reconstruct our beloved nation, We the undersigned Eritreans living in diaspora bring to your attention an issue that has been of great concern to many other Eritreans.

They then petition to have Ruth Simon tried in court or given amnesty "in light of her patriotic contributions during the liberation struggle." Simon was subsequently released, and, according to a senior government official interviewed in 1999, criticism on Dehai was an important factor in this outcome (Koser 2003). Note that the petition describes its signatories as "Eritreans living in diaspora," but casts them as speaking for "many other Eritreans." This sense that the diaspora is speaking on behalf of Eritreans in Eritrea has assumed greater importance as the state has become more repressive.

The audience for Dehai from its beginning in the early nineties to the height of its prominence at the end of the decade was largely confined to the diaspora and government elites. To this day, the government remains an important audience and many people in Eritrea lack access to the internet. This lends particular significance to the online activities of the diaspora who use websites, in part, as a line of communication to the Eritrean leadership. As I write this in 2013, the website of the PFDJ, shaebia.org, displays a link to Dehai on its home page. This recent development reflects the degree to which Dehai is now dominated by progovernment posters in contrast to Asmarino and Awate, but it also reflects the fact that the online public sphere is not simply meaningful for the diaspora, but is recognized by Eritrea's leaders as significant for national politics.

A deeper understanding of Dehai was conveyed to me by one of the most well-known and prolific posters on Dehai throughout the 1990s (whom I call by the pseudonym Yakob). Yakob is an Eritrean who was then in his thirties. He is college-educated and was working as a taxi driver during the height of his internet activity. He married an Eritrean woman in diaspora, started a family, and was also supporting several relatives in his extended family household. His circumstances as a former student, as someone employed in the service sector, living under difficult economic circumstances, and assuming responsibility for siblings and other relatives are typical of many Eritreans in diaspora. As one of Dehai's major posters, Yakob is, by definition, not a typical Dehaier, since he is one of the fifteen to twenty people who emerged as media personalities on Dehai, and who, through their posts, helped define the contours of Eritrean online culture (Bernal 2005a, 2005b). The celebrity of these posters in Eritrean diaspora circles is such that people are excited to meet them in person at social gatherings, and they are sometimes invited as special guests to weddings and other occasions. Posters achieve this kind of status and recognition through their analytical and writing skills, and their wit and insight, as well as their commitment to frequent posting. They also display courage in putting their views on the line and exposing themselves to public vitriol. Among the reasons for Yakob's eventual withdrawal from high-profile posting in recent years is the stress involved in the constant give and take of public criticism and debate, as well as the sheer effort involved in constant reading and posting.

In a conversation we had in 2001, Yakob told me he first became involved in Dehai in 1995. Like many Eritreans at the time, he did not have a personal computer in his home; therefore, in order to read and write on Dehai, he had to go to public places, mainly libraries, where he could go online for free. But this, as he pointed out, added to the time commitment involved. Significantly, although the founders and some of the earliest participants in Dehai were self-described "techies" employed or studying in computer-related fields, Yakob had no other interest or involvement in computing or the internet except for Dehai:

> I didn't do anything else on the internet. I just went to Dehai. It is a big commitment of time. In fact, even when I heard about Asmarino.com and the other sites [that Eritreans developed later], I resisted for a long time, because I can't do more than Dehai. I was totally engaged with Dehai. From 1995 to 2000 I read Dehai every day, and I posted something two or three times a week. (material in brackets added)

Yakob saw himself as communicating not only with fellow Eritreans wherever they might be located but also with the Eritrean government:

> The government never directly addresses it [political criticism on Dehai], but it has an impact on Eritrea. Sometimes after you critique you see the policy change. People feel that they can influence the government. I hoped that a bigger picture would emerge, like a conference or a think tank before policy could be made without your notice on a whim.

He added that, "Eritreans would be more than glad to volunteer their time as a sounding board." Yakob, thus, saw Dehai as a means of participating in Eritrean politics and even advising the government, and he wished that the government would formalize the informal influence of Dehai through creating some institutional framework for the kinds of brainstorming, critique, and debate that take place online. These sentiments are very much in keeping with the ways that Eritreans had been using the internet up to that point as a means for the diaspora to shape Eritrea's emerging institutions and policies and maintain close links to the government. Their citizenship in Eritrea was virtual in two ways; first, they were not literally citizens but were recognized officially as Eritrean nationals by the government, and second, they regularly exercised their "citizenship" and experienced their participation in the nation through the internet.

Not only do Eritreans in diaspora participate in national debates online, but the opinions expressed online influence opinions in other venues so that the lines between the diaspora and Eritrea, and between posts and other forms of national discourse, are blurred. For example, during the development of Eritrea's constitution, which entailed a three-year process of public education and debate within Eritrea and in the diaspora, Rude (1996, 19) observed that "since some members of the constitutional commission actively present their views on Dehai, while others silently 'lurk,' the virtual debate and the real one overlap." Online debates are as real as any, I contend. The conclusion to be drawn here is that the online public sphere is not sealed off from other circuits and its public extends, moreover, beyond those who post and beyond the internet. As Warner (2005, 90) argues, "A public is the social space created by the reflexive circulation of discourse." Such notions of "public" and of "space" are especially relevant to cyberspace where audiences are not clearly bounded and where space is metaphorical rather than territorial. On Dehai, Eritreans created national space in cyberspace, but their activities there were not limited to the virtual; they had wider effects.

## DISCURSIVE COMMUNITY AND VIRTUAL POLITICS

Dehai established cyberspace as a meaningful space for Eritreans; and on Dehai, Eritrean posters established Eritrean online culture. To fully make sense of posts, one must be familiar not only with Eritrean politics and history but also with the culture of the website. This culture is revealed in the histories of posts, the characteristic modes of expression and interaction, the known perspectives of prolific posters, and the kinds of topics that are normally addressed. Posts and the Dehai Charter establish norms and standards, and patterns of exchanges create the atmosphere that shapes the form and content of continued communication on the website. Posters police one another and sometimes explicitly articulate the values and principles of the public sphere. A distinctive Eritrean online culture thus emerged from the sustained engagement of posters with Dehai over many years.

A common feature of Dehai posts is that they are addressed to Dehaiers as a community or sometimes addressed directly to a particular poster or posters in response to specific posts. In these ways, individual posts invoke the larger context of Dehai, as posters respond to the general tenor of sentiments that have been previously expressed regarding a particular topic or take issue with specific statements posted by a particular author. The acceptable boundaries of reasonable debate and the intolerance expressed by some posters can themselves become the subjects of postings. In this way, a self-critical, reflexive mode is built into communications.

The character of the online public sphere, which now includes Asmarino, Awate, and other websites, is not just a product of the interactivity of the internet where readers can generate content as well as consume it. The public sphere is self-reflexive, in that posts reflect on other posts and on the larger history and context of previous posts. Since the establishment of Asmarino and Awate, interactivity and reflexivity take place not just among posters on a given website, but also through crosstalk among websites when posters on any of the sites discuss activities on one of the other websites. This reflexivity can be understood in infopolitical terms because posters are not merely offering information or commentary on Eritrean issues and events, but rather commenting on how those issues and events are being represented, discussed, and analyzed in the online public sphere. Posters are thus actively *constructing* a public sphere, not simply expressing themselves in it, as they debate the very terms in which debates can take place and struggle over the parameters of what constitutes legitimate discourse.

The character and content of posts are diverse. A post may be a simple and sincere statement of opinion about a current event or policy issue in Eritrea or a long argument with previous posters on a political issue. Some posters write poetry about Eritrea or, more rarely, short fiction. Posts that go on for more than five single-spaced pages of complex political and historical analyses are not uncommon. These posts are referred to as "articles" by Eritreans, suggesting the seriousness with which they are written and read, while shorter posts are more likely to be called "messages." Some of the most entertaining posts use witty repartee, parody, and satire to get their points across. While some posters advance reasoned arguments in a dispassionate tone, others, often using exclamation points, capitalization, and hyperbole, convey their emotional responses to the subject matter, whether writing about conditions in Eritrea or what another poster said. The variety of language, style, and tone, as well as occasional outbursts of insults, help to keep the online public sphere fresh and lively and create a sense of curiosity and anticipation since one never knows what might be posted.

While Eritreans may have been drawn to the website through their shared traumatic history as Eritreans, Dehai in turn created community through a shared discursive history of online discussions. This history is, moreover, archived and accessible to Dehai's members. The discursive history of past posts and exchanges, whether lyrical, analytical, troubling, or argumentative, becomes part of the collective memory of Dehai readers that can be invoked by posters in meaningful ways. It is not unusual for posters to weave elements of previous posts into their own posts as they discuss them. The messages themselves construct a context in which the continued communications take place online.

The way that Dehai creates a sense of community through a shared discursive history is revealed in the following post that expresses nostalgia for better times on Dehai. The poster laments, "the trend dehai is going. *BizeyQeleAlem* [frankly], it's regressing. I had no choice but to revisit the old archive and here is what I thought deserved a second chance of reading" (italics added). He has selected a poem by a woman he says is a student at Stanford University, which includes the following lines:

> Look at me . . .
> Stare into my eyes . . .
> See my anger and misery . . .
> A second class citizen in my own country . . .
> Invisible in higher industry and political society . . .
> Look at me . . .
> I am standing, demanding, and screaming . . .
> Do not fear my power, strength or militancy . . .
> I am an Eritrean woman with independent dreams . . .
> That is the new me . . .
>
> (Dehai post, May 12, 1997;
> ellipses in poem are original)

The poem is interesting in its own right for the way it reflects the multiple positioning of self that runs through many Dehai posts. The author is an Eritrean student at Stanford, but, within the poem, she expresses herself as if she were located in Eritrea, "a second class citizen in my own country." Cyberspace and diaspora are not so much outside of Eritrea in such formulations as they are extensions of Eritrea.

Culture and history may be shared by Eritreans, but they are also contested. Although the websites foster community by serving as a cyber-space where Eritreans can gather, conflict is what keeps the public sphere vital and draws posters and readers back time and again. Kadende-Kaiser similarly observes that "Burundinet brings together many different subgroupings with competing assumptions and beliefs about the crisis in Burundi. This does not mean that these groups do not have anything in common or do not have any shared perspectives" (2000, 128). She draws attention, moreover, to the ways that communication in such fora is a creative process in which meanings are constructed and contested through successive postings, so that "as messages are reflected upon or commented on, different versions of a particular story or set of facts emerge" (Kadende-Kaiser 2000, 142). Conflict is not the antithesis of community, and may even be an expression of it. As Werbner (2004, 896) points out, "Diasporas are full of division and dissent. At the same time they recognise collective responsibilities, not only to the home country but to co-ethnics in far-flung places." The internet brings Eritreans together in novel ways, allowing people to participate in (or eavesdrop on as lurkers) conversations and debates with interlocutors outside their own social networks, which, within Eritrea, are largely shaped by region, ethnicity, and religion.

At one level Dehai grew out of existing transnational networks on the ground, yet it also made possible new connections, which were not limited to virtual encounters. A sense of community developed because people felt they had gotten to know others through reading their posts on Dehai, which created a basis for further relationships when they met. At the conference in Asmara in 2001, Ghidewon proudly stated, "We have managed to change a virtual community into a real one. We communicate for a year or two, then when we meet it is amazing. It can be from the U.S. to Sweden or Norway, but it is amazing when we meet." People sometimes respond to posts by sending private emails to the author rather than posting a public response, and thus posts can lead to more personal exchanges. Beginning in 1995, Dehai organized yearly retreats to facilitate face-to-face interactions. Yakob described his experience of a Dehai retreat to me this way: "I attended the 1997 retreat in Virginia. There were about 100 of us, mostly young university students, though some families came. I went because I wanted to meet some of the main people, like Ghidewon." He added, "One of the reasons I went to retreats was to put the face behind the writers, so they become friends. As a result of that we stayed at Berekhet's house. Friendship was being developed with people you never knew before, so it went outside the realm of Dehai. You [already] know them through their ideas."

When talking about Dehai retreats, Ghidewon gave some sense of Eritrean experiences in diaspora when he explained to the audience in Asmara, "So far there have been seven annual retreats, every June or end of May, held in West Virginia where most people, let alone knowing Eritrea, they haven't even seen a black person" (Asmerom et al. 2001). Ghidewon's references to Americans' ignorance of Eritrea and to places where seeing "a black person" is something out of the ordinary hint at the feelings of racialization and of being out of place that, coupled with Eritreans' sense of belonging to Eritrea, constitute them as a diaspora. In 1997, hopes of holding the Dehai retreat in Eritrea were discussed online, but such a plan did not come to fruition then, nor has it since.

Dehai's founders and posters never saw virtual communication or even creating a Dehai community as ends in themselves, but rather as part of a wider Eritrean national imaginary that encompassed Eritrea and the diaspora. Dehai-related activities both reflected and helped to produce this Eritrean national community. In this sense, Dehai has always been much larger than its actual membership. In 2001, Dehai had over two thousand registered members (Asmerom et al. 2001). (By comparison, Burundinet, another African diaspora website that has been the subject of research, had only two hundred members around that time [Kadende-Kaiser 2000; Turner 2008a, 2008b].) As is typical of discussion sites, readers greatly outnumber writers on Dehai and, since there is no need to join as a member in order to read, the audience for Dehai posts is much larger than its paying membership. Ghidewon reports that from its inception in 1992 to 2001, Dehai averaged thirty-seven posts per day (Asmerom et al. 2001). The growing availability of computers, the rise of the internet, and the proliferation of cybercafes over that period mean that this daily average hides the increasing number of posts as Dehai became more accessible. In the late 1990s when I began to study Dehai, there were about fifty new posts every day. In those days one had to skim the list of subject lines or author's names to decide which posts to read and which to skip, and there was no indication of how many people might be reading the posts. Dehai recently introduced a new feature, "top articles," that directs readers' attention to the two hundred most popular pages of posts in a prior month and reports the number of page views each garnered. (In April 2013 it was showing statistics for January 2013.) According to those data, popular Dehai pages (which include more than one post) now commonly receive between two thousand and three thousand views. It is difficult to know how to read this data backward in time, however, because Dehai's popularity has declined, readers now have more Eritrean websites to choose from, and yet at the same time access to the internet has increased so the pool of potential readers has grown. Whether any one of these trends dominates the other or they cancel each other out is difficult to determine.

Clearly, participation that requires some knowledge of English and the use of a computer is exclusive in practice if not in ideals. However, interesting ideas and controversies that surface on Dehai and the other diaspora websites are spread further by email, telephone, word of mouth, and printouts, as well as in face-to-face meetings off-line. In these ways the websites serve a far larger public than indicated by their registered members or even their online readers. The extent of this larger audience cannot be known. In fact, the ambiguity and open-ended nature of the potential audience for posts is an important characteristic of the internet as a global media platform. On Dehai, people who read but do not post anything are called "silent readers." Such people are more commonly referred to as "lurkers," by internet scholars and others. The anonymity of "silent readers" is significant in the Eritrean context, particularly because the president and government cadres are thought to be among them.

The ambiguity of who constitutes the public of the Eritrean online public sphere contributes to a heightened sense of the influence that can be exercised through posting. For example, Eritreans gathered in other venues, whether tea shops in Asmara or coffee shops in Los Angeles, do not have the same sense that their conversations have the ear of government leaders (or if they do, it is only to intimidate and silence them). Moreover, in the context of the culture of censorship and self-censorship that is promoted by the Eritrean state, the very fact that an opinion, analysis, or observation is stated publicly online gives it a certain weight and importance. The fact that posts are not ephemeral but are kept and publicly archived on Dehai (and on Awate and Asmarino as well, though less extensively) reflects the significance that is invested in what is expressed publicly online, and amplifies its impact. The fact that long posts are commonly referred to as "articles" further attests to the seriousness with which some posts are written and read. Posters think their online activities have real-world effects, whether mobilizing public opinion or actions; swaying, pressuring or protesting against Eritrea's leaders; or prefiguring online the kind of open and participatory political debates they hope to see take place within Eritrea. One poster, for example, cautioned that "[i]f even among lay people like us we cannot tolerate dissenting voices, how much more can we expect from Government officials with their vested interests?" (Dehai post, October 6, 1998).

To the extent that Dehai gave Eritreans a "voice" (one translation of *dehai*), that voice was heavily inflected by the national political culture forged by the EPLF and later by the state. A three-page, single-spaced post from January 27, 1998, discusses Dehai's "silent readers" in a way that shows how their silence is produced by this political context. The poster writes that, like him, other readers of Dehai may be silent for distinct reasons:

> I question whether I am qualified enough, whether I have contributed enough, to have the privilege of speaking out. . . . I suspect there are also many people like me in dehai and in the general public. . . . We are silent because of too much "frHi" [fear] lest we seem to disrespect the "Hdri" [legacy] of our mar-

tyrs by our dfret [audacity] to criticize. (Dehai post, January 27, 1998, ellipses and material in brackets added)

The post connects Eritrean infopolitics and sacrificial citizenship when it suggests that Eritreans may not feel entitled to express their views because they have not contributed enough to Eritrea to meet the standards set by the martyrs. However, after reiterating these national values and presenting himself as one of "many people like me in dehai and in the general public," and therefore as part of, and perhaps speaking for, a larger Eritrean community, the poster then turns around and questions these core values. He reclaims the martyrs' sacrifices for all Eritreans, not simply for the state, and asserts that silence is not what the martyrs fought for. In a paragraph written in capital letters and sprinkled with exclamation points, the poster plays on the double-meaning of "dehai": "OUR BROTHERS AND SISTERS BACK HOME ARE WAITING TO HEAR OUR DEHAI!" He writes that just when he feels trapped in silence, he hears voices in the distance, and, as they get nearer, he hears

> their songs, their cries, their hopes. They are voices like mine. They are voices in dehai. . . . In our excitement at having found each other, we raise a lot of noise, we shout at each other. . . . The noise gets so loud that our declaration of love [for Eritrea] sounds too possessive, too exclusive, and we start to argue, to justify, to testify, to rectify, to quantify, and before we know it we are hurling insults at each other. (ellipses and material in brackets added)

The poster thus addresses the joys and pitfalls of communicating in the public sphere where the passions that connect people can also make them bitter opponents who sink to character assassination and personal insults.

In this way the post sheds light on another form of silencing in addition to the self-silencing with which it began. This second kind of silencing is performed by other posters who hurl insults and cast suspicion on people with whom they disagree, creating an intimidating climate. Through the 1990s such responses particularly targeted posters who criticized the president, the ruling party, or the EPLF. Thus, discourse on Dehai is shaped not only by the political culture of the PFDJ and the self-censorship and self-silencing it promotes, but also through active silencing by fellow posters. The online public sphere is not censored by the government, but rather by "citizens" taking it upon themselves to defend the state by attacking its critics.

A poster who expressed disgust about name-calling on Dehai, collected and reposted within his message some of the offensive posts as examples.

These include statements, such as "May be you want to talk about Derg's or Haile Slasie's ministers which, I would guess, would have enticed you very much" [in other words, you are really a supporter of Ethiopia]; "you are a liability in the process of development for Eritrea"; "I hope you will clear all the smog from your brain and refrain from polluting the net"; and "Brother, may be your exposure to the Eritrean history is not that genuine, or at least you are trying to dress it up with buzzwords" (Dehai post, January 13, 1998). On that same day, another poster responded harshly in verse to a poet who had posted about a political prisoner in Eritrea:

> Are you in a day dream or amnesia
> What is your beef against Eritrea
> What a shame the writer of nine flowers
> [a previous poem by the poet he is taking to task]
> Throwing dart at her brothers & sisters
> Is this a personal problem or to the contrary
> What is your grudge against the leadership & the country
> (Dehai post, January 13, 1998).

As these excerpts illustrate, insults are not simply about personal attributes, such as stupidity or any other individual flaw, but commonly involve political accusations. Critics are accused of not being Eritrean enough in loyalty to the government and/or in the knowledge, understanding, and experience of Eritrea's independence struggle, and sometimes they are even accused of being allied with enemies of the Eritrean state, such as the Ethiopians, the ELF, or Muslim extremists.

On Dehai, many posters reiterate and disseminate national discourses, including the martyrs' legacy and the value of sacrifice as promoted by the Eritrean state. Some posters go further, heaping insults on other posters who criticize the government. The online public sphere of Dehai thus served not only to create national space online, but also to extend the nation and the authority of the state beyond its borders. The ways in which Eritreans in diaspora used the internet to extend and strengthen Eritrea as a nation reached a peak during the 1998–2000 border war with Ethiopia.

### DEFENDING SOVEREIGNTY ONLINE

The link between the virtual diasporic public sphere and life on the ground in Eritrea was brought to the fore dramatically when war broke out along

Eritrea's border with Ethiopia in May 1998. Immediately, Dehai was largely given over to various war-related communications. The war brought to the foreground the instrumental dimension of the virtual public sphere, which Eritreans had always treated as if it could accomplish much more than the exchanging of views and the circulation of information. During the conflict, Dehai became a means for mobilizing and coordinating actions and resources across vast distances to effect real-world outcomes.

The outbreak of war appeared to threaten the very survival of Eritrea as a nation and was regarded by Eritreans in diaspora as a crisis that motivated them to set aside debates and unify against Eritrea's adversary, Ethiopia. A burst of online activity gave Dehai new importance as a key source of breaking war news and as a vehicle for rallying support and publicizing various activities to aid Eritrea's war effort. Online and off-line Eritreans in diaspora came together for the common purpose of ensuring their nation's survival. On Dehai posters pursued several distinct avenues of defending the nation. Posters asserted the value of Eritrea's survival as a sovereign nation, circulated and analyzed news reports of the war, and whipped up anger at Ethiopia. Posters also took the United Nations to task and publicly articulated disappointment in the lack of international response to Eritrea's plight. Dehai served as a means to assert and demonstrate the value of the diaspora as active participants in the defense of Eritrea.

Most significantly, posters used the website to broadcast details of their fund-raising and public relations efforts, and to organize and promote such activities throughout the diaspora. Here is an excerpt from one of the impassioned posts people wrote during the war:

> I know everyone has confidence in our EDF [Eritrean Defense Forces] Lions and Sawa [national service militias] Tigers. They are dripping their bloods to do away with Woyane's [Ethiopians]. The Question hinges on if we [he explicitly addressed the post to Eritreans in diaspora] are doing enough . . . If our lions and tigers are giving their life why not our money. . . . Every dollar we pull out of our pocket will kill a Woyane. Let's do it and make a difference. The world is siding with Woyanes. (Dehai post, February 27, 1999; ellipses and material in brackets added)

The author signed off with the phrases, "Lasting glory to our Martyrs, Victory to our Defense Forces, Demise to the Woyanes." This message captures several common themes of wartime posts. Posters expressed intense nationalism, asserted the idea that Eritreans living abroad have an obligation to come to the aid of Eritrea, and some of them, like this one calling for funds to kill more Ethiopians, openly called for bloodshed.

The post above, furthermore, reflects the understanding that money contributed by the diaspora serves as a substitute for giving their lives. Sacrificial citizenship takes a particular form for the diaspora, as discussed earlier. The post suggests that Eritrean lives lost on the battlefront can be matched by financial sacrifices on the part of Eritreans in diaspora. The money they send, in turn, is equated with the Ethiopian lives that will be lost, as "each dollar . . . will kill." The image of a dollar killing Ethiopians makes the act of giving money a powerful form of agency. Here we see money metaphorically in action as it stands in for a diaspora fighter who kills enemy soldiers.

In fact, Eritreans around the world sent millions of dollars to the government in support of Eritrea's war effort during the 1998–2000 border conflict. As posts like the one above made explicit, moreover, these funds were not earmarked for humanitarian relief or reconstruction, but intended to strengthen the capacity of the state to wage war. Instructions about the national defense bank account set up by the government specifically for these remittances were posted on Dehai.

One of the outstanding characteristics of Dehai posts during the war was their intense emotional tenor. Some posters were vehement in the hatred they expressed toward Ethiopia. Most of the outpourings of emotion were passionate calls to action to support the war effort, especially through sending funds. Some posters signed off with exhortations to "remember our martyrs," exclamations of "Victory to the Eritrean People," and the more chilling "Death to the Ethiopian Oppressors!" A June 16, 1998, post from an Eritrean in St. Louis reported that people there had pledged fifty-five thousand dollars in two hours, with fifteen thousand dollars of it collected on the spot, adding that

> Eritreans are most creative problem solvers. When something really bad happens, like the Ethiopian aggression, who are the first people to be there, offering help and assistance for their mother land. Eritreans are. The old self-reliance mentality is still there. (Dehai post, June 16, 1998)

Posts on Dehai not only communicated the surge of nationalist passions and the flow of money from Eritreans around the globe, but served to intensify these emotions and heighten the sense of emergency, fueling the diaspora's fevered engagement in war-related activities. The immediacy, interactivity, and speed of the internet worked to magnify the powerful feelings of fear, anger, and grief, creating a cascade effect as one moving post led to another. Throughout June 1998, post followed post reporting on money raised. A post from Denmark said that Eritreans met in Copenhagen and pledged one thousand dollars per household. A June 12, 1998, post detailed various activities at a gathering of Eritreans at their community center in Sommerville, Massachusetts, to celebrate Martyr's Day, reporting that "our children, through their own initiatives, by holding bake sales and lottery on gifts (courtesy to Eritrean business establishments), were able to raise $1041.00 for the Eritrean National Martyrs Park." The post noted that pledges for the defense of Eritrea were still being solicited. Showing a knowledge of American democracy, the Sommerville gathering also collected the names of Eritreans who had been arrested in Ethiopia following the outbreak of hostilities and drafted some one hundred twenty letters to be faxed to senators from Massachusetts and Rhode Island on behalf of relatives of the detainees. Other posts detailed fund-raising efforts elsewhere: Eritreans in Riyadh pledged one month's salary each; and in Edmonton, Canada, they donated twenty-six thousand dollars on the spot at a single meeting. Posters boasted about the results of local fund-raising efforts, while urging others to follow suit. A post about fund-raising in St. Louis boldly asserted, "This is something that all Eritreans need to emulate."

Many of these local efforts were coordinated with PFDJ representatives and officials from Eritrean embassies and consulates. The outpouring of diaspora support thus was not independent of the state. The state's reach extended into the diaspora and the diaspora reached into Eritrea. In Eritrea, the head of the Bank of Eritrea described the diaspora contributions as "beyond anybody's imagination" (Tekie Beyene quoted in Voice of America 1998). A mainstream media account immediately posted on Dehai reported that in 1997 Eritrean remittances amounted to $300 million, but said that authorities in Eritrea expected that amount to triple in 1998, "as Eritrean nationals stand by their government in time of conflict" (Alexander Last, *Reuters*, June 22, 1998, posted on Dehai). These figures indicate how vital the money transfers from the diaspora to Eritrea have been in times of peace as well as war.

On June 25, 1998, less than a month after the start of the war, a Dehai post, which included the Voice of America report on the remittances, proclaimed, "To all eritrean heroes abroad: read this and rejoice! This remittance is a torrential blow to the ultra-nationalists of ethiopia" (Dehai post, June 25, 1998). In the report, Tekie Beyene, head of the Bank of Eritrea, explains the diaspora's behavior as rooted in Eritrean history:

During the struggle when EPLF was fighting the war, it has never been supported by the East, never been supported by the West, nor by the Arabs. So
everything was from an Eritrean citizen inside or outside.... So every Eritrean
is used to contribute and that is why the war was won. (Voice of America 1998,
reposted on Dehai, June 25, 1998)

Mr. Tekie thus constructs the diaspora as Eritrean citizens who are outside the
country but long accustomed to supporting it financially. Indeed, while Eritreans in diaspora made particular wartime sacrifices in sending money to the
Eritrean government, their activities grew out of the already well-established
sense of involvement in national politics and obligation to take part in Eritrea's struggles from their new homes abroad.

To be sure, the mobilization of funds from the diaspora to support the war
effort during 1998–2000 could have taken place even without the internet.
However, through cyberspace such activities are validated and made visible to
wider audiences. The fact that Eritreans in different cities and countries could
learn immediately through Dehai of the fund-raising, demonstrations, and
other activities carried out by Eritreans elsewhere transformed what otherwise might have been scattered efforts, in effect, into a collective undertaking
across the wider diaspora. Furthermore, through the public accounting that
took place online, posters implicitly and sometimes explicitly pressured others to match or exceed the efforts they described. In this way, the stream of
posts contributed to an intensification of effort as well as to the amplification
of emotions and sense of emergency described above. Thus, it is not simply
that communication among Eritreans occurs in a variety of ways including
via websites, but that communication via websites changed the conditions of
diaspora—transforming local activities into a visible and collective global effort, stoking passions, and serving as a vehicle to intensify pressure on Eritreans everywhere to "do their part" and sacrifice their hard-earned cash for
the nation.

To play a part in the border war, Eritreans in diaspora also organized public relations campaigns and staged demonstrations in various North American
and European cities to draw international attention to the plight of Eritrea.
They sought to counter Ethiopian claims, as well as any reports in the international media perceived as biased, incorrect, or pro-Ethiopian. Dehai was
an integral part of all these activities and helped to construct meaningful roles
for the diaspora in the defense of the nation. Online Eritreans outlined and
promoted various war-related activities, posting about sending money to fund
the state's war effort, and about acting as citizen diplomats and as a public

relations corps lobbying Western governments and drawing the attention of international media and organizations. In June 2000, Eritreans organized a demonstration in front of United Nations headquarters in New York to protest what they saw as the United Nation's failure to respond to Ethiopia's attack on Eritrea. The call to participate was posted on Dehai (Dehai post, June 14, 2000). Telephone, fax, and word of mouth also were used to spread the call to demonstrate, but the speed and reach of Dehai played a role in publicizing the event to Eritreans around the world. The continual breaking news of the war kept readers constantly coming back to Dehai for further information and analysis of the war as well as for updates on the latest diaspora initiatives.

In the conflict, Eritrea and Ethiopia treated the international press as an important battleground, making claims and counterclaims about attacks, victories, and losses. Eritreans in diaspora saw a clear role for Dehai in these infopolitical battles. Commenting on that period of Dehai, Ghidewon stated in 2001 that "our main aim was to saturate the web with Eritrean information because the lie machine in Addis was operating nonstop, so we thought it was our national duty" (Asmerom et al. 2001). Ghidewon clearly positioned himself and Eritreans in diaspora as part of the Eritrean nation with obligations of national duty. His phrase "Eritrean information" is interesting in that it conveys the sense that information is not a neutral good, but dependent on who is producing it and from what perspective. The website was thus an important means for the production of information by Eritreans, presented from an Eritrean perspective. In defending Eritrea's sovereignty online and seeking to "saturate the web with Eritrean information," Dehai was taking part in the infopolitical project of the state.

During the war, Dehai's home page was redesigned to give prominence to the border conflict and a link labeled "Ethiopian lies" was added that focused on Ethiopia's claims and its representation in the media. As the war raged on, Eritrean and Ethiopian government spokespeople struggled to have their versions of reality given the imprimatur of truth by Western reporting. When the poster quoted earlier says "the world is siding with the Woyane," he is reflecting, among other things, the Eritrean perception that the Ethiopians were winning the media war. Indeed, it seemed to many observers, including myself, that Ethiopia possessed more sophisticated government spokespeople who were better skilled than their Eritrean counterparts in manipulating Western media to accept their accounts of the war.

Even as the border war brought the diaspora together to insure Eritrea's survival as a nation, some posters dared to criticize the government's actions and the extreme nationalism of Dehai posts. A post with the subject heading

"Classified Ad: Cyberspace Border Patrol Needed" parodied the overblown patriotism of some posters who could be seen as policing Eritrea's borders in cyberspace by silencing others. The post listed the qualifications sought, including the following: "1. Support anything the prevailing government of Eritrea does at all times"; and "2. Never miss *Awet NHaffash* [victory to the masses—an EPLF slogan] along your signature line when you communicate in writing"; and "4. Remember to always black mail individuals with dissenting views on any issue that prevailing government upholds—Question their ID if you must, this is important, at all cost, by any means necessary, just defame" (Dehai post October 26, 1998). This post describes the kind of behavior that rendered the website an extension of the nation where the sovereignty of the ruling regime was reproduced by posters.

The idea of policing Eritrea's borders in cyberspace is ridiculous, yet thought provoking. It raises questions about what territorial borders mean and about how the limits of sovereignty are determined. It also provokes questions about the limits of virtual freedom. There lies a paradox in the apparent unbounded and open nature of the internet which led some scholars to liken it to a new frontier, and its operation, in practice, which is structured and limited by the ways people use it. Though many have theorized the democratizing potential of the fact that, in principle, anyone can post and read online, the post quoted above draws attention to the operation of power relations in cyberspace and to what I call infopolitics. The Eritrean online public sphere is not boundless and completely free of constraints. Even though websites are not administered or regulated by the state, or even censored by webmanagers, posters impose political norms on themselves and on others that construct the boundaries of what is expressed and what is suppressed. Through such practices on Dehai, the website can be understood as part of the national field of Eritrean politics dominated by the Eritrean state.

The vehemence with which Dehaiers supported the war effort in words and in deeds not only displayed the strength of their feelings about their homeland and the depth of their concern for relatives in Eritrea; it also showed their continuing engagement with the Eritrean state. The funds they sent expressed the economic might of Eritreans in the diaspora and demonstrated their capacity to effectively intervene in faraway events. The threat to Eritrea's survival shifted the emphasis of Dehai away from its role as a space of social imaginary around nation-building and the future of Eritrea, and made tangible the instrumentality of the internet as a tool for the diaspora to affect events on the ground in real time. While the consequences of much online activity is intangible, whether swaying public opinion or influencing government officials, wartime posts were clearly linked to actions and achieved concrete results.

On Dehai, the diaspora's need to come to Eritrea's aid could be expressed and, more importantly, acted on collectively. Here the coupling of new digital communications and a transnational population combined to help a small, poor nation successfully wage war on the ground. Eritrea did not triumph in the border war by any means, however. Indeed the human losses, as well as the political costs to President Isaias's regime, proved to be substantial. But, with the diaspora's support, Eritrea literally and figuratively held its ground against a potentially overpowering adversary.

The diaspora's online activities redefine what the nation is and change the experience of diaspora. The diaspora used cyberspace to construct a new kind of national space and one that blurred the boundaries between Eritrea and Eritreans settled abroad. They created a website where they established a transnational public sphere that they used in ways that reproduced and extended Eritrean sovereignty into the virtual and over the diaspora. This online public sphere served, moreover, as vehicle to help defend Eritrean sovereignty on the ground.

The border war was a crucial turning point in Eritrean politics and cyberspace. Chapter 3 explores how, in the aftermath of the border war, the online public sphere fluoresced and split, spawning new websites like Asmarino and Awate. I argue that, on these websites, the diaspora used cyberspace, not to extend the nation-state, but, rather, as an off-shore platform where civil society and dissent could develop to challenge the state.

CHAPTER 3

# The Mouse that Roars: Websites as an
# Offshore Platform for Civil Society

We need to have an open and honest debate. At the moment this isn't possible inside
Eritrea, because it is simply impossible for citizens to air their views without fearing that
they will be arrested and imprisoned, and accused of treason. This isn't what we fought
and paid dear lives for. We fought for liberation, which means far more than simply the
independent sovereign existence of the state of Eritrea.

(Awate post, August 9, 2002)

[On Asmarino] we have carved out an experimental space for a wide range of voices to
be heard, all sorts of passionate writers to advance the art of self-expression and civil society activists and aspiring lobbyists for democracy and human rights to appeal directly
to the people without any filtering or restrictions.

(Asmarino post, March 4, 2007)

The websites created by Eritreans in diaspora are the most politically significant Eritrean public spaces outside the borders of Eritrea. Cyberspace is
a unique space, a transborder political space that can be used in ways that
change the meaning of territorial sovereignty. Eritreans' engagement in politics online both extends and challenges state authority. To the extent that
Dehai, Asmarino, Awate, and similar websites make innovative forms of political participation possible, they do not simply reproduce something Eritrean
outside of Eritrea's borders; they bring something new into being. Chapter 2
revealed how websites can work to extend national sovereignty elastically to
encompass the diaspora and the online public sphere. This was exemplified
by the website Dehai (www.dehai.org), serving as Eritrean national space
online. This chapter explores the ways that diaspora websites, particularly
Asmarino and Awate, have come to be used as an offshore platform for civil
society where Eritreans engage in national politics outside the authority of the
state. In doing so, the websites are not merely supporting the Eritrean nation
as an auxiliary through which the diaspora participates but, rather, providing

something for the nation, for Eritreans (in diaspora and "at home") that the state has refused to provide—an open public sphere and a public Eritrean gathering space independent of the government. Websites offer novel spaces for political experimentation, as well as for the cultivation and expression of new subjectivities. In these online spaces, politically independent perspectives are developed collectively as posters conduct activities not possible on Eritrean soil—publicly criticizing the government, mobilizing action, constructing alternative histories, and revising national narratives.

The nation as network always has the potential to become less centralized since the relationship among its parts is flexible and connections may be added or broken, strengthened or weakened. The internet, moreover, facilitates fragmentation, as well as connection. As Eickelman notes about the role of new media in the Middle East, "The 'migration' of messages, media, writers, and styles of discourse is part of an increasing fragmentation of authority" (2003, 41). Circulation can be disruptive. What Ferguson (2006) points out with regard to globalization, that the process does not seamlessly create connections, but creates disjunctures as well, is true of new media. The connectivity of the internet, thus, offers new possibilities for reordering relationships, and new divisions are produced along with connections.

Within Eritrea's borders, there is no public space for independent media and civil society to develop. Power is tightly controlled by an autocratic regime that permits no rival parties and does not tolerate dissent. As the Eritrean state has grown ever more repressive, diaspora websites can be understood as offering the opportunity for Eritreans to practice the kind of participatory citizenship and free expression that are denied Eritreans in spaces under state control. For different reasons, many Eritreans in diaspora do not fully participate in politics in the lands where they have made their new homes, where they feel like outsiders in various ways. Websites thus serve as important political spaces that have no off-line counterpart either in Eritrea or outside it. On websites like Asmarino and Awate the diaspora are using the internet to create an offshore platform for civil society that is animated by ordinary Eritreans rather than by national leaders.

This development arose in the aftermath of the border war with Ethiopia that appeared to many Eritreans to demonstrate the carelessness of the state toward the lives of its citizens. That war contributed to a tidal shift in political sentiments. In Eritrea anyone who openly voiced criticism was severely punished. Journalists and others, including members of government who criticized the president were imprisoned, and the independent press that had briefly flourished was completely closed down in September 2001. The internet and the diaspora took on new roles as Asmarino and Awate, in particular, emerged as counterpoints to the Eritrean state.

I argue that posters in diaspora can be seen as producing national media from outside the nation's borders and, most significantly, doing so without the state's authorization or censorship. Since 2001 Eritrean websites have become vital sources of alternative perspectives on the nation, dissent, and even leaked government documents. Posters openly question the legitimacy of President Isaias and the PFDJ, foster critical subjectivities, and generate counternarratives to the state's dominant monologue. The websites provide Eritreans in diaspora and some segments of society in Eritrea, especially urban, educated people, with independent analyses and perspectives that have no public outlet within Eritrea. Ironically, because of the government's own repressive measures against free expression, Eritrean websites also offer the state an important conduit through which the leadership can gain insights about the criticisms being leveled at it and the perspectives of Eritreans on various issues. According to the journalist Dan Connell, government officials in Asmara routinely checked Awate on a daily basis when he was spending time with them in 2001 (2011, personal communication). Much as the diaspora can be conceived of as "outsourced citizens" who contribute resources to the state without consuming any state services, the online public sphere created by Eritreans in diaspora can be considered to be a form of "offshore" civil society.

Until December 2000, when a few public and private cybercafes opened in Eritrea, government elites were the primary audience in Eritrea for diaspora websites. Diaspora posters were very conscious that their ideas could reach and possibly influence the government. As access to the internet increased in Eritrea, it became possible for more Eritreans inside the country to join the ranks of readers and writers in Eritrean cyberspace. Youth appeared to be the primary customers of cybercafes in 2001 from my own observations. A January 27, 2001, news report on visafric, titled "First Cyber Café Opens in Asmara," finds Eritreans in the capital city reading Dehai:

"This cyber café is very useful to many of us," says Solomon Haile, a second year computer science student from the University of Asmara who was checking Dehai, the first Eritrean website based in the U.S. (visafric, January 27, 2001)

With greater access to the internet, the development of software for writing Ge'ez script, and the use of English as the language of instruction in Eritrean secondary schools, the possibility of reaching ever-wider audiences in Eritrea and attracting posters from inside Eritrea continues to grow. However, until now, although there are some citizen posters from inside Eritrea, the content of Eritrean cyberspace remains generated largely by posters in diaspora. In 2001, Ghidewon scolded his audience in Asmara saying words to the effect that "we know you are reading Dehai, you should be posting, too" (Asmerom et al. 2001). Posters continue to feel they are communicating with others in diaspora as well as to the government, but since 2000 they have a growing sense of being able to communicate with a wider public of Eritrean citizens. Because of intensifying repression inside Eritrea through the 2000s, posters, moreover, began to cast themselves as speaking *for* Eritrea's citizens who have been silenced.

### STATE VIOLENCE AND INFOPOLITICS

The years from independence until the outbreak of the new war with Ethiopia in 1998 had been understood by Eritreans as a period of transition for a new nation whose political economy and defining institutions were still in process and, therefore, remained open to many possibilities. Disappointment in Eritrea's progress and with government policies could be interpreted as delays in Eritrea's political development, rather than as failures or betrayals on the part of the state. President Isaias has often promoted this perspective in speeches and interviews where he insists that progress is being made, but cannot be rushed without endangering the nation. The ruling party uses the tortoise as a symbol intended to represent its deliberate, intrepid perseverance on behalf of the nation. The recklessness with which the state embarked on the border war, putting at risk so many Eritrean lives, and perhaps the nation itself, shattered that worldview for many people.

A key political watershed came in October 2000 when thirteen respected Eritrean academics and professionals in diaspora sent an open letter to President Isaias from Berlin, Germany. A central theme of their critique is the lack of an open public sphere in Eritrea and the limited scope for popular political participation. Dated October 3, the letter (excerpted below) was posted on Dehai four days later. The letter states that the border war "has raised grave questions about the conduct of Eritrean affairs both domestic and foreign, and about the nature and style of our leadership in the post-independence period." The letter writers refer to themselves as "concerned citizens who made modest contributions to our national struggle." They write that, despite "disquieting developments, we remained remarkably silent. The reason for our silence was not due to apathy or lack of interest but rather due to the pervasive phenomenon of self-censorship."

Putting in writing what many Eritreans apparently felt, they boldly asserted that "the government has failed the nation in some important respect." Among the things they call for are that "[t]he EPLF [Eritrean People's Liberation Front] (PFDJ) leadership should be willing now to provide political space for groups or individuals." They decry the advent of "one-man dominance" that "has had the effect of suffocating a variety of ideas from blossoming and denied meaningful popular participation." They assert that "[t]he absence of any record of protest is also a function of the absence of freedom of expression." They call for the implementation of the constitution, asserting that it "is the people's document and no one has the right to suspend it or otherwise tamper with it." And they say, "Let the leadership and the entire nation conduct an open debate. People should not be denied this right which they have paid for with their, blood, sweat and tears." In closing, the signatories state that they will "spare no effort to help secure Eritrea's territorial integrity and national sovereignty," but that at the same time they will seek to promote "a culture of openness" and to broaden their base "to begin and institutionalize a government/civil society dialogue on a continuing basis" (Dehai post, October 7, 2000). What is striking in the Berlin Manifesto, as the letter came to be known, is the extent to which its demands are consistent with the goals and practices of the diaspora websites. These websites "provide political space for groups and individuals," allow "a variety of ideas" to blossom, and promote "freedom of expression," among other things.

On the national scene, political rifts emerged within the ruling circles of Eritrea's leadership. Some members of the Eritrean government may have been emboldened by the Berlin Manifesto. In May 2001, fifteen members of President Isaias's own government, later known as the G15, wrote an open letter outlining a series of criticisms. At that time, independent newspapers were appearing in Eritrea and publishing diverse viewpoints, including views critical of the government. When the president accused the G15 of trying to destabilize the country, they published a response in an independent Eritrean newspaper in September 2001. That very month the government launched a major crackdown on its critics, perceived enemies, and the press. The G15 were arrested and imprisoned, except for three who were out of the country at the time. Only one was later released. The government shut down all the independent newspapers and jailed journalists and others indefinitely without trial (Tronvoll 2009). The extreme lengths to which President Isaias and his allies in the PFDJ were willing to go in order to retain centralized control over public discourse were starkly revealed in widespread violations of human rights that have continued until the present (Amnesty International 2004).

While the state's actions against its own citizens were brutal, and came as shock to many, government repression in Eritrea did not come out of nowhere in 2001, but had roots in the centralized practices developed by the EPLF. Dan Connell, who has chronicled Eritrean affairs from the early years of the liberation struggle, described the absence of an open public sphere in Eritrea this way in 1997:

> There is no tradition of signed articles outlining positions not yet adopted by the Front, for example, nor is there any outlet for them, no sections set aside for debate in PFDJ (People's Front for Democracy and Justice) publications, no space for op-eds in the newspaper, no panel discussions of contending perspectives broadcast over radio or TV. Positions on controversial issues are thrashed out within the movement, with input from the membership through forums and seminars convened for that purpose. (Connell 1997, 69)

The political culture institutionalized by the Eritrean state has been highly effective in creating subjects who are self-censoring, as well as in producing some private individuals who take it on themselves to police others. One scholar summed up Eritrea's political climate thus: "Critics are labeled traitors and pro-Ethiopian, and any opinion contesting the narrative of national unity is construed as threatening Eritrea's existence" (Bundegaard 2004, 55). The government deals harshly with any perceived critics, subjecting them to indefinite detentions, torture, and, in some cases, death. A 2009 report estimated the number of political prisoners as between ten and thirty thousand (Tronvoll 2009, 76).

### CONSTRUCTING CIVIL SOCIETY IN CYBERSPACE

In light of the repression within Eritrea, Eritreans' activities online are important for the way they create space for and engage in the kinds of public discussions that cannot take place in Eritrea. As Ghidewon Asmerom, one of Dehai's founders, commented pointedly at his presentation about Dehai in Asmara in summer 2001, before the crackdown, but when it was already clear that even though liberation had been achieved, democracy still remained a distant hope for Eritreans: "That's what democracy is. It is not 'Shut up. I will talk. You listen.'"

As political conditions worsened in Eritrea, Dehai lost its centrality, however. Asmarino and Awate rose rapidly, competing for the same readers and writers as Dehai. These sites transformed and diversified the online public sphere, providing a platform where "citizens'" views are paramount, rather than serving as an extension of national politics as defined by the state. While Dehai's tagline for many years had been "Eritrea online," Asmarino's tagline is, in fact, "Independent," signaling its stance of separateness from the Eritrean state. The motto on Awate's home page is "Inform. Inspire. Embolden," and its tagline includes the phrase "fearless news." These phrases announce and reflect a profound shift in the dynamics of Eritrean cyberspace.

The shifting role of the internet in Eritrean politics is reflected in Asmarino's history. Asmarino is now characterized by many as an opposition website devoted to bringing down the current regime in Eritrea. Yet, according to its founder, Tesfaledet, Asmarino did not start out that way but grew out of an effort to bring the benefits of new communications technology to Eritrea. In a 2008 conversation, Tesfaledet told me that he founded Asmarino.com in 1997 after visiting independent Eritrea for the first time. Like many of his generation in diaspora, Tesfaledet fled Eritrea in the mid-1970s and spent years in Sudan as a refugee before finding a way out and eventually settling in the United States. In 1997, twenty-two years after leaving home, he was working as an engineer in computer communications. The rapid developments in information technologies, he thought, held out great possibilities for Eritrea. "My heart was still there," he says.

Tesfaledet traveled to Eritrea, arranging meetings with Eritrean officials and American experts, in the hopes of helping Eritrea take advantage of these new digital technologies. He explains:

> The internet was developing. I wanted to establish something there. I met with economic advisors in the US Embassy. In those days you would have to go see Yemane Gebreab [still Isaias's right-hand man and a top PFDJ official today]. The Eritrean government rejected the initiative. In Eritrea the telephone system was bad. You really couldn't do anything because communications were so bad. In 1998 I went to Eritrea again with a laptop. . . . I tried to tell people in government, "Here is a technology that would get Eritrea connected to the world, for development and other things." There was no interest. . . . They [the government] wanted to control. (Personal interview 2008; material in brackets added)

Tesfaledet founded Asmarino in the United States in October 1997. It was not until after the border war, however, that Asmarino began to successfully rival Dehai, drawing posters and readers to the website through its tolerant atmosphere for critical posts. In contrast to the histories of state censorship and self-censorship among Eritreans, Tesfaledet asserted that, from the start, Asmarino "would post anything. We never censored." In hindsight, he added, "It is a good thing I didn't build Asmarino in Eritrea." He added, somewhat sadly: "I am not by profession a journalist. I do this because it has to be done."

Awate.com was founded on September 1, 2000, a few months before the end of the border war in December of that year, and quickly gained attention from Eritreans. Awate is named after Hamid Idris Awate, a Muslim Eritrean who is reputed to be one of the first Eritreans to take up the armed struggle for freedom from Ethiopian rule. The date of September 1 is significant, moreover, because the historic battle in which Hamid Idris Awate fought took place on that day in 1961. The founders of Awate are themselves Eritrean Muslims. On Dehai, posters who could be identified as Muslims by their names, sometimes expressed the feeling that their Eritreanness was particularly called into question any time they posted views critical of the government. The establishment of Awate, thus, can be understood in part as a response to the treatment of Muslim posters on Dehai where their national loyalties were sometimes impugned and they were treated as less authentically Eritrean. Awate is, however, an entirely secular endeavor in spirit and practice as are the websites dominated by Eritreans of Christian heritage.

At issue are not religious beliefs or practices per se, but rather that secular nationalism in Eritrea, as in many other contexts, can conceal the extent to which Christian populations monopolize power, and stigmatize and marginalize Muslims. Although Muslims constitute roughly half the population, they are divided among numerous ethnic groups and are treated like a minority in Eritrea where they continue to be underrepresented in the national leadership (Woldemikael 2005). A Dehai post by Saleh Gadi, one of the Dehaiers who later founded Awate, is revealing:

> I am not going to feel ashamed by the deeds of loonies like Turabi and Taliban simply because I share the same faith with them. I am not going to change my conviction because someone tries to intimidate me by throwing "fundamentalist" branding, left right and center. (Dehai post, June 9, 1997)

Further along in the post he writes that Dehai is dominated by "Tigrinya speakers," (which in the Eritrean context is nearly synonymous with Christians since Tigrinya is the mother tongue of highland Christian populations).

Saleh then asks: "Have you ever read anything '*nara, baza, hidareb, saho*' in this medium?" Here Saleh presumably is referring to the perspectives of minority ethnolinguistic groups, some of whom are Muslim, rather than to languages per se, since all posts at that time were written in English, albeit with occasional transliterated Tigrinya words or phrases. Saleh's larger point is that the views expressed on Dehai generally represent the perspective of the historically Christian, Tigrinya-speaking population that has long dominated the political economy of Eritrea.

The establishment of Awate took place when the government's handling of the border conflict had already begun to strain people's loyalties. As any voices raised within Eritrea were brutally silenced, critiques started to appear more openly online. A writer on Awate used humor about the ruling party's use of the tortoise as a symbol to suggest that there is a darker side to the PFDJ:

> Refering to the PFDJ as a "turtle" or a "tortoise" is meant to be a compliment: one with a slow, steady pace who always gets to its destination. . . . Well, let's also look at the other attributes of a Turtle. A Turtle: is a cold-blooded reptile who . . . has a shell that is not transparent . . . has a good eyesight, excellent sense of smell. But can't hear well (too busy sniffing out suspects to hear the cries of its citizens). (Awate post, September 8, 2001, ellipses added)

On February 2, 2002, a five-page, single-spaced, small-font post appeared on Dehai criticizing what its author called "PFDJ propaganda" as well as the progovernment "zealots" posting on Dehai. Titled "The Cycle of Deception," the post begins: "The theme of this posting revolves around this question: Are we turning into a culture of deception?," and goes on to ask, "Do we care anymore about truth and historical facts? Or are we willing to distort any historical fact- however obvious it is—if we feel it will serve our purposes?" The poster argues that "the GoE" [government of Eritrea] and "GoE zealots" on Dehai "have reached that chronic stage of self-deception where they have started believing their own lies." He then gives examples of what he sees as government propaganda and distortions, before directly criticizing "PIA" [President Isaias Afewerki] for cracking down on critics: "He condemns frail old men in their seventies and eighties to prison. . . . He puts thousands of students into mass detention in one of the most inhospitable areas in Eritrea for having dared air their grievances" (Dehai post, February 2, 2002, ellipses added).

By 2000 the role of cyberspace as a significant sphere of Eritrean politics had already been well established through Dehai. Numerous posters, moreover, had honed their writing and analytical talents online and some had established reputations as internet intellectuals or media personalities through their posts (Bernal 2005a). Some of these posters turned their talents to Asmarino and Awate. These websites thus clearly built on the foundation of Eritrean cyberculture established by Dehai, but they did not simply replicate it.

Asmarino and Awate asserted independence from the national leadership. They innovated in other ways as well. While Dehai has remained largely true to its original message-board design, which seems dated in appearance today, Awate and Asmarino have continually added new technical features, such as digital photos, Arabic and Ge'ez script, and streaming video as these have become available. Asmarino and Awate also organize contributed content in distinct ways. Whereas content on Dehai is not organized by the site managers in any way, but simply listed in reverse chronological order, Awate uses its home page to foreground selected posts that it calls "featured articles." Awate also invited talented writers, some of whom were already well known as media personalities on Dehai, to contribute content regularly as columnists. The home page of Awate bears some resemblance to and functions somewhat like the front page of a newspaper, often displaying photos along with the titles and the opening paragraphs of various "featured articles" that one can click on in order to read further. The author's name is listed under the title along with the date it was posted, and sometimes authors include the country where they are living.

Awate's focus and purposes are summarized in its motto: "Inform. Inspire. Embolden." Thus, while the website aims to serve as a source of information ("inform"), it is also meant to motivate and mobilize Eritreans ("inspire"), and, moreover, to "embolden" them. In the context of Eritrean politics, to "embolden" must be understood as encouraging people to voice their criticisms of the government and not be silenced or self-censored in the face of an increasingly repressive regime. In addition to these three words, "Reconcile" appears as part of Awate's heading on its home page. This word signals that dissent and criticism are not to be taken as attacks that imperil the nation by undermining unity, encouraging violence, or promoting civil war. Indeed, the fact that opposing interlocutors can confront each other to express conflicting views and interpretations of reality and clash online without violence is a distinctive property of the internet. Given Eritrea's histories of warfare, civil strife, and state violence, the capacity for nonviolent conflict that websites offer is valued by Eritrean webmanagers and posters.

Awate describes itself as "a free public forum that provides a platform to

Eritreans, friends of Eritrea, or anyone curious about Eritrea, to express their views and to read the views of others" (Awate Registration/Posting Protocols, accessed October 20, 2008). Awate's posting protocols, like those of Dehai, emphasize civility. However, Awate's go further, asserting the value of including "viewpoints that are as diverse as possible" and explicitly stating that "[w]ithin the Eritrean context, this means that the viewpoints can be pro-government or anti-government; pro-opposition or anti-opposition" (Awate Registration/Posting Protocols, accessed October 20, 2008). Like Dehai's managers, the "Awate team," as the site's founders and managers call themselves, asserts that it does not censor posts or act as moderators of online debates. The Awate team, through selecting regular columnists and through designating some posts as featured articles and displaying them prominently on the home page, takes an active role in curating the content that is showcased on the website.

Asmarino describes itself as "not only an information center, but also a meeting point . . . that provides an open forum for the presentation and refinement of ideas relevant to Eritrean communities" (Asmarino Posting Policy, June 14, 2004). Asmarino, like Awate, has regular columnists in addition to posters of all kinds. In 2004 Asmarino posted an announcement informing readers and posters about the establishment of an editorial board that would screen "articles" according to five basic quality criteria. The five criteria emphasize qualities such as interest and originality but do not refer to political content per se. Thus, like the other two websites being discussed, Asmarino represents itself as completely uncensored. Both Awate's curating of posts as "featured articles" and the establishment of editorial quality standards by Asmarino appear to be forms of professionalization of these Eritrean websites rather than efforts designed to constrain political expression.

As posters began to feel empowered to publicly voice their doubts about Eritrea's leadership, the relationship of the online public sphere to the state of Eritrea changed. The Eritrean internet as pioneered by Dehai had been used in ways that extended the nation-state beyond its territorial borders and blurred the boundaries between the nation and the diaspora. Posters' focus on the nation left the distinction between the people and the state ambiguous and undefined. These effects were created when, for example, posters living in diaspora wrote as if they were located in Eritrea, and when posters wrote about Eritrea as if the citizens, the diaspora, and the state were all one entity. These practices have not entirely disappeared from all posts, even on Awate and Asmarino, but they are no longer pervasive.

As dissenting voices began to seek outlets for their trenchant critiques, posters and readers drifted away from Dehai to Asmarino and Awate where the atmosphere was more hospitable to critical posts. These rival websites thrived, decentralizing and diversifying the public sphere. Awate and Asmarino have come to serve as spaces notably distinct and separate from the nation-state and the ruling party. Rather than extending the reach of Eritrean sovereignty beyond its borders, these websites disrupt the seamlessness of the state's control over Eritrean politics.

## THE NATION BEYOND THE STATE

The Eritrean space created online made it possible for the distinction between the state and the people to emerge into political daylight. The existence of this distinction is sometimes taken for granted in scholarship on civil society, but its active construction by Eritreans online is extremely significant in the context of Eritrea because for decades such divisions had been masked and suppressed. The EPLF in the past and the PFDJ today speak on behalf of the people, often referred to as "the masses" [*hafash* in Tigrinya]. PFDJ slogans such as "*hade hizbi, hade lbi*" ["one people, one heart" in Tigrinya] that represent the Eritrean nation as unified into a single body reflect this ethos. A poster on Awate writing near the end of the border war used irony to convey the sense of how President Isaias embodies the nation. His post is framed as an attempt to explain Eritrean politics to his elderly mother, as follows:

> We are endowed with an "Excellency" who is disgusted, angry, happy or sick on our behalf. Mothers should know that; all the Eritrean people have to know it; they are spared the trouble of crying or laughing since their great son will do it for them. They have only to fight our internal and external enemies if they are in the country and pay what so ever cash they own if they are abroad. (Awate post, November 24, 2000)

The founder of Asmarino, Tesfaledet, looking back in 2008 on the government's negative response to his early attempts to bring digital communications technology to Eritrea in 1997 and 1998, told me, "they would just feed you one thing, that's it. That is why they resisted the internet." Even online, Tesfaledet recalls: "At the time, you didn't see anything except what the government is saying. We are brainwashed where what the government is saying is like what God is saying" (personal communication 2008). As one scholar observed, moreover, the regime's hold on the diaspora was such that "Eritreans in diaspora have been unable to create long-lasting, autonomous, diasporic transnational institutions that reflect their desires and interests" (Woldemikael 2005, 162). On Asmarino and Awate, however, they have.

Over the course of the 2000s posters increasingly used the internet to challenge the infopolitics of the Eritrean state and expose its internal logics to critical analysis. A good example of the kinds of alternative national narratives and complex analyses of Eritrean politics developed by posters is a ten-page, single-spaced featured article on Awate in 2009 that begins with the euphoria of independence, then notes that

> The present gap between yesterday's lofty promises and what is actually delivered, between words and deeds, between the declared intentions and the actual performance of the regime, is so wide, that people greet the public pronouncements of the regime with either apathy or ridicule. (Awate post, January, 6, 2009)

Among the numerous insights the author offers to explain the difficulties faced in trying to organize opposition is a powerful analysis of how the regime creates complicity:

> Like all repressive regimes, the regime in Eritrea tries to "popularize" violence by spreading violence-promoting norms and thereby broadening the numbers of perpetrators. In order to secure compliance it uses the motto that "you are either with us or against us"—the latter by implication against the nation. Collective punishment and coercion is used to ensure social cohesion and conformity and to set frightening examples. . . . Critics and nonconformists abroad are subjected to social "quarantine," isolation and character assassination. The regime has a vested interest in making culprits of everybody and involving as many as possible in its acts of violence. Loyalty is ensured when people are entangled in the web of violence spun by the regime. Likewise, their credibility is tarnished and put in question if they at a later date decide to oppose the regime and expose its crimes. (Awate post, January, 6, 2009)

The author also notes that "[m]any are still grateful to the regime for deliverance from foreign occupation and others continue to be loyal to it for fear that their actions or open criticism might undermine Eritrean sovereignty or tarnish the memories of their martyred children and relatives." This text provides, among other things, some sense of the dangers and the profound social and emotional challenges Eritreans had to face in order to publicly criticize the government.

The shift of the online public sphere toward independence and even opposition to the regime, thus, was not a simple process. This shift, moreover, was not prompted by technological advances. The internet could have been used to create critical distance from the state and to generate and circulate independent perspectives from the start. Technology did not determine the motives and meanings of Eritreans' online activities in the first phase of the online public sphere, nor did technology instigate the process of its transformation. Rather, the ways Eritreans in diaspora used the possibilities offered by the internet changed as new political conditions arose in Eritrea. This suggests the need for greater caution on the part of scholars and others who assume digital media are inherently liberating and democratizing.

The transformation of the Eritrean online public sphere shows that in a sense there were always two kinds of networks, the digital one, created independently by Eritreans outside of Eritrea, and the transnational political network, fostered by the EPLF and the PFDJ that also worked to connect the diaspora to Eritrea. The distinction between these two networks was inconsequential and largely invisible until the relationship between the two shifted. As critical perspectives on the state began to emerge publicly and those who expressed them in Eritrea were crushed by the state, the websites became a platform for civil society where a process of reassessing Eritrean politics and history could be conducted independently from national authorities. Online new political subjectivities could be developed among Eritreans in communication with each other, rather than cultivated from the top-down through the various forms of political education and mobilization carried out by national leaders.

Central to the emergence of a new political subjectivity has been a process of building an understanding that the expression of dissent need not mean betraying the nation. For this perspective to develop, the distinction between the nation and the people, and between the state and the citizens, needed to be articulated and given public recognition. For all these processes, the existence of a public space not dominated by the government was crucial. Eritreans in diaspora created that space in cyberspace.

## THE NATION INSIDE OUT

When a new political era dawned as Eritreans' questions about the handling of the border conflict were met with government repression, those in diaspora were able to express themselves much more openly than were people in Eritrea. Diaspora websites expanded and made visible the cracks in the facade of Eritrean unity that had concealed the people's growing disappointment and distrust of the state. Something vital to democracy, a public sphere where Eritreans could express and develop their critiques, and mobilize themselves independently of the state could only exist outside Eritrea's national borders. The diaspora websites, particularly Asmarino and Awate, in this sense turned the nation inside out, since the political activities crucial to Eritrea's political development as a society could not take place within the country but were lead by the diaspora outside it on the internet.

Awate's rapid success in attracting posters and reaching a wider public is documented in a report posted on September 1, 2001, by Saleh Gadi on behalf of the Awate team. Addressed "To Our Readers," the report states:

> When we launched awate.com a year ago, we had no idea that we will be where we are today. Limited resources, and limited know-how of running a Web site, but determination to leave a mark is what made us embark on this project. . . . Since awate.com is all about communication, today we would like to share with you some statistics for the first year of our operation. (Awate post, September 1, 2001)

The report details the rise of Awate's popularity, claiming that three hundred people visited the website on its first day and the number of visitors tripled by the next month, reaching 145,000 by June 2001 and continuing to rise. (Of course, these numbers must be interpreted in light of the fact that many visitors are repeat visitors.) The report asserts, moreover, that the readership is far larger than those who visit the website: "The number of people who read us on printed paper is four-fold" the number who read online. The report adds, furthermore, that in Eritrea the ratio of off-line to online readers is at least fourteen to one. At the time, there were independent newspapers in Eritrea that published material from Awate.

While it is not possible to confirm these figures about off-line readership, which are clearly estimates on Awate's part in any case, they tell us a number of things. Such claims indicate how important audiences are to the Awate team, and reflect its confidence in the website's ability to reach audiences in Eritrea, including even those who do not or cannot go online. These claims also remind us that digital media never operate in a vacuum. New and old media intertwine and cross over each other, connecting online and off-line publics. Those with access to computers can make printouts that can be circulated physically. Readers also draw attention to particular posts by forwarding them to others via email. In 2103 I noticed that Awate had made it even easier to convert its content from the web into other formats, providing a button for printing and another for converting a post into a PDF file. Since printing and saving web content often proves difficult, reducing the friction between media formats clearly enhances circulation, not only beyond the website per se but also beyond the internet. Since Eritreans also communicate by telephone and word of mouth, content accessed by someone online is passed on to others by various means, including face-to-face conversations. As one Awate columnist wrote, "You can combine this with the usual I just-spoke-with-my-neighbor's-aunt-who-just-came-back-from Eritrea analysis to update you" (Awate post, November 30, 2004). The amplification of the reach of digital media via established communication practices and old media might be particularly significant in contexts like Eritrea where both free press and digital access are limited; this lack creates a great hunger for ideas and information that is continually met by various informal means across extensive social networks and geographic distances.

Asmarino's founder, Tesfaledet, strategically uses other media to reach wider audiences in Eritrea. He has been working with Eritreans in South Africa to broadcast satellite radio to listeners in Eritrea. He also uses faxes to get political messages through to people in Eritrea, as he explained to me in our 2008 conversation:

> I sent a fax to all [government] offices on the anniversary of November 4, 2004 when 50 people were killed in Adi Abeto. [The government reportedly shot people escaping from this detention center.] Maybe the ministers to whom it is addressed won't pay attention, but—who gets the faxes? —secretaries. Secretaries will see them and they will spread the word. The people will know they are not forgotten.

The 2001 report by the Awate team to its readers explicitly addresses its political relationship to the government:

> Though we maintain cordial relations with some of the ruling PFDJ members and leaders, government officials have declined our invitation for interviews and communications. As many before us who have tried to establish a dialogue with the government, we have failed. (Awate post, September 1, 2001)

The perspective expressed here, of standing apart from the state in a dialogic relationship, can be read in sharp contrast to the earlier sense among Dehaiers that they had the government's attention for their ideas and therefore could

contribute seamlessly to the Eritrean national project. Moreover, whereas Dehai's stated mission was to help Eritrea develop and prosper, Awate emphasizes the role of the website as one of promoting communication itself:

> We invite all Eritreans to use this medium to promote their ideas and enrich
> dialogue and understanding among Eritreans. When the element of dialogue
> is given a new life, we firmly believe that Eritrea will be safe, stable and embrac-
> ing. (Awate post, September 1, 2001)

It is significant that the invitation for "all Eritreans to use this medium to . . .
enrich dialogue and understanding among Eritreans" is not only an inclusive message, but one that empowers ordinary people, since the focus is on
Eritrean-to-Eritrean communication and understanding, rather than on Eritreans supporting the nation. Saleh does say that ultimately the ideas are for
the "beloved country" when, at the end of the post, he adds the hope that "all
will be rewarded when all the best ideas are realized in our beloved country Eritrea in a new era of unity, dignity, peace, stability and prosperity." The
choice of "country" rather than nation is a subtle shift, and the reference to "a
new era" would be understood by Eritreans as a call for a new government.

The language used here is important. It involves a discursive shift from
the focus on the nation and the state that dominated the ethos of the public sphere established by Dehai to a focus on the people and the country of
Eritrea. This shift is subtle but represents an important change in the political subjectivity being expressed and fostered online. It is noteworthy that
neither Awate's self-description as a "platform for Eritreans" nor Asmarino's
statement that it provides a forum of ideas relevant to "Eritrean communities"
makes any mention of the nation. Their formulations thus suggest a virtual
platform/forum where Eritreans anywhere can connect and communicate in
an Eritrean context that is defined by the Eritrean participants themselves
(posters and readers) rather than by the nation or its leaders. This, then, is not
a virtual Eritrea, not an "Eritrea online" in Dehai's terms, but an expression
and recognition of Eritreanness as something distinct from the nation, President Isaias Afewerki, and the PFDJ, and perhaps as something even greater
than any of those. In the Eritrean political context, this constitutes a profound
re-envisioning of the nation.

If, in some sense, the EPLF saw itself as bringing Eritrea and Eritreans into
being, and, under President Isaias's regime, the people of Eritrea were sub-
sumed under the state into a unified political body, then the emerging political
subjectivity fostered by Asmarino and Awate expresses a rupture and even a

reversal. In this new perspective, Eritreans have an existence distinct from the nation-state. Moreover, instead of the government being all-encompassing and over and above the people, the people come first and the government is something they can decide on.

A post on Awate asserts the distinction between the government and the people that has so often been rendered invisible in Eritrean politics, and at the same time constructs a distinct, new interpretation of the diaspora's obligations to Eritrea:

> I don't subscribe to the view that believes the sky will rain milk and honey if Eritreans worshipped their government. . . . I believe that any government is the servant of the people. If it doesn't do a good job, it has got to be fired. . . . Somebody has to speak up on behalf of those who are cornered and helpless. (Awate post, February 21, 2001, ellipses added)

Here the sense of duty on the part of the diaspora to serve the nation, which was synonymous with serving the state in the culture of sacrificial citizenship promoted by the Isaais regime, is turned around, to become instead an obligation of the diaspora to people living under dictatorship in Eritrea.

Through Asmarino and Awate, Eritrean space online came to offer a unique platform for Eritrean politics. Websites operate outside state authority, offering important counterpoints to the national media it controls and to the state's monolithic public representations of the nation and its definitions of what it means to be Eritrean. The virtual space of websites and the diasporic locations of posters outside the country thus became vital spaces for national politics and political participation that were not orchestrated by the state.

As the euphoria of national independence waned and prospects for peace and prosperity under President Isaias grew increasingly doubtful, posters did not simply become disaffected and lose their enthusiasm for participating in national politics. Rather, they altered the terms of their involvement, transforming Eritrean cyberspace as they sought to promote political change in Eritrea. Posters have remained passionately engaged in Eritrean politics from their locations outside Eritrea, even as their relationship with the regime has gone from one of loyalty to one of distrust and even antagonism. Critics of the PFDJ and President Isaias are intensely committed to national politics as they continue to articulate their views, develop analyses, and generate alternative national narratives and people's histories, in order to sway public opinion, mobilize Eritreans at home and abroad, expose injustice, and exert pressure on government authorities.

The Eritrean government followed the diaspora's lead into cyberspace. The PFDJ established www.shaebia.org in 2000, and the Ministry of Information launched www.shabait.com in 2003. The diaspora, thus, pioneered a political innovation that the state later adopted. The launching of these official websites indicates that the regime recognized the significance of cyberspace as a venue for Eritrean politics. The party's and the ministry's websites also constitute efforts to bring state infopolitics into the twenty-first century of digital media. The official websites, along with government-controlled media in Eritrea, disseminate information that puts the regime in a positive light. The availability of satellite television means that Eri-TV also reaches international audiences and some of its programming appears to be specifically directed to Eritreans in diaspora. Government websites, in particular, serve as a mechanism to compete with the critical views expressed on the independent websites. The time lag between the launching of Dehai in the early 1990s and the launching of the government websites is interesting. It suggests that the state had little need for official websites when the online public sphere, as represented by Dehai, largely facilitated expressions of support for President Isaias's government, and served to coordinate Eritrean nationalist efforts across the diaspora. Once Eritreans began to use websites as a platform for civil society and dissent, the state needed its own websites where it was fully in control. Government websites can be seen as part of the ongoing efforts of the regime to extend its sovereignty over Eritreans in diaspora and into cyberspace. The state strives to bring the outside back into the nation under its authority, while diaspora websites are turning the nation inside out, producing national media and conducting national politics from independent positions outside the nation.

## DIGITAL DISSENT AND TECHNOLOGIES OF CENSORSHIP

Creating a climate where critical perspectives could be articulated and feelings of disappointment could be mobilized into dissent was not something that occurred simply because people had access to the internet. Eritrean communications online and off-line are governed by self-censorship that arises from a climate of fear, distrust, and uncertainty about what is permissible or safe to communicate to whom. Eritreans have experienced the pervasive politicization of all domains of life under the PFDJ coupled with government practices of secrecy and surveillance. Neither the founding of the online public sphere on Dehai nor the fluorescence of rival websites and the alternative spaces they

opened up for expression immediately or totally transformed the infopolitical culture created by the Isaias regime. The lack of political openness and
government transparency within Eritrea, furthermore, does not stand in simple contrast to the online public sphere because there is also considerable
opaqueness in online communications.

For example, allegations of censorship by webmanagers circulate around
all the websites, even though Dehai, Asmarino, and Awate each champion
the ideal of an open public sphere in their statements of purpose and posting guidelines, and the site managers themselves insist that they do not censor. Online, however, readers of any website can only see what is posted, so
the existence of a realm of rejected or immediately deleted posts can seem
plausible and is impossible to conclusively disprove. Issues of censorship
online, furthermore, must be considered in cultural, as well as technological, terms. In the Eritrean context, the national leadership from the EPLF
to the present has been highly centralized and top-down, thinking on behalf
of the people and communicating to them, while exhibiting little tolerance
for deviation from the national script or for spontaneous public expression.
There are thus entrenched patterns of secrecy, mistrust, and self-censorship
among Eritreans, and the suspicions aimed at webmanagers reflect this infopolitical culture. From my extensive readings on these websites, I conclude
that censorship, if indeed it is practiced by any of the website managers to
exclude posts, is far less powerful in these forums than are the practices of
self-censorship and peer censorship through the effect of scathing posts that
intimidate people from posting at all or serve as warnings to stay away from
some topics or viewpoints. There are, moreover, processes of self-selection
that determine who posts or does not post what and on which website they
choose to post. One cannot know what is censored through omission or exclusion from the websites, but one can read on all three sites outrageous statements, vulgar language, personal insults and accusations, and disrespectful
language toward the state, government figures, and the President as well as
towards fellow posters.

Despite any suspicions about the roles played by webmanagers, the websites offer a space where Eritreans are able to build trust in each other through
communicating openly in a public way. This is, nonetheless, a fraught process. As chapter 5 explores in detail, intimidation and silencing are carried out
by posters who write extreme responses to others' posts. Accusations of censorship, patterns of self-censorship, mistrust, and the harsh rejection meted
out by some posters to others should cause us to reflect on just how difficult a

project it is to build an open public sphere. It is by no means solely a technological feat. A poster on Asmarino writing under the pseudonym Dr. Anonymous explained his choice to conceal his name thus:

> I decided to stay anonymous because I believe I can exercise my freedom of speech and writing without fear. . . . Besides I am not "Isayas Afewerke" or any government official. I am just a concerned Eritrean. Why should my name mean anything to you anyway! I am sick and tired of people who cannot stand any idea that does not agree with their perspective. . . . I am going to deny them a chance to call me Woyane [Ethiopian], EPLF, ELF, CIA and what have you. . . . In this millennium we have a priceless media called internet and let us use it for a genuine and truthful discussion. (Asmarino post, November 20, 2000, ellipses and material in brackets added)

Some posters openly challenge site managers on the issue of censorship and the websites' mission. Three months into Awate's existence, a poster began his message by saying, "I am forwarding this short piece to see if I can make it past the 'sifting process' of Awate 'team.' Why am I disinclined to believe the assertion made by the Awate kahuna does not censor at all" (Awate post December 3, 2000). Further on he writes: "As for the noble mission of this website . . . I don't see how one can narrow 'the Eritrean political divide' and bring about reconciliation among Eritreans, if one zeroes obsessively on the weak points of an Eritrean body politic, GoE/PFDJ and ignores other facets of the Eritrean political realities." At this point in the post, the Awate team members interject themselves into the text with humor, writing "we interrupt this message," before getting serious and stating, "The piece is posted as received." They then take the opportunity to explain the rationale for their screening: "we do not accept articles without substance. . . . No one visits a site to read none sense. . . . Furthermore, not everyone considers GoE a divine entity" (Awate post, December 3, 2000, ellipses added).

No one can know for sure that website managers are not censoring any posts. Nor can they know for certain who is reading posts or, in some cases, who is writing them and whether the author is doing so independently or in service to the state. This opacity, coupled with the tight control over information by the state, fosters a climate that allows suspicions to develop, rumors to circulate, and conspiracy theories to be generated. Although most posters use their real names, people speculate about whether some names are fake names, as well as whether particular posters are stooges or proxy posters who are actually government mouthpieces. People wonder what clandestine roles the government plays in online political discussions. There is often a sense among Eritreans that in politics nothing is what it seems. One rumor had it that, under assumed names, President Isaias Afewerki himself and his critics within the Eritrean government used diaspora websites to debate freely with one another. When I was unable to get a visa for Eritrea in summer 2012 and sometime later someone posted something positive about my research on De-hai, I was told by an Eritrean that this was meant as a good sign to me from the Eritrean government. These ways of reading are evidence of the powerful infopolitical effects of the Isaias regime that span a transnational political field that traverses online and off-line contexts.

A five-page, single-spaced post by the Awate team gives a sense of the re-luctance among Eritreans to criticize the regime in the first years of Awate. The post addresses in particular the hesitation among Eritreans in diaspora to protest despite their relative safety. The post opens with a quote from George Orwell that says, "In a time of universal deceit, telling the truth is a revolution-ary act."

> One cannot help but be disgusted at those who enjoy the freedoms that the West accords to them, yet they do not wish the same freedom for their peo-ple. . . . We fled the country hoping that someday we will return to it after helping to rid it of all the ill elements that made it unlivable. We fought, we killed. We died. And we physically liberated our country. But we never freed our people. It hurts to see that we, the victims of dictatorship and injustice, cannot raise a voice in condemnation of injustice. . . . "Follow without ques-tion" is the recipe prepared by the weaklings. . . . The free . . . will always shout: "No to proxy thinking." No to unwanted guardians. Free the people. (Awate post, February 21, 2001, ellipses added)

Later the Awate team refers to what its calls "the alien political culture that the PFDJ instilled in our people." This can be read as turning the standard accusation—that critics of the government are not true Eritreans—on its head. Here the post suggests that it is in fact the political culture of the leadership that is "alien" and not authentically Eritrean. This rhetorical move opens an important space between Eritreanness and the regime and, in effect, makes Eritrean people arbiters of what is Eritrean, rather than legitimizing the state as the master definer.

In 2002 the Awate team posted what it claimed was a leaked government document, arguing that it "exposes the fact that Dehai is a PFDJ propaganda outlet" (Awate post, April 3, 2002). In a subsequent post on the topic, the

Awate team explains that it "wanted to expose Dehai's pretense of being a 'neutral' website" (Awate post, May 8, 2002). The leaked document is a proposal written at the request of Yemane Gegreab, the PFDJ's political director and President Isaias's close ally, by one of Dehai's administrators for "upgrading and re-designing" the PFDJ website, shaebia.org. The proposal can be interpreted in different ways, one of which is that it is consistent with Dehai's original mission of contributing to Eritrean nation-building under the leadership of President Isaias and the PFDJ. What I find most interesting about the leaked proposal is not that Dehai administrators might support the regime, but that the Eritrean government would rely on expertise from a diaspora website to improve an official website. This is a further testament to the government's perception, not just of the of the power internet as a communications technology, but of the political power of Dehai, in particular.

The proposal itself, read through a different lense than that of the Awate team, could be interpreted as pushing the government toward more openness. It argues, among other things, that "[p]erhaps the most important lesson to be learnt from the turmoil of the past three years is the central necessity of delivering timely **information and news** to our people and the rest of the world at large" (emphasis original). Dehai remains a source of progovernment posts, although it stands by its claims of being unedited, uncensored, and uncurated. Often accused in recent years of being tied to the regime, Dehai in 2013 is featured as a link on the home page of the PFDJ's website, shaebia.org, an endorsement that suggests the regime perceives Dehai as a source of political support. Clearly it is in the interest of the ruling party to steer traffic away from Asmarino and Awate where its most outspoken critics post.

The difficult project of establishing dissent as a legitimate activity, building a momentum of critical opinion, and creating a body of counterknowledge and counternarratives becomes visible as one reads posts like the ones quoted earlier in this chapter. This process is further revealed in "a tribute to the writers of Awate.com," a thirty-six-page compendium of excerpts from selected posts from the preceding year posted by the Awate team at the start of 2003. The act of reposting highlights from a year's worth of commentary and analysis is an important infopolitical strategy. The tribute, whether by design or chance, seemed destined to propel the political momentum against the regime further by collecting and, in a sense, codifying these disparate, dissident texts. This is another example of how (as described with reference to Dehai in chapter 2) discourse and past patterns of online activity construct the context in which present and future exchanges take place. Several themes emerge from these posts. Many address directly the importance of breaking the silence and the significance of public opinion. Posters also articulate the need to speak on behalf of Eritreans abused by the state. In thanking the many writers (103 posters are listed by name), the Awate team contends that "[i]n 2002, thanks to their efforts, there isn't a single government in the world, a single human rights agency, a single NGO, a single international reporter that doesn't know about the injustice of the PFDJ" (Awate post, January 2, 2003).

One of the more powerful posts in the compendium raises the case of political prisoners in Eritrea and decries the "silence and ambivalence" of the diaspora:

> After six months of our silence and ambivalence, our brothers, our parts, are asking shouting unto us. They are loudly crying unto our ears. They are knocking the closed doors of our conscience. They are nagging us not to forget them. They are calling us by our very names, Eritreans, that we should not look away. They are literally pulling our ears to pay attention to the sad fact of their incarceration without charge. (originally posted April 3, 2002, excerpted and reposted on Awate, January 2, 2003)

Another post in the compendium similarly questions the reluctance of the diaspora to speak out against the regime:

> I am wondering what kind of tyrannical act of the regime are we waiting for to unfold that would prompt us to support all means necessary to salvage the nation. The Eritrean People need us now and [if] not now when, if not us who?" (originally posted October 15, 2002, reposted on Awate, January 2, 2003)

The power of public opinion in the face of dictatorship is asserted in another post: "Do not forget that it is possible to ban Press Law, close newspapers and jail journalists, but is impossible to ban public opinion regarding the leadership" (originally posted August 21, 2002, reposted on Awate January 2, 2003).

Such posts indicate how difficult it was to turn the tide of support for President Isaias and the PFDJ regime into open expressions of criticism and dissent, even with the ostensible freedom offered by the online public sphere and by living abroad. The following post conveys some sense of the social penalties associated with voicing dissent: "Because I opposed the government of PFDJ, I find myself condemned, isolated and ostracized by my children, my wife, my family, my relatives, my compatriots, my friends and my loved ones. For I spoke the truth" (originally posted December 30, 2002, reposted on Awate January 2, 2003). Such posts make visible the struggles among Eritreans themselves to establish the legitimacy of dissent. This was a wrenching process because for decades people's identification with the national leadership had been tightly tied to understandings of what it means to be Eritrean.

As disillusionment grew and spread, counternarratives and new perspectives on the Eritrean state were developed online. One of Awate's columnists asked readers to consider Eritrea's leadership from two contrasting points of view. While the government represents itself as cautious in protecting Eritrea's sovereignty, the author argues the opposite:

> Is President Isaias Afwerki an able captain, patiently and calmly steering our ship of state to a safe harbor, while all around him people are losing their head? Or, is he more like Eve [*sic*] Knievel who treats Eritrea as his personal bike, jumping her from canyon to a river, while all around him there is nothing but fire, crashes and the howling of adoring fans? (Awate post, November 30, 2004)

He later continues this metaphor:

> I subscribe to the Evel Kneivel theorem of Isaias Afwerki. More precisely, it is the Harry Houdini model: the president as an escape artist. . . . It is a thrilling show: you pay your ticket, catch your breath, applause and go home. But when the magician is the head of state, well that is enough to give one a heart attack. Because the line between *just in time* and *just missed it* is so fine. (Awate post, November 30, 2004, italics original, ellipses added)

The six-page post specifically makes reference to the border war. The president is thus portrayed as a daredevilish risk-taker who thinks nothing of putting Eritrean lives in peril. The poster also points to the government's failure to resolve the issue of the demarcation of the border and put an end to the simmering hostilities years after the fighting ended.

> Often, when one talks about the cost of time, one is reminded of our armed struggle: it took us 30 years. . . . Therefore, we should have no time limit and a similar defiance attitude to safeguard its independence and sovereignty. But . . . during the armed struggle, we had nothing to lose and everything to gain . . . now, we have little to gain and much to lose. (Awate post, November 30, 2004, ellipses added)

Posts like these are politically important because of their dialogic construction: the government's claims and narratives are specifically restated and then refuted. Given the enormous time and resources that the EPLF and the PFDJ had at their disposal to forge national myths and discourses that became core components of Eritrean identities and subjectivities, these legacies could not simply be dismissed and swept away but had to be addressed and reinterpreted. Posts like these are significant social texts that serve to legitimize dissent as a valid Eritrean perspective and to generate new meanings and alternative histories that are potentially subversive. In order to develop new subjectivities and mobilize others, Eritreans had to fight the all-encompassing prevailing narratives of the state by developing and disseminating alternative narratives. In this fight, the independent media of diaspora websites is a powerful weapon. Momentum is built as posters debate and contribute to a collective body of critical analyses.

Posters, moreover, are empowered by the positive comments their posts receive, and in this way posters encourage others and reinforce each other's efforts, collectively creating a climate of tolerance for dissent. An example of positive feedback is this message responding to a six-page, single-spaced critique of the government's "self-reliance" policy:

> Just a magnificent piece! I can't wait to read your next installment. Indeed, GOE [government of Eritrea] has blown "self reliance," whatever that means, beyond proportion. Keep up the good work! (Asmarino post, August 30, 2005)

Posters' efforts constituted a public and collective process of changing the political culture, a process that is ongoing. It is a deeply infopolitical process not simply because of censorship and repression but because the EPLF and the Isaias regime have been so successful in defining the terms of Eritrean existence, not only materially but also ideologically and subjectively. The overdetermination of language by the state is noted by a poster on Awate who writes: "Thanks to the PFDJ, the words 'sovereignty' 'unity' and 'diversity' have lost all meaning" (Awate post, August 17, 2009). Thus, the very language for discussing politics has to be reinvented or reclaimed in order to break the state's hold.

A series of long posts by one writer on Asmarino in 2012 presents a wide-ranging analysis of Eritrean history and current events as well as a pointed critique of views expressed on rival website Awate. Here is how the poster explains the power of the political culture created by the EPLF and sustained under the PFDJ:

> The mass dislocation of the *ghedli* [lit. "struggle," but here "nationalist struggle"] generation started earlier than the revolution in urban centers of Eritrea, in general, and Asmara, in particular, when they identified themselves with "Asmara modernity" and tried everything possible to distance themselves from backward *Habesha*—the Ethiopian, the *hagereseb*, the Orthodox Church, their own fathers, etc. Once dislodged from their roots, they became easy preys to the luring of *ghedli*. In *ghedli*, with every value from the past degraded to the lowest level possible, the uprooting was carried to its nihilist logical conclusion. After independence, this nihilist project went unabated both among the civilian population and the National Service. Now that this perpetual dislocation of *ghedli*'s making has been going on for 50 years, the young generation didn't even get a glimpse of the normal world that would have served them as a reservoir of reference points with which to compare their abnormal position. Having grown in a completely abnormal world, the yard stick by which they assess their situation comes from none other but that abnormal world itself. (Asmarino post, December 2, 2012)

The author's reassessment of the liberation struggle stands out because rewriting the history of Eritrea's independence is fundamental to charting Eritrea's future, and yet this task has been very difficult to approach, given the profound sacrifices the war exacted and the myth-making about martyrs' sacrifices by the national leadership.

Posters engage in a range of infopolitical projects. They not only criticize the government and respond to official discourses, they collectively construct alternative histories and new meanings for core values such as service to the nation. The helter-skelter of posts and debates among posters and even across the three websites, moreover, ends up providing a kind of transparency that is lacking in Eritrea, where the public political participation of citizens is mobilized from the top-down and orchestrated to show unity and support for the government. Many posts, furthermore, explicitly address issues of state infopolitics, the lack of transparency, the absence of freedom of expression, and the repression of independent political expression and participation in Eritrea. Posters contest the parameters of what can and cannot be openly stated, engaging in infopolitical struggles as some seek to expand the range of what can be expressed, to generate alternative histories, and to articulate new understandings.

A poster on Asmarino defends the legitimacy of engaging in criticizing the government and discussing with fellow Eritreans, while making reference to the location of many posters in the United States:

> what is wrong with getting to gother to critic your own government? . . . what is wrong to ask each other's opinion about current or past condition of your own people we might have different opinion about it but it is ok after all you and I are living in the land of the free the great U.S.A. let us learn something. (Asmarino post, February 5, 2007)

Some posts specifically champion the power and significance of diaspora websites in Eritrean politics. Among a series of posts on Asmarino celebrating the website's ninth anniversary in 2006, one proclaimed: "Asmarino scares the PFDJ cadres and its gangster leader more than any other entity. Long live Asmarino" (Asmarino post, August 24, 2006). A post titled "Injustice and the PFDJ Way" used a humorous tone to criticize the lack of transparency in Eritrean politics. This post, like so many, is far too long to quote in its entirety, but includes the following paragraph:

> Ask the hardest-core supporter of the PFDJ what Eritrea's justice system is based on, and he will have to stumble and repeat what Isaias Afwerki, Yemane Gebreab, and the entire PFDJ hierarchy has said, "**we have our own way, our own culture of dealing with things.**" The Catch-22 here is that part of the culture of dealing with things is not telling people how you deal with things. (Awate post, November 2, 2009, emphasis original)

Humor, particularly parody and satire, is an important genre for critical perspectives (Bernal 2013b; Haugerud 2013; Scott 1992). The ruling party's acronym, PFDJ, has been parodied as "Please Forget Democracy and Justice" and "Pests Front for Despots and Jailers," among others.

Asmarino's explanation of its purpose and achievements in a call for financial support to sustain and expand its media efforts in 2007 makes a powerful statement about the online public sphere:

> We have persevered under the most difficult circumstances for 10 years to provide an alternative democratic space for all Eritreans suffering under the absolute control of an authoritarian regime. . . . We have been lucky enough to witness firsthand the birth and growth of a burgeoning Eritrean democratic movement. . . . [W]e have tried to encourage and expand this growing passion

for democracy and human rights. . . . In short we have been motivated by one fundamental principle: to expand democratic space and allow all information, opinions, and views to flow unfettered. As to how much we have succeeded in this endeavor, we will leave to the people and to history. (Asmarino post, March 4, 2007)

## CONCLUSION

These uses of the internet are significant in reframing what the nation is and how it functions and is experienced in practice. The spaces created first by Dehai, and later by Asmarino and Awate, and the subjectivities Eritreans in diaspora have cultivated online are politically transformative. Through producing unauthorized national media and exercising rights in the online public sphere denied citizens in Eritrea, the diaspora decenters state authority and relocates the nation from the power center in Asmara to Eritrean people wherever they are located. While earlier activities online hinted at this, the full implications were made clear when posters shifted from using the internet to extend Eritrean nationalism as defined by leaders in Eritrea into the virtual and throughout the diaspora, and began instead to use the online public space they had created as Eritrean political space that is not under Eritrean sovereignty. As such, the websites came to serve as a platform from which Eritreans could challenge national leaders, call their legitimacy into question, and raise demands for accountability of the national leadership to Eritrean people.

At one level the online public sphere is organized around the existential question, "what does it mean to be Eritrean?," a question that connects individual identity, community, and the nation. The fundamental subtext running through the websites, however, concerns questions of power and infopolitical struggles over who has the right to define Eritrea and its people. A post on Dehai from April 12, 2008, yields insights into how Eritreans understand the significance of the internet. While posting on Dehai, the writer is responding, not to Dehai posts, but to the website Awate and, particularly, one of the founding members of the Awate team. The post opens with the statement that "[t]he purpose of this article is to help expose Dr. Saleh A. A. Younis." Saleh Younis is a well-known internet figure among Eritreans who gained much attention over the years for his marvelous and often humorous posts on Dehai, before breaking away to help form Awate where he continues to post as a featured columnist. The Dehai post consists of five pages of criticism, including: "He operates as a conduit, facilitator, motivator and a smart navigator/leader who provides a place for all anti Eritrean Elements to spew venom freely and unbound."

While focusing on one individual and one website, this critique reveals, among other things, the distinct kinds of power associated with the online public sphere. The labels used—"conduit," "facilitator," and "motivator"— describe the various effects that the websites have in Eritrean circles. The websites created by the Eritrean diaspora are not simply sources of information or merely places to express oneself, or to make social connections with fellow Eritreans. Rather, they facilitate and motivate; they enable new leaders and forms of leadership, "smart navigator/leader," to develop outside of official channels. The websites, furthermore, are understood (even by their critics) as places to communicate "freely and unbound." And certainly they are free, compared to other Eritrean venues that are more effectively policed by the state or directly under its control. This Dehai post also offers a view of the kind of cross-talk among Eritrean websites that connects them as a national public sphere, where posters with diverse concerns and perspectives can seek audiences and where readers can access a range of sources and competing arguments. Online the nature of Eritrean identity, citizenship, and governance are not simply reproduced but are actively being questioned, constructed, and transformed.

As this analysis of digital dissent has shown, what is powerful about the access opened by the internet and by online public spheres is the ways they allow diverse actors to call into question the terms of knowledge production, relations of authority, and the politics of representation, as well as the ways that they make possible the collaborative production and circulation of alternative knowledges and the emergence of counterpublics. These are not events but processes that are inherently political and involve conflict. Such an understanding helps explain why some experiments to create digital public spaces have failed, because a public sphere (and by extension citizenship and democracy) cannot be reduced to access to technology or to information. The public sphere, civil society, and democracy require forms of social engagement and exchange that are not captured by simple concepts of transparency or access.

The next chapter examines how the Awate team used leaked government documents to create an unauthorized online war memorial, thereby seizing infopolitical power from the state.

# CHAPTER 4

# Mourning Becomes Electronic:
# Representing the Nation in
# a Virtual War Memorial

[W]e believe that a big portion of the Eritrean culture glorifies warriors. However, at the same time, the Eritrean culture considers life very precious. One indicator is the grieving process in Eritrea. In some traditions, the dead are mourned for forty days and forty nights. Even people of very modest means spare no resources to pay their respects. There has been a great deal of criticism of the "excess" of this tradition; now, however, we have reverted to an opposite extreme where we are supposed to "ululate" and celebrate the dead—but not mourn them. Each hero listed in the Martyr's Album, each number represented in the statistics represents a loss of Eritrea—a loss that should be mourned and grieved by all of us.—The Awate team

(Awate post, January 16, 2005)

In 2005 a virtual national war memorial, called the Martyrs Album, was established on awate.com. The unauthorized memorial used leaked government records to commemorate and document the Eritrean lives lost in the 1998–2000 border war with Ethiopia. The Martyrs Album is a prime example of the ways that the internet facilitates political experimentation and makes possible the development of novel forms of political engagement that have no off-line counterpart. This online memorial represents a creative form of political protest. In this chapter I explore how Eritreans in diaspora used digital media to act on behalf of the nation as a surrogate for the state, and in so doing, seized infopolitical power from the state.

This act of commemoration by the Awate team reminds us that losses, absences, deaths, and displacement are not simply sources of human suffering, but are generative of identities, social relations, and subjectivities (Feldman 1991; Theidon 2013; Bay and Donham 2006). Eritreans are defined to a great extent by their losses and shared sacrifices. The war memorial is important because all Eritreans are essentially survivors whose lives and families have been irrevocably harmed by decades of war fought on Eritrean soil. Eritreans' connections to the nation have been constructed through compelling narratives in which martyrs are accorded a central role. Martyrs, as I have argued, are a potent national symbol deployed by the state to exact sacrifices from Eritreans, a symbol that I argue represents the social contract of sacrificial citizenship between citizens and the Eritrean state.

From the early 1990s until today Eritreans in diaspora have used the internet not simply to discuss or observe national politics, but to actively participate. The Martyrs Album is a distinct intervention, however, because the diaspora used the internet to act like the state and carry out statelike responsibilities. In the pages of the memorial the Awate team emulates state practices, wielding the state's own symbols, rhetoric, and national narratives as infopolitical weapons to decenter the state. The establishment of the war memorial on Awate, thus, stands as another element of the transformations described in this book in which the Eritrean diaspora has gone from using the internet as an arm of Eritrean nationalism reaching beyond Eritrea's borders to using websites as an offshore platform where a transnational civil society could develop to challenge the Eritrean state. Through the Martyrs Album, the diaspora constructed a national institution outside the nation and performed duties on behalf of the nation that the government had failed to fulfill. It is significant, moreover, that the construction of the online memorial involved cooperation between Eritreans in diaspora and government insiders in Eritrea who leaked the information to them, as well as cooperation between the Awate team and Asmarino's webmanager, who provided some technical assistance to the project (as recounted in an editorial on Asmarino, December 28, 2012).

## STATE SECRECY AND RAISING THE DEAD

How does it happen that a group of Eritreans based in the United States construct an online memorial commemorating Eritrea's war dead? Any analysis of Awate's war memorial must set it in the infopolitical context that connects this online project with wider Eritrean histories and conditions. The most significant elements of this context are the histories of warfare, mourning, and silence that emerged during the liberation struggle and, since then, have been fostered by the Eritrean state. At the same time that the Eritrean People's Liberation Front (EPLF) and later the ruling party, the People's Front for Democracy and Justice (PFDJ) sacralized dying for the nation and called the war dead "martyrs," these authorities maintained secrecy about the actual numbers and identities of those killed in war. During the thirty-year liberation struggle, the EPLF did not release information about guerilla fighters' deaths. The Eritrean government likewise honored and celebrated the sacrifice of martyrs for their country in the border war, yet for years it withheld information about the number of lives lost and the identities of the dead. The Isaias regime's treatment of deaths in the border war thus echoed earlier losses and earlier silences on the part of national leaders. State secrecy about the war dead, moreover, reflects an important dimension of the regime's infopolitics, which is that it operates as a guardian of information in relation to its citizens, treating the public as not to be trusted with too much knowledge.

The national holiday Martyr's Day, observed every June 20 in Eritrea, is set aside as a time of national mourning that serves to acknowledge the losses of lives cut short and provides an occasion for families to remember and grieve. However, Martyr's Day, I argue, is also an expression of power whereby the state officially authorizes mourning as a national activity once a year and thereby orchestrates and delimits its practice. In calling the war dead "martyrs" and making Martyr's Day a public, national observance, moreover, the state claims all losses for itself, foregrounding the significance of losses sustained by the nation, while obscuring the private dimensions of loss experienced by Eritreans. In withholding information about the casualties of the border war long after the fighting had ended, the state denied families access to the personal information about the dead they needed to mourn. Judith Butler (2004, 34) recognizes the political significance of memorializing the dead when she asserts that "we have to consider the obituary as an act of nation-building." Butler (2004, 36) contends that failure to accord public recognition to deaths can be equivalent to a denial: "In the silence . . . there was no event, no loss." In consequence, she argues "violence is derealized and diffused," which shores up nationalism and suppresses internal dissent "that would expose the concrete, human effects of its [the nation's] violence" (2004, 38). The unauthorized online memorial arises from and makes visible the contradiction between the state's public veneration of martyrs and its efforts to keep actual deaths secret.

The Martyrs Album is complex in its dynamics as a political action as well as in the various texts, images, and documents that comprise it. In creating the memorial, the Awate team used digital media not only to protest and criticize the state, but to perform a national service in a statelike manner. Throughout the pages of the memorial the Awate team employs statist language and practices to speak in a national voice on behalf of the nation and to the nation. The tone and presentation of the Martyrs Album stand in stark contrast to the irreverent posts slamming or spoofing government policies on the main pages of Awate. The dominant genre or modality of the Martyrs Album is not that of dissidence, but that of official nationalism. Within the webpages of the memorial, protest and critique of the government are for the most part expressed obliquely through the very act of stepping into the void left by the Eritrean state, and thereby making the state's silence and inaction publicly visible.

By establishing a memorial in cyberspace, a group of Eritreans in diaspora offered a virtual surrogate for what the state had failed to provide its citizens. In doing so, they did more than simply challenge the secrecy of the Isaias regime. The unauthorized, but official-like, action taken by the Awate team on behalf of the nation worked to decenter state power from the seat of government in Asmara to Eritreans everywhere, revealing the inadequacy of the Eritrean state and foregrounding Eritrean people as the true essence of the nation. By taking leaked government documents and using the information to construct a virtual national memorial, Eritreans in diaspora, thus, not only challenged the infopolitical power of the state but also actively and publicly diminished that power, claiming some of it for Awate and the Eritrean people the website seeks to serve. The Martyrs Album was a response not only to the fact that the Eritrean state refused to provide citizens with information about the losses sustained in the war, but to the greater failure of the state to fully acknowledge the terrible human costs of the war and the unwillingness of the national leadership to hold themselves accountable to the people for the devastation and suffering the war caused. Stepping into the void created by state secrecy, Eritreans in diaspora constructed a memorial on behalf of the nation, raising the dead to make the failure of the nation's leaders publicly visible and, in the process, presenting a new version of the nation as based on connections among Eritrean people rather than on people's relationships to the state.

## THE MARTYRS ALBUM

The Martyrs Album first appeared on Awate in late 2004 and was completed in January 2005. It was featured in the main menu of links on the left side of Awate's home page. Clicking on this link opened the memorial home page. Looking at this page, one was immediately struck by the visual contrast between it and the colorful, lively main home page of Awate, where images and text appear on a white background. On the home page of the Martyrs Album one confronts a black page on which a few images appear along with some lines of text in white type. A further contrast between the main web pages of

Awate and those of the Martyrs Ablum is that all elements of the memorial are unchanging and fixed throughout, whereas the rest of Awate is continually changing as it is updated with new posts and photos. Posters' contributions of various kinds of content to Awate create its in-the-moment feeling of timeliness and interactivity. The starkness and fixity of the Martyrs Album create an opposite feeling of timelessness. Within the pages of the memorial there is no means provided for posters to add any content or comments. The only interactivity allowed within the Martyrs Album is the viewer's choice to click or not to click on the several links displayed on the memorial's home page. The Martyrs Album is comprised of three distinct components: the memorial home page, a statistical report, and a FAQs page.

The design of the home page of the Martyrs Album makes clear that it is intended as a national memorial. Its lack of interactivity contributes to its aura of authoritativeness. Across the top of the page, the phrase "Eternal Glory to Our Martyrs" appears in Arabic, Tigrinya, and English. This text is framed on each side by the image of a burning candle. The overall effect of this stark, black page with images of burning candles is very somber, still, and sad. Along the bottom of the page, "Liberty, Security, and Martyrdom" is written in English, Arabic, and Tigrinya. These three words can be read as an assertion of core Eritrean national values, values which have been promoted by the state and have deep resonance in Eritrean history. Eritreans are understood to value liberty as evidenced by their long struggle for independence. They demonstrated the value they place on security in their defense of the Eritrean border against Ethiopia in the border war. Finally, Eritreans are understood to value martyrdom, since the liberty and security of Eritrea were achieved through the sacrifice of lives that liberated Eritrea and through the lives lost to preserve the security of the nation after independence, particularly during the border war. The mention of martyrdom places the deaths in the border war into the wider context of Eritrean history and echoes state rhetoric. In these ways, the message of the memorial is not limited to the border war but represents the nation and addresses Eritrean conditions more broadly.

The language and design of the Martyrs Album emulate official practices and discourses in numerous ways. For example, the home page is devoid of any explicit religious imagery, discourse, or iconography, which is in keeping with the state's adherence to secular nationalism in a country that is nearly evenly divided between Christianity and Islam. The use of the term "martyr" also is consistent with the use of this term by the state that has, in fact, redefined and secularized the meaning of this term in the Eritrean context. The use of Tigrinya, Arabic, and English echoes government forms since, from the time it was a nationalist movement, the EPLF used all three languages, and, after independence, this practice has continued under President Isaias and the PFDJ. The image of burning candles reflects the practice of candlelight processions that mark Martyr's Day in Eritrea.

The two slogans—"Eternal Glory to Our Martyrs" and "Liberty, Security, Martyrdom"—form the head and foot of the page. In between them, reading down from the top, is the logo of Awate, which depicts a rider on horseback. This is followed by an introductory statement, which in its entirety reads:

> This website is designed for many purposes. First and foremost, it is to pay tribute to the heroes who fell. Second, it is to humanize war and chronicle the cost of war and, in doing so, to prevent future wars. Heroes die for the sake of a cause, a country, but mostly they die to protect their comrades. This is a living monument to them.

(This passage appears only in English, like most of the text on the page, as well as in the statistical report and FAQs pages that can be accessed via links on the memorial home page.)

This text by the Awate team performs a subtle yet significant departure from the state's national narrative about martyrs when it claims that "mostly they die to protect their comrades." This, along with other statements in the memorial, presents a new vision of the nation and its war dead; a vision that runs counter to the state's assertion that martyrs die for the nation. Dying to protect their comrades constructs Eritrean nationalism, not as a bond of people to their state but as the bonds that tie Eritreans to one another. This reformulation of national loyalty is politically meaningful because it suggests that loyalty on the part of Eritreans need not be defined as loyalty to the state or to national leaders, but can instead mean loyalty to fellow Eritreans. This distinction has profound ramifications in the highly centralized political context of Eritrea.

The main content of the memorial home page is a box containing a link for each year from the start of the border war with Ethiopia in 1998 to 2003. (As is explained elsewhere in the Martyrs Album, although the war ended in 2000, deaths resulting from war injuries continued into 2003.) By clicking on a specific year, a visitor can see a list of the names of those who died that year, along with their rank, service assignment, year of birth, and age at death. Except for numbers, this information is written in Tigrinya and is not displayed correctly unless one has downloaded the appropriate software. The links to the lists of martyrs' names are accompanied by a disclaimer that reads:

> This page contains the names of Eritrean martyrs who died between 1998 and 2003, as a consequence of the 1998–2000 border war that broke out between Eritrea and Ethiopia. This page is designed as a tribute. If you think seeing the names would cause you stress and/or anxiety, please don't continue any further.

This disclaimer can be interpreted as a statement designed to foreground the seriousness of the content of the memorial, indicating to visitors that neither they nor the Awate team should take the information presented lightly. The warning further makes clear to readers the break between the memorial and the other pages of Awate where posts may be humorous, vulgar, playful, and insulting. The Awate team's descriptions of the Martyrs Album as a "living monument" and a "tribute" also serve this purpose.

## INSTITUTIONS OF POWER AND INFOPOLITICAL CITIZENSHIP

In his influential book on nationalism, Benedict Anderson points to the map, the census, and the museum as "three institutions of power" key to the formation of national imaginaries (2006, 163). It can be argued that a war memorial is also an institution of power, particularly for a nation like Eritrea where national identity has been forged through warfare and martyrdom. War memorials, like museums, are partly concerned with representing the nation and narrating national history. In practice, memorials are often part of or linked to museums. Moreover, as White (1997, 8) notes: "Museums may—and often do—*act* as memorials. Likewise memorials and monuments often include historical displays and exhibitions" [italics original]. From this perspective, the unauthorized cybermemorial created by the Awate team constitutes an intervention of "citizens" in diaspora into a form of representing the nation that is normally the prerogative of government. Like the other institutions of power identified by Anderson—the map, the census, and the museum—a war memorial is very much about the kind of power I have called "infopolitical."

By establishing the memorial, the Awate team goes beyond criticizing the state to actually take for itself and for the Eritrean people some of the power of the state. The infopolitics of the online memorial has multiple dimensions. At one level, the Martyrs Album is an infopolitical intervention, because it is an act of symbolic and communicative power rather than an act of seizing control over territory, material objects, or people. Because the memorial makes public information from leaked government documents, it is also an exposé of state secrets and state practices of secrecy. The memorial is part of a struggle with the state over what could be termed "infopolitical citizenship," the people's rights of access to information and freedom from state censorship and secrecy. The memorial is also infopolitical in the specific tactics of its composition. The methods of the Awate team in the design and composition of the Martyrs Album involve using the state's own national symbols, practices, and official discourses. These elements give the memorial its recognizable national character, lending this unofficial construct a stately, authoritative aura. From an infopolitical perspective, authoritative power is, among other things, the power of authorship. In authoring the Martyrs Album in this way, the Awate team stepped into the state's role, thereby taking some of the state's power. In the close analysis that follows, I show that in the pages of the memorial the Awate team speaks not only from a position of Eritreanness but also speaks to and for the Eritrean people in the way that the national leadership does. This works to decenter the nation from the state's authoritative power.

The location of the memorial in cyberspace contributes to a distinctive representation of the nation that is conducive to decentering it from the seat of authority in Asmara. Museums and maps emphasize the territorial boundaries of the nation, and thus, foreground the division between everything and everyone internal to the nation and all that lies outside it. While a museum usually requires a building in a physical location, memorials are more conceptual in nature, "a memorial may be a day, a conference, or a space" (Young 1993, cited in Khleif and Slymovics 2008, 187). An online memorial obscures borders and distances. Given the dispersion and displacement Eritreans have experienced, it is particularly significant that, no matter where they were located (if they could access a computer), Eritreans could experience the memorial firsthand once it appeared on Awate.

The digital memorial, thus, by virtue of the qualities of cyberspace as well as through its content, then, contributes to a sense of the nation as a social formation rather than as a territorial state. This construction of the nation is made explicit in the texts composed by the Awate team for the memorial, including the one quoted earlier on the Martyrs Album home page. In the FAQs section, the Awate team explains that in order to assess how complete the data it had obtained were, "we conducted a small sampling: we searched for names of martyrs, those of our family members and friends." In this way, the members of the Awate team connect themselves through kinship and social relations to the dead and thus to the nation. Intimate ties to martyrs rather than residence in Eritrea or legal status define the Awate team as Eritreans by making clear that they have personally shared the pain of losses caused by war. Their statement about martyred family members and friends positions the Awate team as insiders to Eritrean experience who speak from within the Eritrean national community, even if located outside of Eritrea. This is an example of how the ambiguity of cyberspace and of diaspora make it possible to be simultaneously outside and inside the nation. The vision of the nation as constituted through social bonds among Eritreans marginalizes the state and challenges its role as that which defines the nation. At the same time, the Awate team reclaims the martyrs from the state, by situating their deaths in relation to ordinary people ("family members and friends"), rather than simply in relation to the nation.

If the memorial works to decenter state power through the way it represents the nation as fundamentally based in Eritrean people rather than in the state or national territory, the way in which the Awate team acts in place of the Eritrean state, taking on responsibilities on behalf of the nation, serves to further displace state power. Explaining their actions on the FAQs page, the Awate team states that the Vietnam Memorial in Washington, DC, served as its model. The team even provides a link to the Vietnam Memorial's online counterpart. This comparison highlights the statelike qualities of Awate's actions and makes visible the lack of appropriate action on the part of the Eritrean state. The Vietnam Memorial is an official memorial created by the American government to honor and remember its dead soldiers, whereas, in the Eritrean case, the Martyrs Album was established online by Eritreans in diaspora stepping in to take statelike actions that the government of Eritrea had failed to take.

There are important similarities between the Vietnam War and the Eritrean-Ethiopian border war that make this more than a random comparison. Both wars were deeply controversial in the eyes of citizens; moreover, neither war ended with a decisive victory. There are clearly aesthetic similarities between the Vietnam Memorial and the Martyrs Album whose stark design and foregrounding of the names of the dead work to emphasize the human losses caused by war, rather than to celebrate heroism or victory. Though not mentioned by the Awate team, there are some key distinctions between the virtual Vietnam War Memorial and the Martyrs Album, however. Awate's memorial is purely a digital artifact that has no offline counterpart. In contrast, the Vietnam Memorial has a material existence on the ground, and significantly is located in the nation's capital. Its website is not the Vietnam Veterans Memorial but better understood as an adjunct, companion piece, or a virtual surrogate for the actual memorial. To say that the Martyrs Album is purely a digital construct with no offline counterpart does not in any sense mean it did not have off-line effects, of course. In addition to generating discussion and controversy, the Martyrs Album led to further actions. In June 2005, for example, Eritrean volunteers around the world read out the martyrs' names in a radio broadcast organized by Asmarino.

## MEMORIALS, POLITICS, AND PROTEST

States may create war memorials as national symbols designed to emphasize unity, while rendering invisible the political struggles surrounding warfare. Yet, memorials always resonate with multiple political meanings. It is not uncommon for unofficial memorials to be staged as forms of protest and for official memorials to be used as sites for protests. Memorialization is deployed in diverse ways as part of political struggles (see Khleif and Slymovics 2008, for a Palestinian example; see Jelin and Kaufman 2002, for an Argentinian example). Memorials themselves are often controversial, and their form and content subjects of contestation. As White (1997, 8) observes, "Perhaps because of the role of history as an idiom of collective identity, representations of the shared past have been among the most intensely debated." He further notes that "when historic events remain within living memory, such that they continue to be recalled by those who lived them, they are especially likely to become sites of political and emotional conflict" (1997, 9).

These conditions clearly apply to the Eritrean situation since the 1998–2000 border war is a living memory for all but the youngest generation of Eritreans. For many Eritreans, the border war that followed so closely on the heels of the long struggle for independence from Ethiopia, was a powerful aftershock of the liberation struggle that visited new traumas on this war-torn population. Making sense of both of these wars and coming to terms with what was gained and what was lost in the fighting is still very much an ongoing process for Eritreans individually and collectively. This context adds layers of emotional and political significance to the Martyrs Album.

The border war and the war of liberation hold quite different implications for the Eritrean state and it treats them dissimilarly. The history of the independence struggle is officially celebrated as having established Eritrea as a nation and as having produced and therefore certified the legitimacy of Eritrea's current leadership. By contrast, there is little for the state to celebrate in the case of the border war, which gained no territory for Eritrea yet nearly cost Eritreans their hard-won sovereignty. The 1998–2000 war terrorized the entire population and caused massive displacements of Eritreans including those expelled from Ethiopia, as well as those living near the border. The war destroyed homes, schools, and hospitals, and left much land unsuitable for farming or habitation due to landmines. Not only did the conflict exact a great toll in lives lost and economic progress postponed, many Eritreans regard it as having been avoidable. The border war, thus, could not be easily claimed as a source of pride by President Isaias and the PFDJ. Therefore, while the meaning of the liberation struggle has been defined, mythologized, and articulated powerfully and pervasively by the state in ways that have left little space for contest and reinterpretation, the meaning of the border war, fundamentally more ambiguous in the rationale for its origins, as well as in its outcomes, remains ill-defined. The border war, thus, has been much more open to various interpretations on the part of Eritreans themselves, many of which are critical of Eritrea's leaders.

Awate's war memorial, therefore, contributes to a national dialogue (one that has been largely repressed within Eritrea) about how to come to terms with Eritrea's history of violence and how to justify the lives that have been sacrificed. As Eritreans embark on the project of reassessing the official version of their history and question the relations of sacrificial citizenship defined by the state, they confront a disturbing question: What does it mean if sacrifices were made on behalf of an oppressive state rather than on behalf of the nation? This question is never posed in such bold terms in the Martyrs Album, but it is a question the memorial seems likely to raise in people's minds.

Memorialization is a deeply political act. Jelin and Kaufman (2002, 41) observe that "the political arena of memory struggles is not simply a confrontation between memory and oblivion . . . [there are] struggles over appropriate means and forms of commemoration, about the content of what should be remembered publicly, and also about the legitimacy of different actors to embody memory." All these issues are raised by the Martyrs Album. Within the context of a national infopolitics of war in which the government has resisted acknowledging and accounting for the devastation experienced by so many Eritreans and has withheld information and silenced debate and dissent, the action by Eritreans in diaspora in establishing the memorial is audacious and powerful.

While the creation of the memorial constitutes an act of political protest against the Eritrean government, the way the online memorial is designed to emulate state practices and official forms is particularly remarkable. Whitaker (2007) describes how Tamil.net, the online journalism site that links Tamils reporting on the ground in Sri Lanka with Tamils in diaspora, purposefully mimics the tone and rhetoric of mainstream Western media in order to gain journalistic authority and credibility. The choices made by the Awate team similarly create an aura of authority and legitimacy. This is done on the memorial home page through the use of the three languages used by the government and through references to core national values (liberty, security, martyrdom) that are central to state rhetoric. The fact that the Awate team states that the memorial is patterned after an American government memorial is also significant in this regard. The other major component of the Martyrs Album, the statistical report, also mimics state forms.

The statistical report, accessed through a link on the memorial home page, titled "Profiling our martyrs—a statistical report," is essentially a census, albeit a census of the dead that documents the diversity of the martyrs in terms of their regions of origin, gender, rank, and so on. The statistical report, thus, constitutes one of the national "institutions of power" identified by Anderson (2006). Instead of this data being published officially by the Eritrean state, however, it was published in unauthorized form, virtually, by a group of Eritreans in diaspora. The Awate team, thus, takes on another form of statelike action on behalf of the nation, constructing a public representation of the nation through a censuslike survey of the nation's war dead. In the report, the Awate team notes, moreover, that the Eritrean government has never published a national census. This calls attention to the regime's practice of withholding information from its citizens and helps to position the Awate team as performing a national service. Ironically, the infopolitics of the state created a vacuum that Awate could fill.

By constructing a national war memorial, as well as by publishing a census (of the war dead), and by likening their unauthorized virtual memorial to a well-known US government memorial, the Awate team gains authority for the information it presents and gains legitimacy for its unauthorized assumption of functions normally carried out by the state. In taking such actions, these Eritreans in diaspora take some power away from the state, not simply by obtaining leaked government documents and making public information the state had withheld, but also by presenting that information in the form of institutions of power normally used by states, and by usurping the power of the Eritrean state's own symbols and practices to create an authoritative memorial that presents an alternative view of the nation.

## DEATH COUNTS AND ACCOUNTABILITY

The statistical report is not simply a presentation of information suppressed by the government, which in itself would be a powerful act; it is a political document crafted with care by the Awate team. Clicking on the link to the statistical report opens an ordinary-looking page of black type on a white background that could easily be a report produced by a government, nongovernmental organization, corporation, or scholar. This component of the Martyrs Album is thus clearly distinguished from the black memorial home page with its image of burning candles. The actual statistical data on the war dead are presented much like official census data, with tables, maps and various statistical breakdowns, such as martyrs by region, by cause of death, by gender, etc. (That portion of the content may be simply a reproduction of a leaked government document; the extent of the Awate team's editorial contribution to the statistical presentation of the data is unclear. Awate does state, however, that it chose not to make public all the information it had obtained.)

What is most interesting are the texts the Awate team composed to frame this data and interpret its significance for Eritreans. The report starts with a quote from an American politician and an explanatory text written by the Awate team that compares the US government's response to the 9/11 attacks in 2001 with the Eritrean government's response to the loss of Eritrean lives in the 1998–2000 border war. The quote reads: "'The number of casualties will be more than any of us can bear.'—Rudy Guiliani, Mayor of New York, 9/11/2001." The choice of comparison with 9/11, like that of the Vietnam Veterans Memorial, draws on the Awate team's location in and knowledge of the United States. The references to American political practices also can be read as allusions to democracy. By implication, the US comparisons suggest that what the Awate team has done in creating the memorial and what its actions are indirectly calling upon the Eritrean government to do are not radical or extreme, but the kinds of things that democratic governments do for their citizens.

The 9/11 attacks on the United States followed closely on the end of Eritrea's border war with Ethiopia; for Eritreans, this contemporaneity provides a certain logic to the comparison. In 2001 Eritreans in Eritrea and around the world were still struggling on their own to find out about the soldiers and civilians killed in the border war and to ascertain and come to terms with the death and displacement it caused. Many, moreover, were feeling let down or even betrayed by their leaders' handling of the conflict. This was evident at the time from newspapers within Eritrea (that were shut down by the government in September 2001), as well as from posts on Awate and other diaspora websites. Whereas the earlier comparison to the Vietnam Memorial seems apt, however, in that it commemorates soldiers who died in a controversial war that was not a great victory for the United States, which parallels the Eritrean border war experience; the 9/11 attacks, in contrast, were not part of a war, and the lives lost were not soldiers fighting for their country but civilians caught by a surprise attack. The comparison with 9/11 that the Awate team develops explicitly, however, concerns governments' attitudes toward their citizens' lives as revealed in the official responses to their deaths. In my view there is also a significant comparison to be made between the worldwide attention given to the American lives lost on 9/11 and the lack of global attention given to lives lost in African conflicts, such as the Eritrean-Ethiopian border war. But the focus of Awate's attention is on the relationship of the Eritrean state to its people and not on the responses of international audiences or institutions.

The Awate team points out that the loss of life on 9/11 in the United States was publicly acknowledged as a national tragedy and great efforts were made to provide a complete accounting of the losses. In their text, the Awate team juxtaposes the American and Eritrean states' reactions to the killing of their citizens and sums up this contrast with the phrase "life is precious in the U.S." They write that, although the number of lives lost in the 9/11 attacks

> accounts for *one thousandth of one percent of US population*, because life is precious in the US, we know their names, their gender, their ethnicity, their nationality, their religion, their occupation, their age. We know how many died in which airline, how many died in the towers, how many at the Pentagon. We know how many were firefighters, how many were police officers and how many were ordinary civilians. We know the impact of their death: a series of hearings, a restructuring of the US government, a total change in US foreign policy and US way of life. To Americans, the deaths—however miniscule percentage wise—were, indeed, "more than any of us can bear." (emphasis original)

The wording of this text emphasizes cultural values and emotions—"life is precious" and the loss is "more than any of us can bear," yet in practical terms the real contrast that emerges from the American-Eritrean comparison is not one between American and Eritrean attitudes toward life, but rather the contrasting attitudes of the American and Eritrean governments toward their citizens.

As the text above shows, even while writing from and about the United

States, the members of the Awate team do not position themselves as Americans but instead as close observers of Americans. For example, they write, "to Americans, the deaths," whereas, in reference to Eritrean affairs, the team members speak as insiders, "we Eritreans." After describing the immediate US government response to 9/11, they turn to the border war:

> Between 1998–2000, we Eritreans lost, according to the government, 19,000 lives. That is almost *one half of one percent of Eritrea's population.* Yet, we don't know who these children of Eritrea were: neither their names, nor their ages, nor their gender, nor how they died. We don't know what kind of impact, if any, their death is to have on the lives of the living Eritreans or on the policies of their government. In fact, given the government's habitual politicizing of everything and its tendency to view every subject from the standpoint of "will this information benefit our enemies," we didn't even know if the 19,000 that was officially cited on June 20, 2003 was an accurate number. (emphasis original)

June 20, 2003, was three years after the fighting stopped and, significantly, is Martyr's Day in Eritrea, indicating how carefully the government controlled the information and how strategically it timed its release. In fact, losses are now known to have been far higher.

The fundamental differences exposed by this comparison with the US concern access to information, public acknowledgement of the extent of the losses, and accountability of the leadership, including taking responsibility for the deaths and for learning from the mistakes that contributed to them. The issue of the state's accountability to Eritreans is also addressed on the FAQs page. There, the Awate team explains that it was able to obtain the information about martyrs because "Eritrean patriots who believe that the Eritrean people should have the information provided it to us. Given the prevailing situation in Eritrea, we cannot say anything further about the subject." The Awate team writes that its objective is "to provide as full accounting as possible, *to provide information so we can demand accountability* from those responsible for the policies that resulted in this tragedy and, finally, to promote a culture of peace" (emphasis added). This statement acknowledges the role of the memorial as a political protest and indicates that Awate is not providing information simply as a service to the nation, but with the goal of mobilizing Eritreans to hold the Eritrean state accountable.

In answer to the FAQ, "Why Now? Do you have a political objective? What do you hope to accomplish?," the Awate team replies:

Unlike our War of Independence, which had unanimous support among Eritreans, the Eritrea-Ethiopia border war of 1998–2000 was controversial. Some believed it was avoidable, some thought it was not. Some vocalized their positions, some were silent. But we all were caught by surprise. We all agree that the martyrs, regardless of the political decisions that led to their martyrdom, should be honored. And one way to honor them is to tell their story and do everything we can to make martyrdom rare. We also hope that this will help prevent future destructive wars.

They then pose the question: "Is this a political position?" and answer it as follows: "Yes. But so is the position that says we should not disclose the information." The Awate team's discussion of their intervention in terms of the politics of information and the relationship between access to information and the accountability of governments to their citizens speaks to the wider infopolitical struggles examined in this book.

The Awate team goes on to explicitly address the question of the legitimacy of their actions in creating the Martyrs Album, as follows:

When we said that **the martyrs do not belong to the Eritrean government**, we were reminded that they don't belong to Awate, either. This rejoinder came from two groups of Eritreans: those who felt that we, without a clear mandate, had no right to publish any of the information, as well as from Eritreans who felt we had no right to censor any of the information. In the process, we do not want to disclose information that we deem is sensitive, either because it endangers national security or violates social norms or promotes disharmony. We understand that many of our readers consider our parameters arbitrary but we *are sticking by our decision and we will let history judge whether our decision is right or wrong.* (Awate team, January 16, 2005, emphasis in bold added, italics original)

The Awate team presents the case for why such an unauthorized memorial based on leaked government documents is nonetheless legitimate. It directly addresses criticisms it says some Eritreans raised concerning Awate's "mandate," "right to publish," and "right to censor" information related to the martyrs. These legalistic terms reflect a tone, not of radical dissidence or passion but of measured and impartial official language, a further example of the statelike discourse used throughout much of the memorial.

Information, the Awate team asserts—in this case information about the dead—is necessary for accountability. It is notable, however, that in constructing a national war memorial online, these webmanagers did much more than simply reveal secret government documents. They crafted a digital artifact that represented the nation and the state in ways that challenged central authority. The memorial, thus, brings infopolitics to the fore and suggests the creative potentials of the internet as a political tool. The Awate team explicitly address the role of the internet on the FAQs page, where the third question is "Is the internet really the right medium to publish such emotional and sensitive issue?" Awate's reply is:

> More important than the medium is the presentation. To those who doubt the ability of the internet to handle such an solemn issue, we invite you to visit the Vietnam Veterans Memorial website, which we used as our inspiration when designing the special page. http://thewall-usa.com/. By converting the data into an image file, we have taken some care to make it harder for malicious people to manipulate the information. Harder, but not impossible.

Later, on the FAQs page they make clear that they have nothing personal to gain stating, "Using erroneous assumptions, most of it promoted by the government and its supporters, some have drawn erroneous conclusions about Awate. First of all, Awate has no vested interest, financial or otherwise, in drawing "traffic" to its website."

They also address the question of why Awate should be the ones to publish this information:

> Awate is an independent organization serves no agent, governmental or nongovernmental, foreign or domestic, now, in the past, or in the future. Period. Second, we reject the notion of stratified citizenship: we are all equal stakeholders.

The line "we are all equal stakeholders" can be read in a number of ways, but the very use of the term "stakeholders," rather than "citizens," blurs the distinction that might separate Eritreans in diaspora from Eritreans in Eritrea who are in fact different kinds of citizens and stand in very different relations to the Eritrean state. However, in minimizing the distinction between themselves and Eritreans in Eritrea, the Awate team is not unusual. As previous chapters have demonstrated, it is common for Eritreans in diaspora to see themselves as stakeholders in Eritrea, even though they have established new lives and new legal citizenships abroad. It is also common for posters in diaspora to write as if they were still in Eritrea.

At the same time, elements of the memorial make clear its roots in diaspora. The quote from New York's Mayor Guiliani and other references in the memorial's pages are examples of how the media-savvy, technologically skilled, US-based diaspora that created and manage Awate, Asmarino, and Dehai are shaped by their new country of residence and are able to use their transnational location in the United States as a position of strength and authority in relation to Eritrean affairs. They are not only beyond the state sanctions that restrict citizens within Eritrea from voicing dissent but also, by virtue of residence in the United States, "experts" on democracy to some degree. In creating a war memorial, however, the Awate team went beyond acting as transnational citizens or even as an offshore civil society, to take on a national responsibility that normally would be an official activity of the state.

## CONCLUSION

The Awate team's actions are simultaneously acts of protest that criticize the current government of Eritrea and a usurpation of the state's role. The Martyrs Album exposes the failure of the Eritrean state to act in the best interests of its citizens, in engaging in warfare, and in responding to the deaths that resulted from putting its citizens in harm's way. In establishing the Martyrs Album, Eritreans living outside Eritrea performed national duties in a manner similar to a state. They used the internet as a medium to bridge the geographic distances that separate Eritreans, and used cyberspace as a space outside of the government's control. The Awate team constructed online a war memorial that normally would be established by the government and located within national borders. This act constitutes a direct challenge to state authority, moreover, because the website revealed to a transnational public information that the government had kept secret. More importantly, the memorial implicitly and explicitly criticizes and protests the Eritrean state's management of information about war deaths. At a deeper level, the virtual memorial questions the legitimacy of the border war and ultimately of the state that waged it.

By drawing on examples of what they saw as democratic practices in the United States, the Awate team contextualized its actions in a wider framework than that offered by the Eritrean state and presented the political culture and practices of the Eritrean state in critical perspective. Eritreans based in diaspora used their technological knowledge, their exposure to American political culture and current events, and their distance from the Eritrean state's regulation of media and censorship of information in constructing the memorial. At the same time, they acted on behalf of the public good, providing a service to Eritreans everywhere (inside and outside of Eritrea). The fact that the memorial is based on leaked government documents obtained through the help of government insiders in Eritrea is a telling example of the kinds of cooperation between diasporas and other political actors across national boundaries that have far-reaching consequences for politics.

The Martyrs Album does not simply commemorate the dead but represents the nation and asserts and redefines core national values. Awate's digital memorial reframes national narratives, symbols, and values and establishes a national institution beyond the authority of the state. It challenges the power of the state, constructing the nation as a social network made up of Eritreans rather than an entity defined by the state. This vision of the nation as distinct from national leaders or territory is directly at odds with that of the Eritrean state and the form of sacrificial citizenship it has constructed in which the state is the essence of the nation and citizens belong to the state.

Through the Martyrs Album, the Awate team can be seen as acting like the state they wish to see in Eritrea—making information of national interest available to the public, publishing a census of sorts, constructing a war memorial, and representing collective national values, as well as offering leadership in terms of educating the public on how to read and think about the information they provide by contextualizing it in the various accompanying texts they produced.

In a surprising development, Awate reorganized its website in 2008; the link to the Martyrs Album no longer appeared on the home page, and the memorial was accessible only in Awate's archives. In a subsequent reorganization, Awate changed its practice of maintaining the archives in their entirety and began to delete things from the archive after some time had elapsed. The last time I checked in 2012, the Martyrs Album could be found only in internet archives maintained on other sites, to which some online searching for "Martyrs Album" took me. Memorials, as noted earlier, are not necessarily permanent but may take the form of specific events or activities. The Martyrs Album was, among other things, an innovative political intervention. It was a powerful act of protest at the time of its establishment. A more comprehensive body of data about the lives lost in the border war is now available on Asmarino (http://wall.asmarino.com). But that initiative, titled "the online searchable Martyrs' database 1998–2001," is very much a "database" rather than a memorial. Experientially and politically it is quite different in character and content from the Martyrs Album. The disappearance of the Martyrs Album raises questions about the permanence and transience of digital artifacts, online texts, and virtual constructions. I will return to this issue in the conclusion of the book.

Chapter 5, the next and final chapter before the conclusion, explores issues of citizenship, digital media, and political participation from a feminist perspective, elucidating Eritrean politics of gender, gender online, and the gendering of infopolitics.

# Sex, Lies, and Cyberspace: Political Participation and the "Woman Question"

Ask any Eritrean about the size of the army and he is apt to reply "3 million"—the size of the population.

*The Guardian*, June 17, 1998

Eritrean freedom is a gem to us all that no one could take away before the last person goes six feet under. We will all defend it by eradicating poverty, ignorance, women-oppressing cultural elements, injustices of all sorts, and when necessary by sacrificing our lives.

(Dehai post, August 4, 1998)

Eritrean enemies and traitors . . . have taken up the imaginary issue of "rape in Sawa" in attempt to discredit the government, . . . confuse the Eritrean public, discourage young Eritreans from doing national service, create division between senior officers and trainees, and find sympathetic ears in the West, in the knowledge that rape guarantees attention and sympathy.

(Letter from the Eritrean Embassy, Canberra, Australia, December 12, 2002)

If the story of the Eritrean refugee woman going northward is to be told, it would be a trail of tears that begins with the PFDJ [People's Front for Democracy and Justice] rapists at home and ends with Arab rapists in Libya or Egypt.

(Asmarino post, December 2, 2012)

This chapter brings the nation, diaspora, and the internet into feminist perspective considering the ways women figure in national imaginaries and revealing how websites are constituted as gendered space. Online debates about military rape afford insights into the biopolitics of gender in a militarized nation while simultaneously exposing the gendering of infopolitics. Posts from different historical moments and websites show how gendered struggles are reproduced and transformed in the online public sphere. They suggest the limits as well as the potential of the internet as a vehicle for politically empowering women.

"The woman question" in the title of this chapter refers to the Marxist formulation of gender issues and, more specifically, to the Eritrean People's Liberation Front's (EPLF) approach to gender equality that have shaped the dynamics of gender in the development of Eritrea's national politics (Weber 2011; Bernal 2000; Hale 2001). The woman question also calls up broader histories of women's marginalization in political movements and states because the woman question is first and foremost a question posed *by* men *about* women (Einhorn 1993; Mani 1998). Historically, women have faced obstacles to full participation in states and in public spheres. Women also have been excluded from control over and engagement with new technologies. The internet, however, has been seen as having the potential to empower marginalized groups. The next section frames the discussion of gender and online politics to follow by bringing a feminist perspective to bear on theories of citizenship and sovereignty, particularly Mbembe's necropolitics and Agamben's notion of bare life, which proved their usefulness in revealing the dynamics of state power in Eritrea in chapter 1.

## GENDER AND SOVEREIGNTY

A large body of literature addresses the implications of war, revolution, militarism, and violent conflict for gender relations and for the construction of women as citizens (Yuval-Davis 1997; Giles and Hyndman 2004; Das 2008). A common theme in this literature is the association of the military with manhood and with full citizenship (Jacobs 2000). In this light, the situation of Eritrean women is particularly intriguing. In the course of the thirty-year war for national independence, Eritrean women guerilla fighters participated as combatants to an extent perhaps unrivaled anywhere (Wilson 1991). Women fought side by side with men in mixed units and comprised about one-third of the fighting force by the end of the war. Yet this proved an insufficient answer to the woman question after independence, failing to provide a basis for gender equality in practice whether in public or private life, even though it gave legitimacy to the idea of women's equality (Bernal 2000, 2001; Hale 2001).

The militarization of Eritrean citizenship and the social contract between Eritreans and the state that I have conceptualized as sacrificial citizenship make the theories of politics that accord a central role to violence especially relevant. Thus, as I have already argued, Mbembe's (2003) notion of necropolitics and Agamben's (1998) concept of bare life are useful theoretical frameworks for analyzing Eritrean sovereignty. The Eritrean state is a necropolitical state that is organized around and legitimates itself through militarism, war, and the figure of the "martyr" who dies for the nation. The requirement that all young Eritreans receive military training and perform a period of national service reflects relations of sacrificial citizenship and seeks to reproduce them in successive generations.

But how do women figure in such citizenship when soldiers and martyrs are predominantly male figures in national imaginaries and in actual numbers? Agamben and Mbembe offer little guidance for an analysis of gender and sovereignty. Mbembe uses inclusive wording such as "men and women" and "he or she," but this really is testament to the lack of gender analysis in his theory of sovereignty, since a gendered analysis must deal with the fact that male and female subjects are *not* interchangeable in relation to the state as subjects, soldiers, or citizens (Pateman 1988; Gal and Kligman 2000; Yuval-Davis 1997). Agamben works with a universal notion of "man" that is not inflected by gender. In *Homo Sacer*, he imagines a human being in the abstract that is constructed through power relations into life, *bios* (the socially recognized subject), or bare life, *zoe*, exemplified in the figure of homo sacer (one who is denied social recognition and therefore can be killed with impunity): "The sovereign sphere is the sphere in which it is permitted to kill without committing homicide and without celebrating a sacrifice, and sacred life—that is, life that may be killed but not sacrificed—is the life that has been captured in this sphere" (1998, 83).

Agamben's formulation of sovereignty and sacrifice differs from that which I call sacrificial citizenship in important respects. First, sacrificial citizenship is not established through creating a special category of people, but instead promoted as the basis of the social contract connecting all Eritrean citizens to the state. Moreover, sacrificial citizenship is not predicated on the power of the sovereign to kill, but instead on the citizens' willingness to die. In fact, however, the Eritrean state exercises a great deal of coercion to extract sacrifices from citizens.

The categories of "life" (*bios*) and "bare life" (*zoe*) draw attention to relations of exclusion as central to politics. These categories can be gendered if we consider the different ways women are inscribed in matters of life and death, in reproduction and in war. My feminist reading of Agamben suggests that women can be understood politically as a form of "bare life." In many historical contexts, women have been denied political agency, social citizenship, and full legal status in their own right. Defined by their role as producers of life, women have been included in the nation through exclusion. Women as child bearers, and as reproducers more generally, while often excluded from political recognition and status, are regarded nonetheless as an essential part of the nation, almost in the way that a vital natural resource might be regarded or in the same way that territory is a sine qua non of any nation. That women are associated with the domestic and the private, while the state is gendered male, has been well documented in feminist scholarship (Joseph 2000). Indeed, as Inderpal Grewal and I argue, the widespread association of women and "women's issues" with the *nongovernmental* sector arises in part from the exclusion of women from the state (Bernal and Grewal 2014).

A feminist interpretation of Agamben draws attention to the relations that include women through exclusion, making clear that women are not simply excluded from the political but are constructed as a particular political category of subjects that, like "bare life," constitutes the political through its exclusion. When Agamben (1998, 2) writes that "[i]n the classical world . . . simple natural life is excluded from the polis in the strict sense and remains confined— as merely reproductive life—to the sphere of the . . . 'home,'" and later (1998, 7) explains that "Western politics first constitutes itself through an exclusion (which is simultaneously an inclusion) of bare life," we can read gender into this framework. Women are a form of bare life "excluded from the polis" and associated with "simple natural life" and "reproductive life." Women are treated as subjects of state power, but not as political subjects in their own right. In this sense, women, like bare life in Agamben's terms, are included in the nation as those who are excluded from politics. In fact, it seems to me that this is how it happens that the woman question comes to be posed *about* women by *men*.

## GENDERING ERITREAN POLITICS

The history of the nationalist struggle for independence and the culture of the EPLF provide a context that is taken for granted by Eritreans as the backdrop for current conditions and controversies. Online this history is sometimes referenced by posters explicitly, while at other times its influence in framing the issues and the terms in which they are debated is implicit. The EPLF gained worldwide renown for its inclusion of women in the fighting force and its progressive agenda of social transformation (Wilson 1991). Yet, despite the strides in gender equality made by the EPLF, Eritrean women experienced a different national history than men. The national history that has been reported by scholars and constructed by national leaders is not one told from women's perspectives. The heroic woman fighter figures in national narratives, but not her gendered experiences or those of Eritrean women civilians. As Chait (2011, 203) found, moreover, in her study of Africans from the Horn in the Pacific Northwest, Eritrean women themselves maintain silences: "They fear being ostracized as unpatriotic if they speak about their wartime experiences, disloyal if they disparage their husbands, and shamed if they admit to being raped during the war."

The experiences of Ethiopian rule and the war of liberation were gendered, the experiences of flight are gendered, and the processes of resettlement in new lands are gendered. Even suffering has been gendered—Eritrean women as mothers are understood to be the primary bearers of loss in relation to those killed in war. The state's admonishment of mothers not to mourn their children because they died for the nation simultaneously recognizes mothers' losses while seeking to deny them and suppress women's public expression of grief.

One of the most blatant differences between men's and women's experiences under Ethiopian rule and during the struggle for independence in Eritrea was the fear or experience of rape and other forms of sexual abuse at the hands of Ethiopian soldiers and authorities. Abduction, rape, forced concubinage, and other abuses on the part of Ethiopian troops are well documented in the course of Ethiopia's battle for control of Eritrea (Africa Watch 1991). At the same time, the absence of men from homes and communities as a result of fighting and flight created new responsibilities and opportunities for women as de facto heads of households, providers, and managers of family resources, businesses, and property. At independence, an estimated one-third of Eritrean households were "female-headed" (UNICEF 1994). After independence, women and men guerilla fighters faced distinctly different circumstances upon their reintegration into civilian society, and the lack of success in translating the forms of gender equality practiced among the guerillas to Eritrean society at large has been well documented (Bernal 2001; Hale 2001; Weber 2011). Women fighters were largely reabsorbed into a social fabric of domestic life that emphasized their status as wives, mothers, and daughters. The experiences of the majority of Eritrean women who were not guerilla fighters have received less attention. What I have observed suggests, as we might expect, that the scope of women's agency and responsibilities are contested and sometimes diminished when men return to their families from war or from living abroad.

Wars have caused massive population movements of Eritreans over the past five decades, involving internally displaced people, refugees, migrants (many of whom undertook multiple, serial migrations), people who settled

abroad, people who resettled in Eritrea in locations other than their original communities, demobilized fighters from the EPLF after independence,
Eritreans expelled from Ethiopia during the border war, and the demobili-
zation of two hundred thousand troops after the border war, among other
population movements (Kibreab 2009a). Little attention has been paid to how
the dynamics of these displacements and migrations operate differently for
women than for men (McSpadden and Moussa 1993, Moussa 1995).

During the struggle, women who left Eritrea as refugees faced specific challenges related to their gender. These include "sexual exploitation by bandits,
border guards, camp guards and even refugee organizations" (Matsuoka and
Sorenson 2005, 101). The greatest numbers of Eritreans who fled seeking
safety escaped across the border into Sudan. By the early 1980s when I arrived
in Sudan, Eritrean women were commonly associated with prostitution in the
public mind, a stereotype that put all Eritrean women at risk of sexual assault
since it was assumed they were of loose morals. With few economic opportunities open to them, some Eritrean women operated or worked in brothels or
in the illicit bars where sex work was presumed to occur on the side. Flight
and resettlement also disrupted extended kin groups and compelled women
to become independent decision makers and providers for their dependents.

Men's and women's mobility differed as more men than women left home to
join the liberation fronts, more men than women fled Eritrea, and many more
men than women gained admission to North America and Europe because
of screening criteria that accorded advantages to those with more education
and language skills. Under the rule of Emperor Haile Selassie and the military
junta known as the Dergue that succeeded him, moreover, students sent for
study abroad from Ethiopia were almost exclusively men. On the other hand,
Eritrean women have a long history of migrating for work as domestics and
nannies in Saudi Arabia, Yemen, and the Gulf States and sending remittances
home to their families.

Under Ethiopian rule, during the independence struggle, and in processes
of flight and resettlement, women faced special vulnerabilities and constraints. But each of these processes also opened new spaces in which women
could maneuver and negotiate their familial, communal, and national roles. In
diaspora some women are empowered by being separated from extended kin
groups, by the individualization of their treatment under international legal
frameworks and by host state institutions, as well as by other experiences of
autonomy (McSpadden and Moussa 1993). In Europe and North America,
Eritrean women and men, furthermore, are exposed to ideologies that promote gender equality, not as a tool for the emancipation, defense, or develop-

ment of the nation as the EPLF and the PFDJ have done, but as an end in itself. In addition, the gendering of Western racism is such that African women face less hostility and discrimination in these host societies than men, with the result that women in diaspora are less economically disadvantaged in relation to men than are women in Eritrea. Many working Eritreans in diaspora of both genders are stuck in service-sector jobs, even if they possess higher educational qualifications (Woldemikael 1998). Eritrean women are held back, however, by their lower levels of education and training. The gender gap in education is exacerbated when men who have established themselves abroad choose much younger brides in Eritrea to join them in diaspora. Diaspora men seeking marriage partners from Eritrea results in part from the fact that men greatly outnumber women in the Eritrean diaspora.

While women have made strides individually in terms of personal autonomy in diaspora, this has not translated into public political roles. Women's participation in organized community activities in diaspora often means providing the Eritrean food, whereas the leaders, organizers, key speakers, and activists are men. A report by Eritrean scholars on Eritreans in Canada concludes that

> [a]lthough women are active participants in community activities in Diaspora, it appears that for the most, the roles they take on do not enhance their strategic needs and interests. Often, they are relegated to performing productive (cooking), reproductive (caring of children) and collective roles (help out at weddings, funerals, etc.). (Tezare et al 2006, 23; parentheses original)

The histories and circumstances described above reveal the distinctive experiences of women and men within the larger processes that have defined Eritrean national identity. Some, like the woman guerilla fighter, have been woven into national narratives while others, like sexual violence against women or the secondary roles accorded women in diaspora organizations are rarely acknowledged publicly. All of these gendered experiences constitute the terrain of struggles in which Eritreans and the state construct the terms and significance of citizenship.

## IN THE SERVICE OF THE STATE

Far more than women in most nations, Eritrean women have been incorporated into the nation, not only as bearers of children but also as bearers of arms. While one-third of EPLF fighters were women, since independence all young women have been required to participate in the national program of military training and service. The national service program, often referred to as "Sawa," which is the name of the first remote military camp to which young people were sent for training, thus includes women on a much greater scale than did the nationalist front. Women are thus subject to the relations of sacrificial citizenship under the Isaias regime.

National service has been key to the state's efforts to reproduce the nationalist culture of the EPLF's guerilla movement in successive post-independence generations (see Kibreab 2009b for a detailed history of the policy). In May 1998 national service took on a new meaning with the outbreak of war on the border with Ethiopia. Young people who had already performed their national service were recalled, and the duration of service was extended indefinitely. Although the border war ended in 2000, the practice of open-ended national service continues. Many young people have now served for a decade without being released. When not performing military tasks, they are deployed as labor in various development efforts and state-owned enterprises.

In 2003 the Eritrean government built national service into secondary schooling through the addition of a final year during which all high school students are transferred to remote training camps. Students spend their final year of education getting military training and performing national service work before they are allowed to graduate. Grafting national service directly onto the educational system is a striking example of the militarization of Eritrean society. This practice institutionalized a process designed to create future generations of citizen-soldiers. Not incidentally, the new policy made it much harder for young people to avoid Sawa (Muller 2008; Riggan 2009). State control over youth was a core goal of the national service policy from the start, in keeping with the PFDJ's activities as a vanguard party leading the transformation of Eritrean society. The generation of EPLF leaders who are now top PFDJ officials were shaped in their youth by separation from their families and home communities in the camps of the EPLF. Taking today's youth to remote training camps in some way replicates this formative nationalist experience, breaking (or attempting to loosen) the bonds of local, ethnic, kin, and religious loyalties, as well as forging solidarity on a national basis and instilling discipline under the state's authority.

A post on Asmarino summed up the relation of Eritrea's history to the policy of national service in these critical terms:

> From the very day of independence, DIA's* self-imposed grand project has been how to remold the *Warsai* [postindependence generation] into the image of *teghadalay* [guerrilla fighters]: or put in more general terms, how to trans-

form the Eritrean culture into the nihilistic and abusive culture of *ghedli* [the nationalist struggle]. (Asmarino post, August 7, 2006, translations in brackets added. *DIA is a play on PIA, the shorthand posters use for President Isaias Afewerki, substituting "dictator" for "president.")

Because of the extremely harsh conditions of life in the military training camps and the government's failure to demobilize youth after a fixed period of service, Sawa has come to be dreaded by many Eritrean youths and their families. Many young people seek to escape endless service to the state, and growing numbers continue to flee the country for this reason. It is a cruel irony that a new generation is repeating the flight from homeland that defined an earlier generation of Eritreans and created the original diaspora. Only this time the government Eritreans are fleeing is their own. As a post on Asmarino puts it:

The young generation is trapped in the military mindset and zone that Isaias crafted carefully, and 90% of the youth want to leave the country, many now populating refugee camps, European and North American cities, and daring to die on the tormenting waves of the Mediterranean and the killing sun of the Sahara. (December 27, 2006)

In an effort to stem the flow, the government imposes fines on parents whose children leave the country without having completed Sawa.

In 2010 reports began to surface about Eritreans who were held hostage, tortured, raped, and even killed as they attempted to cross the Sinai from Egypt into Israel seeking asylum. The excerpt from an Asmarino post quoted at the start of this chapter refers to those abuses, among other things. That same post includes the following analysis:

We have seen how the National Service provided *Shaebia* with *Sahel*-like [liberation struggle] environment to mold the young generation in the image of *tehadalay* [fighters]. And it is this search for alien *ghedli* [struggle] identity, whose two defining marks are the "Spartan warrior" (never-ending confrontation) and the "selfless developer" (never-ending slavery), that is to be blamed for the mass exodus of this generation. (Asmarino post, December 2, 2012, material in brackets added, italics and parentheses original)

Although Sawa is intended as a policy of universal citizenship, it has proven to be profoundly gendered in practice. Removing adolescent girls from the supervision of their families is understood in Eritrea as elsewhere to pose different risks than it does for young men. Almost from the beginning, rumors arose of girls being sexually harassed, exploited, and raped in Sawa. Questions about the sexual abuse of women during their national service have spawned heated debates in the online public sphere. The substance of these debates revolves around women's problematic membership in the nation, while the form of the debates raises questions about women's political participation in cyberspace.

## GENDER, EMPOWERMENT, AND THE INTERNET

As Miller and Slater (2000, 16) note:

> Both a premise and a promise of internet development has been a concept of freedom. Discourse encountered on and about the internet has been notoriously libertarian: like the Wild West, it has provided a screen on to which could be projected images of freedom, danger, transformation and transcendence. The internet has both produced new freedoms (of information and of speech) and come to stand as a symbol of potential freedoms.

Because internet communications are seen as disembodied, scholars have particularly celebrated cyberspace as offering the possibility of transcending identity, a view that casts the internet as potentially liberating women from the constraints of gender, at least online (Harcourt 1999; Youngs 2006). This form of liberation, however, places an unequal burden on women to conceal their gender in order to gain equal treatment. Moreover, as Beyer (2012, 154) found in her study of *World of Warcraft*, even when women are not identified as such online, they encounter "the language and values of the male-dominated environment" that has been constructed on websites.

Other characteristics of internet communications besides their disembodied nature are important. The internet is reconfiguring barriers between public and private (Senft 2008). This means in theory that women can benefit from being able to access the public sphere from a variety of locations, such as computers in their homes, public libraries, and offices, as well as other places where women already are located or feel socially comfortable going. Through the internet, women can, thus, engage in politics without having to expose themselves to public scrutiny or to bodily contact, and without drawing attention to their persons in the same way they would if attending or speaking at a public meeting, for example. The internet has been seen as offering an openness of access, as well as a decentralized organization, which make it easy for diverse groups to express themselves (Elmer 2006; Gajjala and Oh 2012), and for the marginalized to challenge hegemonic views (Landzelius 2006b). Despite the apparent openness and ease of access offered to women by the internet, I found relatively few women posters in the Eritrean online public sphere. As noted earlier, most posters to Eritrean websites use their real names, and their gender is usually clear from the name alone. Dehai, Asmarino, and Awate were established by and are managed by groups of men, and most of those who post are men. The overwhelming majority of internet intellectuals and media personalities who have achieved notoriety through the websites are also men. It is not surprising that posters are predominantly male in the Eritrean online public sphere, if one considers that national politics and public spheres are de facto male domains in many societies, including that of the contemporary United States.

In spite of the open aspect of the internet, and even the explicitly democratic goals of these particular websites, the Eritrean online public sphere is a virtual space that is gendered male. The character of exchanges on gender issues reveals that Eritrean cyberspace is a venue where gendered boundaries are maintained and women are excluded from full political participation. This is an important finding in itself, but rather than accepting it as a natural or inevitable outcome, a feminist perspective requires us to question how this situation has come about and to reveal the mechanisms by which it is perpetuated. Online debates about the sexual abuse of women in Sawa bring together questions about women's citizenship in the nation and women's political empowerment through digital media.

## WOMEN AS NATIONAL SUBJECTS

Since, as I have argued, Eritrean citizens are essentially constituted by the state as soldiers and prospective martyrs, the status of women in the paramilitary service program goes to the heart of women's membership in the nation. The policy requiring national service of all young Eritreans cannot be openly debated and criticized within Eritrea, but it has long been a subject of controversy on Eritrean websites. The most intense debates have focused on allegations that girls have been raped during military training.

The sexual exploitation of women in a militarized context is not unique to Eritrea, as recent revelations about the prevalence of rape in the US military make clear. Sexual abuse of women in Sawa, however, echoes particular histories of gendered violence against Eritrean women. Eritrean women were forced into concubinage and raped by Ethiopian forces administering Eritrea during the regime of Mengistu Haile Mariam, as well as by Ethiopian troops in the the war for independence. More recently, Eritrean women were raped by Ethiopian soldiers during the border war. The rapes of women that took place as part of the border war generated significant official and unofficial responses on the part of Eritreans. These responses help to elucidate the national frameworks within which Eritreans are grappling with issues of gender, sexual violence, and citizenship. Therefore, before turning to the online debates over allegations of rape in Sawa, I analyze two essays that were posted on the website Dehai (www.dehai.org) concerning the rape of Eritrean women by enemy soldiers during the 1998–2000 conflict with Ethiopia.

The first essay can be considered to represent the official views of the Eritrean state. Its author is Luul Gebreab, head of the National Union of Eritrean Women (a mass organization begun by the EPLF and now best understood as a GONGO, as government NGOs are sometimes called) under the PFDJ. Luul's essay is the text of a June 9, 2000, speech that she addressed to the UN General Assembly's special session on "Gender, Equality, Development and Peace for the 21st Century." It was posted on Dehai on June 11, 2000, by a regular male contributor to Dehai who posts from Canada. Luul's text states, "It is with great anguish that I inform this august body, that as the current war between Eritrea and Ethiopia goes on unchecked by key actors in the international arena, so does the spiraling violence on civilians in general and women in particular." Luul then makes an interesting parallel between women and Eritrea as a nation, when she says: "we would like to remind the world that silence, in the face of crimes against women and children and against the sovereignty of small nations, triggered instability and wanton destruction." The parallel Luul draws between Eritrean women and the nation as victims of Ethiopian aggression is one in which Eritrean women stand in for the nation. Women are being used by the government of Eritrea to signal Eritrea's plight as a "victim" in order to sway international public opinion and to seek support for intervention on behalf of the nation. The issue of the rape of Eritrean women by Ethiopian troops, as defined here by the Eritrean state, then, is not so much about gender violence in the context of war as it is about the violation of Eritrea, symbolized by the violation of Eritrean women. This is a telling example of the way women can be included and yet simultaneously excluded from politics.

The second essay, posted on Dehai later that summer, is by Abeba Tesfagiorgis, an Eritrean woman who is the author of *A Painful Season and a Stub-*

*born Hope: The Odyssey of an Eritrean Mother* (1992). Abeba's essay, titled "The Plight of Eritrean Women Rape Victims," was posted on Dehai by a man who introduced it, by asking:

> what are we doing about this most urgent plight of the rape victims of the *Weyane* [Ethiopians] marauders (our sisters and mothers) . . . Is dehai just a feel-good-do-nothing talk shop of Eritreans, or can it be used to raise awareness and mobilize people to do something to alleviate the plight of our people? (Dehai post, August 19, 2000; parentheses original, ellipses and materials in brackets added)

His question, "what are we doing about . . . ?," reflects the assumption that Eritreans in diaspora have a collective responsibility and the power to act in Eritrean affairs, and, furthermore, that Dehai can and should be used to have an effect, not just to communicate, or as the poster writes, to "talk" and "feel good."

It is noteworthy that the rape victims are identified by the male poster as "our sisters and mothers" rather than as fellow citizens or fellow Eritreans. Similarly, Abeba identifies herself in the subtitle of her book as "an Eritrean Mother." These kinship terms I argue reflect women's political inclusion through exclusion in that they suggest women are related to the nation not as citizens in their own right but as sisters and mothers of (male) citizens. This implicit construction of women as kin to citizens is likewise reflected in the state's construction of women as grieving mothers in relation to the nation's martyrs.

Abeba's essay on Eritrean women rape victims can be read among other things as a masterful, feminist rewriting of Eritrean history and I quote from it at length here for that reason. Abeba asserts that "Eritrean women have paid dearly for the liberation of their country. . . . Without the monumental sacrifices of our women, we wouldn't have been a nation state today" (ellipses added). She lists numerous sacrifices and struggles on the part of Eritrean women in various walks of life, including raising children under terrible political and economic conditions during the Haile Selassie and Mengistu regimes, as well as active service in "our fronts." She notes that Eritrean women in the diaspora in Europe and the Middle East "worked hard from dawn to dusk in any kind of jobs and gave to the struggle not only their salaries, but their jewelry," and that women in diaspora organized "Eritrean nights" (fundraising events) in support of the liberation struggle. She says that "Eritrean women in North America, who mostly came to pursue their studies, quit school, held menial jobs to earn money," and "opted to live poorly in wealthy America in order to save and send every single sent [*sic*] to the Front and publicize the plight of their people."

Abeba thus establishes the sacrifices made by Eritrean women for the nation and thereby writes women into the established national narrative. Abeba's account can be seen as gendering sacrificial citizenship through describing contributions and suffering distinctive to women, including child rearing and donating their jewelry to the cause. Abeba next turns to the period after Eritrean independence:

> I noticed these gallant Eritrean *mothers, wives, sisters, and daughters* turning to be worthy politicians who very well analyzed the strength and weakness of our government. The discussion and debates were not conducted in our parliament and newspapers; it was discussed in their kitchen, in their compound of their homes over ceremonial coffee, at wedding celebrations, burials, and mourning places, and any such gatherings. Traditionally, these are the places and occasions where our women from different walks of life converge. . . . Yes, Eritrean women who are highly educated through life's experience, or exposed to the Western type of education, or both, are worthy politicians. After all, politics is not about egos, power, or control. It is about discussing and solving public problems equitably and justly—it is about the food we eat, the clothes we wear, the land we till and on which we build our homes. . . . [her list goes on] . . . In all these main issues, women are the main actors—the glue of our nation and our true politicians. (emphasis added)

Abeba Tesfagiorgis makes a number of important observations and claims here. One is that, despite their sacrifices and contributions, women were not given many positions in government after independence. Furthermore, the key issues facing Eritreans were not being dealt with in official arenas or in the public sphere dominated by men, but rather outside these spaces. Abeba, thus makes the excluded space of domesticity ("bare life" in Agamben's terms) one where politics are conducted, even if not recognized as such. Abeba likewise makes the reproductive issues—"the food we eat, the clothes we wear"— that Agamben dismisses as "simple natural life" that is excluded from politics, the very center of what politics are about. Through these repositioning moves, Abeba makes women central to politics, even calling women "our true politicians."

Having first established women's bona fides as Eritreans, through their particular sacrifices and contributions, Abeba turns attention to the rapes of Eritrean women by Ethiopian troops during the border war:

In Senafe [a major Eritrean town near the Ethiopian border] 50 rapes have been reported. God knows the number of women who have encountered these terrible crimes and who have not reported them. . . . Our government has appealed to the UN and some people have been talking and writing about these brutal rapes; but let us raise our voices higher.

Then, as if to preempt the criticism she expects to receive for focusing attention on women, Abeba goes on to mention the importance of other national concerns, such as helping the displaced and working on implementing the constitution, before asserting that "we have to also honor members of our sacred mothers, sisters, wives and daughters by telling the world community about their inexcusable extreme human rights violations." It is striking that here, too, in appealing to her Eritrean audience, Abeba refers to the bond of kinship as what ultimately connects Eritrean women to the national community and creates an obligation to them on the part of other Eritreans. Rather than appearing as citizens whose rights and security should be upheld by the state, women thus figure in the nation as dependents of other Eritreans.

Considered together, Luul's speech and Abeba's essay reveal the fraught dynamics of gendered citizenship in the militarized context of Eritrean politics where women occupy multiple iconic roles, including symbols of the nation itself, guerilla fighters, "sacred mothers," sacrificing citizens, and "true politicians," as well as "victims." It is within these various frameworks that the question of women's obligation to perform national service and the rumors that some women are raped while doing so is debated. The rape of Eritrean women by Ethiopians is acknowledged socially by Eritreans and officially by the state, even if individual rape victims may remain silent due to social stigma. In contrast, rumors of rapes of girls in Sawa are hotly contested. These abuses are much more disturbing for Eritreans to consider because they occur not between enemies, but among fellow citizens and comrades in arms and are even carried out by government authorities against their own female citizens.

### SEX, LIES, AND INFOPOLITICS

Online discussions about the sexual abuse of women in Sawa bring into focus underlying questions about Eritrean citizenship and gender. These discussions also reveal the gendering of infopolitics such that men are authorized to speak publicly on many topics, including about women, while women's statements are treated as unauthorized, unreliable, and possibly even dangerous to the nation. My analysis explores the ways in which such debates are conducted in the online public sphere, the framing of issues and the stakes raised, the practices of inclusion and exclusion, and the silencing and self-censorship that shape the debates. These elements make visible the operation of the public sphere itself and show how infopolitics is gendered. Thus, I am not seeking to evaluate which statements by posters are true, or what is alarmist, or what is a cover-up, but rather to understand how participants in the debates make such claims about their own and about other's posts.

I first look at debates that took place on Dehai in 1997. At that time, Eritrea was not at war, young people were released when their eighteen-month stint of national service ended and support for the government was strong. I then turn to debates that took place during and after the 1998–2000 border war. In these years, as explained in preceding chapters, the online public sphere underwent dramatic changes as Asmarino and Awate emerged to rival and surpass Dehai, and sentiments of dissent became ever more widespread and outspoken online. But those developments had yet to transpire in 1997 when a Dehai post raising a question about rape in Sawa set off a series of impassioned exchanges.

The poster was a woman in diaspora in the United Kingdom who stated in her post that she was a new member of Dehai and wanted to express her concern about hearing that "girls in Sawa are getting raped and abused by the leaders." She added, "I am very sorry to tell such a bad news on my first day. But I don't know I don't really know what to think and believe. The only think I can do is talk with my people" (Dehai post, October 17, 1997). An Eritrean man in Toronto posted this response to her: "I am sorry to tell you that your first post to Dehai was full of rubbish!! You are spreading unfounded rumor about Sawa. Please read the Dehai charter and you will see that it is not allowed to spread rumors in Dehai" (Dehai post, October 17, 1997). In terms of questions about women's access to the public sphere, this exchange is revealing. For one thing, the woman explicitly identifies herself as a newcomer, implying a marginal or liminal status. Moreover, she adopts an apologetic tone, "I am very sorry," rather than expressing outrage or protest. The man's response to her is harsh in content ("rubbish") and tone (exclamation points), and he also uses a legalistic route to delegitimize her entry into the public sphere. His exhortation to "read the charter" seems to draw on the notion that women are unschooled in proper political behavior.

Another man posts with a subject line, "She must be dumm like youRe," and proceeds to argue that if a girl was raped, "I bet you she could have told her parents. Other wise please shutup!" (Dehai post, October 21, 1997). Yet another poster, an Eritrean man posting from Germany, responded to the same woman's post:

> May sister don't propagate completely unbelievable stories about SAWA. Sawa is a great School to be brave and sound ERITREAN CITIZEN. Everybody should think about and proof twice, tentimes such false rumours (*Belabielow*) [lit. "she said, he said," which is a Tigrinya expression for the rumor mill] before you post it on DEHAI. (Dehai post, October 24, 1997, material in brackets added)

Posts like these moved some women, who by their own accounts had previously been silent readers, to post for the first time. An Eritrean woman who includes her location in Ohio posts:

> This is my first time ever writing something in Dehai so bare with me. I have sat here and read all sorts of mail come threw to my home . . . The one that i am replying to about SAWA has really gotten me mad. . . . The person who told the person to shut-up for telling his/her friends story should be ashamed of themselves. I know we didn't fight for 30 years for us to come to this . . . (Dehai post, October 23, 1997)

She adds, "i went to Eritrea in the summer of 96' and i heard a lot of stories myself. But the ones that i do believe are the ones my three female cousins that were there told me. If you want to know just e-mail me privately."

Her post offers a number of points for analysis. For one, her invitation to private emailing brings up the public-private divide and makes clear that Dehai is understood as a public forum, and one where certain things are better left unsaid. Additionally, in common with the first woman poster who said she was a new member of Dehai, this woman states that this is the first time she has ever posted. Her statement that "all sorts of mail come threw to my home" refers to the way some members of Dehai subscribed to receive posts as emails. Her words reposition her, not as someone stepping out into the public sphere, but as located in domestic space, passively on the receiving end of other people's online activities. Her hesitation to reveal the full details of her knowledge in her post may be a response to the accusations of rumor mongering and spreading "rubbish" that were heaped on the first woman poster.

In a very unusual turn, a non-Eritrean woman based in the United States (who identifies herself as American and Bermudian) enters the debate, with this post:

> Instead of immediately condemning them as simply spreading rumours and propaganda, they should be responded to like anyone else on dehai typically is when another disagrees with them—they debate, as[k] questions, presenting other facts in contrast. They have as much right to say anything they want, and to be challenged on it with consideration—not just dismissed like they were gossiping women. . . . If even these women cannot write on the topic openly in Dehai without being accused of spreading rumours, proganda, being dumb, and speaking against the "Great" SAWA . . . [this ellipses is original] Then how difficult it must be for women who have been raped to speak about it? (Dehai post, October 24, 1997)

This prompts a reply from an Eritrean woman who posts:

> Thank you for backing Eritrean women up. . . . You see most of us (Eritrean women) grew up with this kind of treatment and it is hard for us to point out which part of what he is saying is offending us. Most Eritreans aren't sure of themselves, we aren't even sure if our opinion mean something or whether we should even have an opinion to begin with . . . (Dehai post, October 24, 1997, ellipses added)

An Eritrean woman in Canada posts, "I always remember my own mother who thought me not to argue with men and her reason may have validity or not you can see from my brothers they seem closed the door for us" (Dehai post, October 25, 1997).

The posts of these two Eritrean women relate online behavior to long-standing Eritrean cultural patterns. One says, we "grew up with this kind of treatment," and the other says, "my mother taught me." They thus make sense of men's behavior online by putting it in the wider context of Eritrean gender relations where men's views count for more than women's. Infopolitics is gendered since the public sphere is understood as male space and women's statements are not accorded the same weight of authority as men's statements. Where one woman poster mentions that Eritreans may not feel entitled to "even have an opinion to begin with," she also may be referring more generally to the culture of the PFDJ, where leaders do the thinking for the masses and tell people what they should think. Her post reminds us just how significant websites like Dehai, Asmarino, and Awate are in such a political climate, even if the websites also are flawed in some ways.

Later that same month, another woman, who also states that she is a new member of Dehai, posted this:

> after reading the exchange about SAWA and what is happening to some of the women there or allegedly happened. I fell compelled to express my thought. Now before I say what I intend to say. I would like to explain my intention before I make some of you mad and drive you to call me names. My reply is not to confirm or deny that rape do happen in SAWA, I have no direct knowledge of that. What I am responding to is the perception or understanding of rape that is being take lightly by some of the respondents . . .

She goes on to say:

> If we try to hide the sad and bad things about us and our situation under the carpet . . . how does that help us grow or correct our mistakes to be better people and nation? besides the politics and economy there are many social ills in Eritrean communities be it is back home or in Diaspora. (Dehai post, October 25, 1997; ellipsis original)

Another woman posts:

> In the culture I grown up men are the decisions maker as in most society but on top of that our women don't bother to what is going on because there is a strongh belive women should only be at home. I gusse, that why our men on dehaie telling us to shut up about almost anything we want discuss they feel we are taking the power from them. (Dehai post, October 25, 1997)

In these posts, women are protesting the treatment of women posters by men on Dehai, but they choose not to criticize the individual male posters; they focus their critiques instead on Eritrean culture. They imply that the behavior of male posters is best understood as a reflection of conventional Eritrean gender relations in which men are understood as having greater authority. This suggests first, that women experience the online public sphere as an Eritrean cultural space, and second, that the online public sphere poses some of the same challenges to women's full participation as other Eritrean contexts.

As the discussion of sexual violence against women in Sawa continued, a man posted, making a number of arguments, which can be summarized in the following four points: (1) even a good government includes some bad people, therefore don't blame the PFDJ for rapes; (2) the Dergue [Ethiopian regime of Mengistu] damaged Eritrean culture and ethics, therefore the Ethiopians are to blame; (3) there are crimes and bad people everywhere, so rapes should not be blamed on Sawa; and (4) rape is a very serious crime. Then, he turns on those who are raising the issue of rape on Dehai, telling them: "you people who went to Eritrea from Europe or US heard about the crime. You waited til you came out of Eritrea and start to talk about it. Why didn't you . . . try to bring it to some one attention" (ellipsis added). He adds, "From what I heard from my aunt, it is because of this [women's] organization insisted that women and men should be equally trained in SAWA that women were included in the program" (Dehai post, October 26, 1997). With this final salvo, he seems to shift the blame for rape to women for ever wanting equality and political inclusion in the first place. Yet, where citizens and soldiers, nationalism and militarism are entwined, as they are in Eritrea, women are disenfranchised if they are excluded from military activities. Therefore, seeking equality through participation in military activities is one obvious strategy available to women, and all the more obvious given the (now mythologized) history of Eritrean women guerilla fighters.

Taking part in the military appears to offer a way out of women's inclusion in the nation through exclusion. As the issue of military rape suggests, however, women's entry into military service does not open the gate to full political enfranchisement because women's military experiences are themselves gendered. The logic of inclusion is a powerful one, nonetheless. Thus, for example, an Eritrean woman in Canada posted:

> We [in diaspora] have to go home and go to SAWA and give them some encouragement that what they doing is a requirement. Otherewise it may disapprove our capability of doing equal job with our brothers.
> (Dehai post, October 27, 1997)

Her post raises the question of how women can be equal citizens if not serving the nation equally. This perspective is consistent with that of the Eritrean state. Some years later, when President Isaias was asked about the requirement of national service for women on Eri-TV in 2002, he stated, "There cannot be different laws for men and women" (quoted in Kibreab 2009b).

As the debate continued on Dehai in 1997, an Eritrean man posting from Germany questioned the truth of stories about Sawa and the motives behind their circulation, asking a woman poster: "where did you get this information????? Because there are many people try to speak bad things about our Government with their BELA-BELOW INFO" [lit. "she said, he said" in Tigrinya] (Dehai, October 27, 1997). Not all men expressed such critical views of women's posts, however. One man, for example, addressed his post to one of the women posters by name saying, "You and many other Eritrean sisters belong to a community, dehai community, which comprises many people of different opinions. . . . Say what you think is right and the wise will learn from it" (Dehai post, October 27, 1997). His post interestingly does not respond to the issues of rape or women and national service , but rather takes up the operation of the online public sphere itself ("dehai community") and the value of tolerating diverse perspectives.

From these exchanges, it is clear that posters are not simply grappling with the issue of alleged rapes but in various ways are addressing fundamental questions of infopolitics—who is to be trusted as a source of information, who can legitimately circulate what kind of information, and how should information that reflects negatively on the Eritrean government be handled? These infopolitical questions are gendered questions in that women and men stand in different relations to the public sphere, the state, and political power. We see that women posters are viewed by the men who are the majority of posters as spreading rumors, as being too easily led to believe what others tell them, as politically unsophisticated, and possibly as inherently less loyal to the nation than men. For their part, women posters also raise questions about the gendered aspects of infopolitics when they suggest that men are attempting to silence them in ways that are consistent with historical patterns in Eritrean political culture. It is noteworthy that some women were moved to actively participate in politics online because of an issue involving women, yet, even where women's experience was under discussion, men took the authoritative positions and rebuked and ridiculed women posters.

These exchanges also shed light on the ways that Eritreans in diaspora gather, assess, and pass on information from a multiplicity of sources and locations. Posters refer to Eritrean websites, kinship networks, and visits home to Eritrea as sources that inform their views. Whether in diaspora or "at home," Eritreans are largely reduced to obtaining information through rumors and other informal channels, including diaspora websites, because the government exercises such tight control over information and media.

Gendered issues of self-censorship, particularly the shame surrounding sexual violation, were also raised by women posters. For example, an Eritrean woman poster with a Swiss email address begins her message by greeting the first woman whose post started this debate by name and saying, "welcome to Dehai—it feels good to talk about things which preoccupy us." She then goes on to quote an earlier poster who wrote:

> I was in Asmara last summer and I heard few people complain about the same thing but I have yet to meet someone who could tell me that she was raped. I met and talked to girls who have been to SAWA, I have asked them if what I heard was true and they dismissed it with a laugh . . .

Continuing her post, the Eritrean woman from Switzerland writes:

> Would you have told me or anyone that you got raped if that happens to you I don't think so. Without a safe place and emphatic understanding in place we cannot expect women to feel safe and being able to talk about it. . . . So because some women denied knowledge of it doesn't make it a lie. (Dehai post, October 17, 1997)

A similar sentiment is posted by another woman:

> You know if, if you born in Eritrea you know exactlly how it looks like to tell to someone that you have been raped or abused. It is a kind of shame. (Dehai post, October 21, 1997)

An Eritrean woman from Canada contributed this to the discussion:

> I am n't at any point the centre of big storry. But as most of Eritreans women in my age I had my own slice and you right we are strong survivors. . . . I don't have the culture which enables me to talk about myself therefore even though most of these things apply to me but I preserve not talk here. (Dehai post, October 28 1997, ellipses added)

These posts about shame and the need for a "safe place" indirectly raise the question of whether the online public sphere created by Eritreans in diaspora is a "safe place" for women to express themselves. It would seem that it is not a safe place for women in any obvious sense since some women who expressed themselves there were dismissed and insulted, and other women expressed fears, asking not to be "called names," for example. No woman, moreover, felt safe enough to speak openly about her own experience of sexual violence or abuse, only to tell secondhand accounts as well as to say, in the words of one poster, "I preserve not talk here."

Nonetheless, despite the silencing and self-censorship observed, the internet may still offer a forum that is more open to women than the tea rooms of Asmara or the coffee shops favored by Eritreans in diaspora or other public political venues either in Eritrea or in diaspora that are de facto male spaces where women do not spend time. This is particularly true if, as I suggest, we regard reading as a form of participation in online forums. A number of women posters mentioned having been readers and subscribers of Dehai; as such, they form part of Dehai's public. Through reading posts, women are privy to everything being discussed by men in the online public sphere, which is not the case for many face-to-face male gatherings.

The debates about rape during national service draw attention to the ways that silencing is carried out by self-appointed citizens, not simply by repressive state authorities. Infopolitics is not just about state practices but about political culture that establishes shared notions of who is authorized to communicate about what to whom and in what context. The openness of cyberspace and the freedom from centralized state power or other centralized authorities, such as editors or media owners, belies the hegemony of dominant groups and dominant perspectives. Dominant views are often so pervasive, moreover, that they do not require the state to actively police and enforce them online or off. In relation to questions about gender, digital media, and empowerment, the Eritrean online public sphere makes clear that the barriers that prevent or inhibit women from full participation are more complex than gaining access to the internet. The obstacles women face are rooted in gendered understandings of citizenship, politics, and the public sphere. Social barriers can be and are reproduced in novel settings, such as in cyberspace and diaspora. At the same time, as evidenced by the debates on Dehai, the internet may enable some women to express themselves who otherwise may not have spoken in a political forum. The characteristics of digital media and the qualities of the online public sphere made it seem thinkable for these women to engage in public, political discussions.

The October 1997 debates occurred during peace time. Conditions changed significantly once the border war began in 1998. Members of Sawa were sent into battle, and those who had already completed their national service were recalled and also sent to fight. As one Eritrean posting from Australia saw it, this war vindicated the government's controversial national service policy:

When the Eritrean Government disclosed its plan, immediately after the nation had won its independence, to send all capable young Eritreans to Sawa to receive basic military training as well as helping those young Eritreans to develop some self-discipline, the overwhelming reaction to the plan was NOT AGAIN!!! . . . Fast forward to 1998, . . . when the country had its back to the wall . . . it was the kids from SAWA who stepped up to defend the country. . . . In this instance it is fair to say that full credit should go to the Government for their foresight and judgement in putting into place a brilliant contingency plan, SAWA!!!!!!!!! (Dehai post, May 3, 1999, ellipses added)

Throughout the border war, as discussed in chapter 2, most posts were concerned with breaking news of the war and with fundraising and other activities to ensure Eritrea's survival as a nation, while criticism of the government's policies and practices was rare. The post above reflects some of that wartime nationalist fervor.

In December 2002, as dissent began to be voiced in the aftermath of the war, a new controversy about women and Sawa arose. Reports of women being raped in Sawa were picked up by Western media. An article on the Australian news website, *The Age*, titled, "When Rape Is a Requirement of Military Service," got considerable attention in Eritrean cyberspace and a response from the Eritrean state (www.theage.com.au/articles/2002/12/04/1038950095366. html). *The Age* article, in fact, begins with material that appeared on Awate, though it cites the source as "Gedab News, the Eritrean opposition website" (Gedab news is a component of Awate). *The Age* also quotes a post from Asmarino. This suggests that diaspora websites played a role in drawing international attention to the issue. The fact that much of the information in the article comes from Eritreans in diaspora and their websites may also be a reflection of the state's success in scaring people inside Eritrea into silence.

Five days after the publication of *The Age* article, the Awate team posted an editorial linking the sexual exploitation of Eritrean women to Eritrean's history of militarization, starting with Italian colonial domination, through the Ethiopian Dergue, and continuing with the ongoing militarization under President Isaias. Beneath the provocative heading, "Is Sawa a Rape Camp?," the team wrote:

It is a common complaint of every female veteran freedom fighter that the PFDJ employs a use and dispose policy. It is common knowledge that all the egalitarian values that were Developed in Sahel [the region where the EPLF was based] were quickly abandoned once they entered Asmara, with women *tegadelti* [guerilla fighters] now expected to forget their "we are equal" teachings and accept the traditional role of a housewife. It is also common knowledge that some of the male *tegadelti* (the *yeka alo*) [lit. "the capable ones," meaning the liberators of Eritrea], specially the officers, believe that having spent their youth in sacrifices, it is now their time to play. . . . [I]t is not difficult to believe the transformation of the Eritrean woman from the status of first among equals to a sex toy. (Awate team post, December 9, 2002, translations of Tigrinya and explanations in brackets added)

The editorial goes on to focus on those who doubt the reports of rapes in Sawa, asking, "Would they believe the story if they spoke to a rape victim or would they dismiss her as a liar?" This question brings infopolitics to the fore, recognizing the underlying dynamics that determine who can speak about what and with what authority or credibility. The rhetorical nature of the Awate team's question, the fact that it is understood how easily a rape victim's own statements could be dismissed as lies, reflects the gendering of authority and the association of "truth" with positions of power. The power of official authority and men's social authority imbues their statements with an aura of veracity, while there is less willingness to believe those who do not speak from positions of authority, and an unpleasant statement by a woman need not be heeded.

In fact, the postwar debates about rape in Sawa focused largely on issues of truth and deception, particularly on whether a poster was perceived as pro-PFDJ (and therefore predisposed to disbelieve the rape allegations) or as anti-PFDJ (and therefore inclined to believe the allegations). Since a poster's leanings are often divined from whether his or her posts seem to serve or oppose the government's interest, there is somewhat of a tautology involved—that is, if you are posting something critical, it must be because you oppose Isaias's regime and we know you oppose the regime because you posted something that reflects negatively on it. On the other hand, certain frequent posters are already known for their tendencies to toe the party line or scream bloody murder or fall somewhere in between, and their posts are interpreted in light of their prior posting histories.

This reading of posts through the political filter of progovernment versus antigovernment means that, even in discussions about rape, women are incidental to the real battle in which posters are engaged. That battle is essentially an infopolitical struggle over whose information and analysis can be trusted, and over who has a legitimate voice to speak about Eritrea as an Eritrean, whether it is only those who post praise or also those who post damaging information and critiques. I argue that in such cases, women are not the focus of concern, but rather that women serve as a medium through which societal values are defined and contested and the limits of sovereign power are explored. Therefore, debates about the treatment of women or the behavior of women must also be understood as debates about fundamental social questions of morality, authority, and power. In debating questions about women and Sawa, what is at stake for Eritreans is not simply women's rights (and obligations to the state) but rather a vision of the state, society, and the nation. Somewhat paradoxically, this symbolic significance of women makes it harder for women themselves to bring their interests to the fore. This reflects the political position of women as "included through exclusion" in Agamben's terms, where women are necessary to the production of sovereignty and the constitution of politics, but women are constructed as political objects, not subjects.

A Dehai poster seems to grapple with this paradox when he writes:

> If we, the men from Eritrea, could make an effort to show a small portion of love and affection that we have continued to display toward that petit and beautifully shaped country called Eritrea, toward women, a tremendous positive change, not only socially, but economically as well, could be seen in the lives of many Eritreans . . .

The same post continues:

> The issue of Eritrean women being treated like second-class family members by their own husbands . . . is one issue which is rarely touched by the predominately male members of the Dehai Forum. (Dehai post, March 23, 1998, ellipses added)

A post on Asmarino raises the gender contradictions of Eritrean politics very much along the lines of what I have analyzed under the rubric of the woman question. The post takes the form of a parody in which a government official is being interviewed about a watch factory. The interviewer asks him, "Does the law require that there be women in the assembly line of watch manufacturing?" The official replies:

> After a great deal of social engineering, we have perfected our watch factory to a degree that, when discussing the issue of whether we still need women's watches, and what the styles should be, only the men discuss the issue, with-

out pausing for a second to reflect on the absurdity of this. (Asmarino post, March 19, 2002)

This parody, like my analysis of the discussions of rape, points to the underlying contradiction in the terms of women's inclusion in the nation.

The manner in which the Eritrean government deals with criticism is illustrated in its response to *The Age* article. The Eritrean Embassy in Canberra wrote an official letter to *The Age* which *The Age* duly published online. (Part of the official response is quoted on the opening page of this chapter.) The embassy's letter states that "since 1994 over 200,000 young Eritreans (about half female) have completed their Sawa training" and goes on to assert that rape is not a problem in Sawa or anywhere else in Eritrea. It claims that

> Eritrean enemies and traitors . . . have taken up the imaginary issue of "rape in Sawa" in attempt to discredit the government, . . . confuse the Eritrean public, discourage young Eritreans from doing national service, create division between senior officers and trainees, and find sympathetic ears in the West, in the knowledge that rape guarantees attention and sympathy. (Eritrean Embassy quoted in *The Age*, December 12, 2002, ellipses added)

This kind of blanket denial, coupled with claims that enemies and traitors are deceiving and manipulating everyone from young Eritreans to Westerners is a good example of how the Eritrean state clamps down on critical discussions. A response that can be paraphrased as "the issue is based on lies told by traitors—case closed" leaves no space for any dialogue between citizens and the state to develop.

Posts concerning women's service and possible abuse in Sawa and the military have continued to appear from time to time. The views they express reflect the increasing disillusionment of Eritreans with the PFDJ and President Isaias. Outspoken critics began to cast the issue of women and national service as a form of government mistreatment of women. A poster on Asmarino reacted to the government lifting its ban on sexual relationships among soldiers:

> In an astounding reversal of policy, the Isayas regime relaxed its attitude toward sex within the army. . . . The reason provided was an "enlightened one": "It is up to the woman to choose." Imagine the irresponsible recklessness involved in this. They snatch these young women (many teenagers) from their

families—many of them that have hardly ventured outside their homes—and throw them in the fox hole with many men, and expect them to make informed choices on sex . . . we could easily see how criminally irresponsible the government has been. (Asmarino post, July 3, 2006, ellipses added)

Here the poster seems to be indicting the government on the grounds that it failed in its duty to protect women who are assumed to be inherently vulnerable. His perspective thus keeps the frame of the woman question, where women can be central to the debate yet simultaneously marginalized from it. Women, in his approach to this issue, are not so much citizens with rights, as female dependents who need the government to act as a proper male guardian, one that protects them, rather than one that exploits them.

The poster goes on to argue that abuses of women in national service are not simply incidental occurrences but actually serve a political agenda,

[Isaias] could hardly afford to antagonize his colonels and generals. So he literally bought the loyalty of these authorities by letting them do whatever they want to do with the *Warsai* [lit. "my heir," used by the PFDJ to mean the younger generation]—from labor enslavement (building their villas) to sexual enslavement. (Asmarino post, July 3, 2006, parentheses original, material in brackets added)

Another poster writes:

Come to Beirut, Bahrain and other Gulf Countries to see how the regime of DIA [Dictator Isaias Afewerki] has changed the supposed once free women (*Tegadlelti*) to slaves of 21st centuray, and about those girls in the slavery service and how they became tools of entertainment to the ignorant generals of DIA. (Asmarino post, March 7 2006, material in brackets added)

The last poster is presumably referring to accounts he heard from Eritrean women who left the country and are now living in the Middle East where they can express things that would be too politically risky to talk about in Eritrea.

It is significant that, in each of these debates over women's military training and service, the focus is intensely and almost exclusively on the sexual vulnerability and alleged abuse of women, while little or no attention is paid to other aspects of women's lives, aspirations, or health (given the rigors of Sawa) or even to families' need for women's domestic labor or women's responsibilities for childcare. Young women seem to be defined exclusively in terms of sexuality, a sexuality that is, moreover, devoid of any agency and represented only through victimization by masculine sexual agency.

## CONCLUSION

Infopolitics are deeply gendered. In the online discussions, from the late 1990s until now, for the most part, men are speaking about women and speaking for women, if they address gender at all. Tellingly, the 2012 Asmarino post quoted at the beginning of this chapter for its discussion of rape and Sawa, received over forty comments within two days of its appearance. Although some praised the author's critique of the regime, and someone accused him of "insulting our martyrs," and a number of posters expressed agreement with his criticisms of Awate in particular and of Arabs and Muslims in general, not a single poster even mentioned the issue of rape. Rape in Sawa or during flight from Eritrea was apparently seen as a minor issue compared to the other abuses of Eritreans by various actors including their own government.

Exploring how gender relations are reproduced and contested by Eritreans online reveals the contradictions inherent in women's problematic membership in the nation. Exchanges among posters reflect the tensions between notions of universal rights and duties and the gender-specific conditions faced by women, particularly sexual violence and exploitation. The ways in which women are silenced and the terms of these debates make visible gendered struggles over political participation and women's citizenship and indicate the limitations of the internet as a means of transcending gender or empowering women. On the subject of rape, moreover, government infopolitics of tight control over information merges with the silence of "victims" about their experiences since women fear the stigma associated with sexual assault. The lack of available data about the existence and prevalence of rape or other sexually predatory behaviors in Sawa, coupled with the general lack of transparency and accountability of government authorities serve to fuel debates and give rise to conspiracy theories. Debates on Eritrean websites illuminate the vexed relationship of women to the state under ideals of universal citizenship and the complex locations of women in nexuses of family, community, and nation. Analysis of these debates reveals how barriers to political participation are produced online and therefore suggest a critical perspective on theories of digital empowerment. Eritrean cyberspace is not transformative of gender relations simply by virtue of its medium. Even in cyberspace Eritrean women face gender barriers to full "citizenship."

Neither diaspora nor the internet offers escape from gender. Cultural understandings of public/private divides and gendered discourses of citizenship rooted in local and global histories, in fact, shape online practices and participation, including what is posted by whom and how such posts are read and responded to, even as the internet and life in diaspora also reconfigure the experience of social spaces and identities. As earlier chapters have shown in different ways, the "local" context is thus present, even where it seems not to be, in the ambiguous, deterritorialized, and decontextualized spaces of cyberspace.

On the other hand, it would be a mistake to see cyberspace as simply another venue for "politics as usual." The characteristics of the internet and the ways people experience and engage with digital media give online public spheres their own distinctive character. The internet appears to be less transformative of gender relations and less empowering of those excluded from full political participation in society than many first thought. But the dynamics of how cyberspace opens and delimits spaces associated with particular communicative and political opportunities must be revealed through research in specific contexts as I have tried to do here.

While gendered notions of politics that limit women's participation are reproduced online, websites, nonetheless, constitute a unique forum where women and men publically discuss and contest gender issues. Women readers, moreover, have access to these and other political discussions even if they are too intimidated to post. In the online public sphere, furthermore, the practices that exclude women become exposed as posters seek to justify their views and employ tactics designed to discredit and silence others. The online public sphere offers a significant arena in which communication and struggles over gendered belonging and citizenship can take place. Online exchanges among posters also affect readers, exposing diverse audiences to a range of perspectives on the woman question, even if women have not yet escaped its terms.

The practices that silence and exclude women do not simply hurt women; they also constrain the transformative potential of what Eritreans are doing online. There is a missed opportunity since, as Eritreans engage in a collective project of critically evaluating their past, challenging official national narratives, and generating the alternative histories and narratives that could lay the groundwork for a new understanding of the nation and a new basis for a social contract of citizenship, women are not coauthoring these emergent social texts. This means that the narratives being developed will be incomplete, partial, and flawed, unable, therefore, to encompass the perspectives, insights, and experiences of half the population.

Women often figure in national narratives as symbols of the nation and as those whom armies must defend, as well as on behalf of whom laws and policies promoting gender equality are set in place. Yet, women are marginalized from engaging political power directly. Women have participated in Eritrea's nationalist projects from the liberation struggle to the border war and in Sawa where they continue to serve alongside men. To the extent that women have been included, they have been deployed in national projects but largely excluded from defining those projects. We cannot fully understand nations, sovereignty, and citizenship without including in our analyses the absences, silences, and suppression of women, and we must recognize the ways that these very exclusions are part of what constitutes politics. My analysis of the conflict surrounding the issue of women and the military also provides an avenue for exploring the limits of current theories of sovereignty and citizenship that are inadequate to account for women's experiences.

# Conclusion

The landscapes of citizenship and sovereignty are undergoing tectonic shifts. New forms of technological and geographical mobility are giving rise to new political spaces and relationships that transform the meanings of the nation. Diasporas and other mobile populations are altering nations' centers of gravity through the powerful transnational fields they sustain, in part, through the internet. Digital media are central to the shifts in the configurations, expressions, and experiences of political power associated with transnational circuits of people, resources, and ideas. The internet is a political game changer with consequences far beyond increasing people's access to information. Immediate and interactive public communication across institutional barriers, social boundaries, and geographical distances has opened political struggles up to a range of participants who can produce national media, mobilize opinion and action, and construct and contest national narratives and the legitimacy of state authorities from outside the nation.

The internet makes possible unconventional political tactics and collaborations that support as well as challenge states in new ways. Cyberspace offers a site of cultural production and expression where dissenters can not only find outlets free of government control but create them. Websites can serve as an ambiguous political space that is both inside and outside the nation, extending as well as revealing the limits of territorial sovereignty. Through the internet, connections may be created, intensified, and expanded. However, the flexibility offered by digital technology also fosters splitting and diversity, since it is easy for new groups or individuals to establish their own nodes and networks that reflect and contribute to the reconfiguration of relationships.

This is a powerful political dynamic that, along with migration, is producing new kinds of political subjects and strategies of power that cause state-citizen relations to be remade.

The analysis of Eritreans' online activities presented here reveals political power in many forms, showing how sovereignty, militarization, and war, as well as the rights and duties of citizenship, are being defined and redefined through the conjunction of digital media and diaspora. The close, contextual readings of posts in the preceding chapters suggest the ways that political order is established and policed in diaspora and online, as well as the means by which this order is being disrupted and contested. If we see nations as networks, the diaspora websites bring the nation into focus through their separation from the nation, as well as through their connection to it.

Eritreans in diaspora have institutionalized in cyberspace a public sphere of citizenship and belonging more successful in achieving democratic form than any within Eritrea. Online the diaspora are unofficially producing national media from outside the nation. In the beginning, posters largely hewed to the government's line and websites extended the regime's reach outside its borders. Later, posters sought to serve the nation by questioning official narratives, fostering dissent, and even by stepping in to take on statelike duties, activities impossible for ordinary people to undertake on Eritrean soil. It is not simply the location of cyberspace beyond state authority that is significant for these developments, but the distinct characteristics of the internet as a medium. The instantaneousness of communicating with multiple publics as well as the relative informality of posts (as compared to writing a letter to the editor of a newspaper or speaking up at a public meeting) have intensifying and amplifying effects on what is communicated. The rapid interchanges among posters stoke passions, creating a cascade of affect that is effective in mobilizing collective action as Eritreans's responses to the border war illustrate.

The nation as network is revealed in the new political practices and discourses Eritreans have developed to negotiate the deterritorialized relations between citizens and the state. Eritreans in diaspora are experimenting online in ways that suggest that new forms of citizenship, democracy, and the public sphere are emerging from the new technologies and the heightened mobility of our times. The internet is decentralizing control over information and knowledge production, as well as making possible innovative strategies of political expression. New kinds of political realities and subjectivities are being developed through diasporas' engagement with homeland affairs and digital media. Rather than seeing Eritrea and Eritreans in diaspora as exceptions to the norms of politics and civic life, I suggest we see them as exemplars of the kinds of transformations the twenty-first century is bringing about.

The significance of the internet, like earlier technological advances, is not uniform around the world. This variation may be even more pronounced in the case of the internet than for other new technologies because of its highly interactive nature such that users are also creators and content producers, not simply consumers. This study shows that a universal technology is still a cultural artifact. Digital technologies become cultural artifacts through the ways they are used by different populations. Thus, despite their politically deterritorialized locations, diasporas and cyberspace nonetheless have local contexts. The particular histories of diasporas and their states of origin vary greatly and give rise to diversity in the relationships of diasporas to states and in the ways states and diasporas use the spaces of diaspora and cyberspace to experiment with new forms of sovereignty, citizenship, and political participation.

For diasporas, the internet is more than simply a cheap, convenient mode of communication. Cyberspace does more than simply shrink distances; it serves diasporas as a space that is ambiguously located, easily accessed, and in some sense equidistant from all locations on the globe. It is at once neither here nor there (neither located in the new country nor in the homeland), and yet also both here and there simultaneously. The internet, thus, disrupts the homeland/diaspora dichotomy. The political impact of digital media, moreover, appears to be much greater outside of established democracies, in autocratic systems where information and public debate are state-controlled or highly centralized.

What becomes clear from the posts examined in previous chapters is that under regime's like that of President Isaias, information is understood to be inseparable from political ends. Thus, it is never simply a question of whether a given allegation of government abuse or mismanagement is factually true or not, but always also a question of why that information is being brought into the public sphere, by whom, and for what purpose. As a consequence, factual disputes in highly politicized contexts like Eritrea's cannot easily be understood from the theories of knowledge production that underlie Western notions such as "transparency," which presume information to have a freestanding, objective existence. An understanding of infopolitics, thus, helps to shed light on why Eritrean posters accuse others of ulterior motives and/or of lying, even when what was posted is known to be true or cannot be refuted given the absence of evidence. If the effect of the information could diminish Eritrea's standing in the world, or undermine the state's authority, then whether it is true or not is less important than how the information is being used and why. This is certainly the perspective of the Eritrean state, reflected, for example, in the embassy's letter calling Eritreans who spoke about military rape "Eritrean enemies and traitors."

Eritrean politics continue to unfold in surprising ways, and the online public sphere grows and changes. This public sphere will continue to be developed by various participants, diversifying as new groups of posters and readers in Eritrea and around the world start to participate, as new websites are established by Eritreans in diaspora, and one day by Eritreans in Eritrea, and as new technological innovations reconfigure the platforms and potentials of digital media. The project of reassessing the nation's past and constructing new definitions for what it means or could mean in the future to be Eritrean is still very much in flux. I see hope, however, in the ongoing struggles of Eritreans from various locations and walks of life to narrate their own history and to widen the scope of political participation and expand the borders of what can be publicly expressed. The process of reimagining the social contract that binds Eritreans and their leaders is unfinished, and the answers to questions about how to achieve democracy have yet to be found. There is, however, inherent value in the very possibilities for continued questioning, contesting, and creative nonviolent political engagement that the diaspora websites have brought into being.

Digital technologies continue to develop and proliferate rapidly, and politics in the Horn of Africa are likewise dynamic, changing in unpredictable ways. It is possible that by the time you read this, any or all of the websites, Awate (www.awate.org), Asmarino (www.asmarino.com), and Dehai (www .dehai.org), will have changed significantly, or will have been eclipsed in significance by new websites, or even gone offline altogether. The temporality of the digital is fluid and ambiguous just as the space of cyberspace has distinct qualities compared to everyday lived space. Something a poster may have written in haste in 1993 responding to another post or to an event in Eritrea which may now be forgotten can still be found online in Dehai's archives. On the other hand, the Martyrs Album, which possessed such an aura of eternity at its establishment, no longer exists except as a ghost of itself apparently saved as a screenshot somewhere by someone in the recesses of the internet. The speed, transience, and endurance of digital texts and artifacts, as well as their paths of circulation in reaching immediate or intended audiences and also unimagined and eventual audiences, are difficult to determine or predict, and so are their wider effects in the world.

For Eritreans, the political future remains uncertain and unknown. It is possible that by the time you read this the Eritrean state will no longer be under the authority of President Isaias Afewerki and the People's Front for Democracy and Justice. Political and technological conditions certainly will change. What endures is the human quest for belonging, expression, and meaningful participation in the communities and institutions that are important to them. Eritreans in diaspora effectively brought into being and institutionalized a transnational public sphere that offered to fulfill such longings not only for those in diaspora but also for the nation. The relation of the virtual public sphere to politics within Eritrea is varied and complex, and continues to evolve. The meanings of national sovereignty and state power in the lives of Eritreans are fraught and profound as the nation defines them, even in diaspora and cyberspace, and as Eritreans inside and outside of Eritrea also define the nation through their ongoing struggles to realize the promises of democracy, peace, and prosperity once held out by national independence. Clearly, Eritreans in diaspora will not stop engaging in national politics and using digital media among other means to do so, any time soon. The concerns Eritreans express in relation to the state are shared, moreover, by many Africans and others in the global south who seek accountable leadership and freedom from political violence. Recognizing the transience of the digital, the smallness of Eritrea, and the impermanence of particular regimes and historical figures, the arguments, analyses, and concepts in this book should prove relevant beyond the immediate circumstances they describe.

Part of the contribution this study makes lies in getting beyond the newness of "new" media, by situating it in a wider context that makes visible the cultural continuities that traverse and translate across political boundaries and media platforms. While scholarship on digital media tends to focus on innovation and novelty, new technologies do not in themselves revolutionize social organization or political subjectivities. Social and political transformations depend on human actors whose behavior even in novel spaces is shaped by particular historical conditions and contexts. Conservative forces operate online as chapters 1 and 2 demonstrated in relation to sacrificial citizenship and the extension of sovereignty and chapter 5 showed in relation to gender. Yet these chapters also bring into focus more clearly what *is* distinctive about new media. Armbrust (2004, 87) asserts that "mass media, if they do nothing else, extend the boundaries of access to discourses and, in doing so, potentially reshape the ways in which discourses are perpetuated or changed." The internet, far more than mass media, allows ordinary people to take part in the process of constructing knowledge and producing social narratives as well as in circulating, evaluating, and reshaping discourses. At the same time, geographic mobility and websites create new social spaces for politics. Digital media are bringing infopolitical struggles to the fore, providing citizens with new resources in their demands to participate and to coauthor the narratives that govern their lives.

States, for their part, are also developing new mobile forms of sovereignty in their encounters with transnational subjects (Pandolfi 2006). Novel political relationships and strategies emerge from the need to negotiate deterritorialized forms of nationalism and to sustain loyalties and obligations that are not represented by or enforced through legal citizenship. The internet, furthermore, raises new infopolitical questions about state-citizen relations as it increases the methods and opportunities for state surveillance and propaganda, as well as the means of circumventing state secrecy and censorship. As I write this conclusion in 2013, struggles over infopolitical citizenship are lead news stories. The punitive fervor with which even electoral democracies like the United States has pursued leakers Bradley Manning and Ed Snowden, and website manager Julian Assange, reveal how crucial infopolitical power is to state power. These cases also exemplify the power of the internet coupled with geographic mobility as Assange and Snowden at the time of this writing have maintained some degree of liberty through international travel and seeking asylum in foreign countries.

The transformations I have called the "nation as network" are not limited to the migrant-sending or refugee-producing countries of the global south. They are global in scope. While the internet enhances the influence of diasporas in their homelands, at the same time, it may intensify the presence and persistence of the global south in the global north. The dynamics of migration and diaspora in the global north are changing because the ease and immediacy of digital communications makes it more feasible for migrants to collectively sustain deterritorialized belonging and political participation. Moreover, the internet and social media also make it easier for the affective and political ties underpinning these transnational engagements to be reproduced in successive generations. These processes are reconfiguring not only the nation/diaspora dichotomy but also north/south dichotomies. As this study shows, the image of the digital divide and conceptions of information rich and information poor (Norris 2001) are misleading as representations of these relations and their transformations.

The rise of diasporas, digital media, and the nation as network are likely to have other consequences than the kinds of political creativity and democratic activism I found on Eritrean websites. Neither nations nor their diasporas are necessarily benign forces in the world. Eritrean history and experience, in fact, demonstrate the profound and even absurd costs of nationalism borne not only by opposing forces but by the nation's ardent supporters and supposed beneficiaries. There are, moreover, diasporas within diasporas, formed along ethnic, religious, and regional lines whose online activities and homeland influence may further fragment multicultural nations and promote civil strife. One danger of diasporic citizenship is that diasporas do not live in the countries where their political energies are focused and thus do not bear the same risks and consequences of the outcomes they seek as do other citizens. The specific ends and outcomes of diaspora engagement with national politics online, in any case, cannot be predicted from technology. As illustrated by the shifts I tracked over time in Eritrean cyberspace, the internet can be used to vastly different ends. Thus, it may not be possible to generalize about whether the nation as network reflects a strengthening or a weakening of national sovereignty. What is clear thus far is that states continue to remain significant and powerful, even in the midst of global flows and transnational connections of various kinds.

Diasporas and digital media are not fixed, unitary phenomena, but flexible and multifaceted. No single approach, conceptualization, or policy will capture these complex domains and relationships. In this book I chose to focus on one example of how some Eritreans in diaspora are using the internet as a means of political participation, intervention, and protest. By exploring culture and politics in the transnational, ambiguous spaces of diaspora and cyberspace, this study speaks to questions about the fates of the citizen and the nation in our contemporary context which is increasingly constructed through dynamic processes of mobility and dislocation, connection and fragmentation, violence and security, and struggles over the limits of repression and expression.

# REFERENCES

Abu-Lughod, Lila. 2001. *Dramas of Nationhood: The Politics of Television in Egypt*. Chicago: University of Chicago Press.

———. 2012. "Living the 'Revolution' in an Egyptian Village." *American Ethnologist* 1 (39): 21–25.

Abusharaf, Rogaia. 2002. *Wanderings: Sudanese Migrants and Exiles in North America*. Ithaca: Cornell University Press.

Adams, Tessa. 2000. "Whose Reality Is It Anyway: A Psychoanalytic Perspective." In *Digital Desires: Language, Identity and New Technologies*, edited by Cutting Edge, Women's Research Group, 47–58. London: I. B. Tauris.

Africa Watch. 1991. *Evil Days: Thirty Years of War and Famine in Ethiopia*. New York: Human Rights Watch.

Agamben, Giorgio. 1998. *Homo Sacer: Sovereign Power and Bare Life*. Stanford: Stanford University Press.

Al-Ali, Nadje, Richard Black, and Khalid Koser. 2001. "The Limits to 'Transnationalism': Bosnian and Eritrean Refugees in Europe as Emerging Transnational Communities." *Ethnic and Racial Studies* 24: 578–600.

Al-Ali, Nadje, and Khalid Koser, eds. 2002. *New Approaches to Migration?: Transnational Communities and the Transformation of Home*. London: Routledge.

Amnesty International. 2004. *Eritrea: 'You Have No Right to Ask'—Government Resists Scrutiny on Human Rights*.

Anderson, Benedict. 1991. *Imagined Communities: Reflections on the Origin and Spread Of Nationalism*. New York: Verso.

———. 1992. "New World Disorder." *New Left Review* (193): 3–13.

Anone, Anna. 2011. "Talking About Identity: Milanese-Eritreans Describe Themselves." *Journal of Modern Italian Studies* 16 (4): 516–27.

Appadurai, Arjun. 1996. *Modernity at Large: Cultural Dimensions of Globalization*. Minneapolis: University of Minnesota Press.

———. 2003. "Sovereignty Without Territoriality: Notes for a Postnational Geography." In *The Anthropology of Space and Place*, edited by Setha Lo and Denise Lawrence-Zuanisa, 337–50. Malden: Blackwell Publications.

Armbrust, Walter, ed. 2000. *Mass Mediations: New Approaches to Popular Culture in the Middle East and Beyond*. Berkeley: University of California Press.

———. 2004. "Egyptian Cinema On Stage and Off." In *Off-Stage/On Display*, edited by Andrew Shryrock, 69–100. Stanford: Stanford University Press.

Asmerom, Ghidewon, et al. 2001. "The Internet and Computing Environment in Eritrean Cyberspace: Past Experiences and Future Directions." Paper presented at the FirstInternational Meeting of the Eritrean Studies Association, Asmara, Eritrea, July 22–26.

Axel, Brian Keith. 2001. *The Nation's Tortured Body: Violence, Representation, and the Formation of a Sikh Diaspora*. Durham: Duke University Press.

———. 2002. "The Diasporic Imaginary." *Public Culture* 14 (2): 411–28.

———. 2004. "The Context of Diaspora." *Cultural Anthropology* 19 (1): 26–60.

Baker-Cristales, Beth. 2008. "Magical Pursuits: Legitimacy and Representation in a Transnational Political Field." *American Anthropologist* 110 (3): 349–59.

Balibar, Etienne. 2005. "Difference, Otherness, Exclusion." *Parallax* 11 (1): 19–34.

Balsamo, Anne. 2000. "The Virtual Body in Cyberspace." In *The Cybercultures Reader*, edited by David Bell and Barbara M. Kennedy, 489–503. London: Routledge.

Basch, Linda Green, Nina Glick Schiller, and Cristina Szanton Blanc. 1994. *Nations Unbound: Transnational Projects, Post-colonial Predicaments, and De-territorialized Nation-States*. Langhorne: Gordon and Breach.

Bay, Edna, and Donald Donham, eds. 2006. *States of Violence: Politics, Youth, and Memory in Contemporary Africa*. Charlottesville: University of Virginia Press.

Becker, Barbara, and Josef Wehner. 2001. "Electronic Networks and Civil Society: Reflections on Structural Changes in the Public Sphere." In *Culture, Technology, Communication*, edited by Charles Ess, 67–84. Albany: State University of New York Press.

Bernal, Victoria. 2000. "Equality to Die For?: Women Guerilla Fighters and Eritrea's Cultural Revolution." *Political and Legal Anthropology Review* 23 (2): 61–76.

———. 2001 [2006]. "From Warriors to Wives." *Northeast African Studies* 8 (3): 129–54.

———. 2004. "Eritrea Goes Global: Reflections on Nationalism in a Transnational Era." *Cultural Anthropology* 19 (1): 1–25.

———. 2005a. "Digital Diaspora: Conflict, Community, and Celebrity in Virtual Eritrea." *Eritrean Studies Review* 4 (2): 185–210.

———. 2005b. "Eritrea On-Line: Diaspora, Cyberspace, and the Public Sphere." *American Ethnologist* 32 (4): 661–76.

———. 2006. "Diaspora, Cyberspace, and Political Imagination." *Global Networks: A Journal of Transnational Affairs* 6 (2): 161–80.

———. 2013a. "Diaspora, Digital Media, and Death Counts: Eritreans and the Politics of Memorialization." Special issue on diasporas. *African Studies* 72 (2): 246–64.

————. 2013b. "Please Forget Democracy and Justice: Eritrean Politics and the Power of Humor." *American Ethnologist* 40 (2): 300–309.

Bernal, Victoria, and Inderpal Grewal, eds. 2014. *Theorizing NGOs: States, Feminisms, and Neoliberalism*. Durham: Duke University Press.

Beyer, Jessica. 2012. "Women's (Dis)embodied Engagement with Male-Dominated Online Communities" In *cyberfeminism 2.0*, edited by Radhika Gajjala and Yeon Ju Oh, 153–70. New York: Peter Lang.

Boyer, Dominic. 2006. "Conspiracy, History, and Therapy at a Berlin *Stammtisch.*" *American Ethnologist* 33 (3): 327–39.

Boys, Jos. 2000. "Windows on the World: Architecture, Identities, and New Technologies." In *Digital Desires: Language, Identity and New Technologies*, edited by Cutting Edge, Women's Research Group, 125–47. London: I. B. Tauris.

Bozzini, David. 2011. "Low-Tech State Surveillance: The Production of Uncertainty Among Conscripts in Eritrea." *Surveillance and Society* 9 (1/2): 93–113.

Brinkerhoff, Jennifer. 2009. *Digital Diasporas: Identity and Transnational Engagement*. Cambridge University Press: Cambridge.

Bundegaard, Christian. 2004. "The Battalion State: Securitization and Nation-Building in Eritrea." *Program for Strategic and International Security Studies, Occasional Paper No. 2*. Geneva: Graduate Institute of International Studies.

Butler, Judith. 2004. *Precarious Life: The Power of Mourning and Violence*. New York: Verso.

Calhoun, Craig, ed. 1992. *Habermas and the Public Sphere*. Cambridge: MIT Press.

Castells, Manuel. 2001. *The Internet Galaxy: Reflections on the Internet, Business, and Society*. Oxford: Oxford University Press.

Clarke, Kamari Maxine. 2010. "New Spheres of Transnational Formations: Mobilizations of Humanitarian Diasporas." *Transforming Anthropology* 18 (1): 48–65.

Chait, Sandra. 2011. *Seeking Salaam: Ethiopians, Eritreans, and Somalis in the Pacific Northwest*. Seattle: University of Washington Press.

Cliffe, Lionel, and Basil Davidson. 1998. *The Long Struggle of Eritrea for Independence*. Trenton: Red Sea Press.

Clifford, James. 1994. "Diasporas." *Cultural Anthropology* 9 (3): 302–38.

Coleman, E. Gabriella. 2010. "Ethnographic Approaches to Digital Media." *Annual Review of Anthropology* 39: 487–505.

Comaroff, John, and Jean Comaroff. 2005. Presentation to Workshop on Middle Eastern And African Studies, University of California, Irvine, October.

Connell, Dan. 1993. *Against All Odds: A Chronicle of the Eritrean Revolution*. Lawrenceville: Red Sea Press.

————. 1997. "After the Shooting Stops: Revolution in Postwar Eritrea." *Race and Class* 38 (4): 57–78.

Conrad, Bettina. 2003. "Eritreans in Germany: Heading from Exile to Diaspora." In *Hotspot Horn of Africa: Between Integration and Disintegration*, edited by Eva-Maria Bruchhaus. Munster: LIT Verlag.

————. 2005. "'We Are the Prisoners of Our Dreams': Exit, Voice and Loyalty in the Eritrean Diaspora in Germany." *Eritrean Studies Review* 4 (2): 211–61.

————. 2006a. "A Culture of War and a Culture of Exile: Young Eritreans in Germany and Their Relations to Eritrea." *Revue européene des migrations internationales* 22 (1): 59–85.

————. 2006b. "'We are the Warsay of Eritrea in Diaspora': Contested Images of Eritrean-ness in Cyberspace and in Real Life." In *Diasporas Within and Without Africa: Dynamism, Hetereogeneity, Variation*, edited by Leif Manger and Munzoul Assal, 88–104. Uppsala: Nordic Africa Institute.

Coronil, Fernando. 2006. Discussant remarks. Panel on "The Limits of the State." Annual Meeting of the American Anthropological Association, San Jose, November 15–19.

Coutin, Susan. 2007. *Nations of Emigrants: Shifting Boundaries of Citizenship in El Salvador and the United States*. Ithaca: Cornell University Press.

Dahan, Michael, and Gabriel Sheffer. 2001. "Ethnic Groups and Distance Shrinking Communication Technologies." *Nationalism & Ethnic Politics* 7 (1): 85–107.

Das, Veena, and Deborah Poole. 2004. "State and Its Margins: Comparative Ethnographies." In *Anthropology in the Margins of the State*, edited by Veena Das and Deborah Poole, 3–34. Sante Fe: School of American Research Press, and Oxford: James Currey.

Das, Veena. 2008. "Violence, Gender, and Subjectivity." *Annual Review of Anthropology* 37: 283–99.

Dean, Jodi. 2009. *Democracy and Other Neoliberal Fantasies: Communicative Capitalism and Left Politics*. Durham: Duke University Press.

DeHart, Monica. 2004. "'*Hermano* Entrepreneurs!' Constructing a Latino Diaspora across the Digital Divide." *Diaspora* 13 (2/3): 253–78.

Diamandaki, Katerina. 2003. "Virtual Ethnicity and Digital Diasporas: Identity Construction in Cyberspace." *Global Media Journal* 2 (2): not numbered. American Edition, Graduate section, paper 10. Accessed online April 21, 2011.

Diouf, Mamadou. 2000. "The Senegalese Murid Trade Diaspora and the Making of a Vernacular Cosmopolitanism." *Public Culture* 12 (3): 679–702.

Donham, Donald. 2006. "Staring at Suffering: Violence as a Subject." In *States of Violence*, edited by Edna Bay and Donald Donham, 16–33. Charlottesville: University of Virginia Press.

Doornbos, Martin, Lionel Cliffe, Abdel Ghaffar M. Ahmed, and John Markakis, eds. 1992. *Beyond Conflict in the Horn*. Trenton: Red Sea Press.

Doostdar, Alireza. 2004. "'The Vulgar Spirit of Blogging': On Language, Culture, and Power in Persian Weblogistan." *American Anthropologist* 106 (4): 651–62.

Dorman, Sara Rich. 2005. "Narratives of Nationalism in Eritrea: Research and Revisionism." *Nations and Nationalism* 11 (2): 203–22.

Eickelman, Dale F. 2003. "Communication and Control in the Middle East: Publication and Its Discontents." In *New Media in the Muslim World*, edited by Dale F. Eickelman and Jon W. Anderson, 33–44. Bloomington: Indiana University Press.

Eickelman, Dale F., and Jon W. Anderson. 2003. "Redefining Muslim Publics." In *New Media in the Muslim World*, edited by Dale E. Eickelman and Jon W. Anderson, 1–18. Bloomington: Indiana University Press.

Einhorn, Barbara 1993. *Cinderella Goes to Market: Citizenship, Gender and Women's Movements in East Central Europe*. London: Verso.

Elmer, Greg. 2006. "The Vertical (Layered) Net: Interrogating the Conditions of Networked Connectivity." In *Critical Cyber-Culture Studies*, edited by David Silver and Adrienne Masssanari, 159–78. New York: New York University Press.

Escobar, Arturo. 2000. "Welcome to Cyberia." In *The Cybercultures Reader*, edited by David Bell and Barbara M. Kennedy, 56–76. London: Routledge.

Ess, Charles. 2001. "Introduction: What's Culture Got to Do with It? Cultural Collisions in the Electronic Global Village, Creative Interferences, and the Rise of Culturally-Mediated Computing." In *Culture, Technology, Communication: Towards an Intercultural Global Village*, edited by Charles Ess, 1–50. Albany: State University of New York Press.

Ettlinger, Nancy, and Fernando Bosco. 2004. "Thinking Through Networks and Their Spatiality: A Critique of the US (Public) War on Terrorism and its Geographic Discourse." *Antipode* 36 (2): 249–71.

Fandy, Mamoun. 1999. "CyberResistance: Saudi Opposition Between Globalization and Localization." *Comparative Studies in Society and History* 41 (1): 124–47.

Farquhar, Judith, and Qicheng Zhang. 2005. "Biopolitical Beijing: Pleasure, Sovereignty, And Self-Cultivation in China's Capital." *Cultural Anthropology* 20 (3): 303–27.

Feldman, Allen. 1991. *Formations of Violence: The Narrative of the Body and Political Terror in Northern Island*. Chicago: University of Chicago Press.

Ferguson, James. 2006. *Global Shadows: Africa in the Neoliberal World Order*. Durham: Duke University Press.

Fessehatzion, Tekie. 2005. "Eritrea's Remittance-Based Economy: Conjectures and Musings." Special Issue—Eritrea Abroad: Critical Perspectives on the Global Diaspora, edited by Tricia Hepner and Bettina Conrad. *Eritrean Studies Review* 4 (2): 165–84.

Firebrace, James, and Stuart Holland. 1985. *Never Kneel Down*. New Jersey: Red Sea Press.

Foucault, Michel. 1984. "Right of Death and Power Over Life." In *The Foucault Reader*, edited by Paul Rabinow, 258–72. New York: Pantheon Books.

Fraser, Nancy. 1992. "Rethinking the Public Sphere: A Contribution to the Critique of Actually Existing Democracy." In *Habermas and the Public Sphere*, edited by Craig Calhoun, 109–42. Cambridge: MIT Press.

Gajjala, Radhika, and Venkataramana Gajjala, eds. 2008. *South Asian Technospaces*. New York: Peter Lang.

Gajjala, Radhika, and Yeon Ju Oh, eds. *cyberfeminism 2.0*. 2012. New York: Peter Lang.

Gal, Susan, and Gail Kligman. 2000. *The Politics of Gender After Socialism: A Comparative-Historical Essay*. Princeton: Princeton University Press.

Gershon, Ilana. 2010. *The Breakup 2.0: Disconnecting Over New Media*. Ithaca: Cornell University Press.

Giles, Wenona, and Jennifer Hyndman, eds. 2004. *Sites of Violence: Gender and Conflict Zones*. Berkeley: University of California Press.

Gilroy, Paul. 1993. *The Black Atlantic: Modernity and Double Consciousness*. Cambridge: Harvard University Press.

Ginsburg, Faye. 2008. "Rethinking the Digital Age." In *Media and Social Theory*, edited by D. Hesmondhalgh and J. Toynbee, 127–44. London: Routledge.

Glick-Schiller, Nina. 2005. "Transborder Citizenship: An Outcome of Legal Pluralism within Transnational Fields." In *Mobile People, Mobile Law*, edited by Franz von Benda-Beckman, Keebot von Benda-Beckman, and Anne Griffiths. London: Ashgate.

Greenhalgh, Susan, and Edwin Winckler. 2005. *Governing China's Population*. Palo Alto: Stanford University Press.

Habermas, Jurgen. 1992. "Further Reflections on the Public Sphere." In *Habermas and the Public Sphere*, edited by Craig Calhoun, 421–61. Cambridge: MIT Press.

Habte Selassie, Bereket. 1989. *Eritrea and the United Nations and Other Essays*. Trenton: Red Sea Press.

Hagos, Asgede. 2002. "Eritrea: Wiring Africa's Newest Nation." In *Beyond Boundaries: Cyberspace in Africa*, edited by Melinda Robins and Robert Hilliard, 59–76. Portsmouth: Heinemann.

Hale, Sondra. 2001 [2006]. "The State of the Women's Movement in Eritrea." *Northeast African Studies* 8 (3): 155–78.

Hall, Stuart. 1990. "Cultural Identity and Diaspora." In *Identity, Community, Culture, Difference*, edited by Jonathan Rutherford, 222–37. London: Lawrence and Wishart.

Hannerz, Ulf. 1996. *Transnational Connections: Culture, People, Places*. London: Routledge.

Hansen, Thomas Blom, and Finn Stepputat. 2005. "Introduction." In *Sovereign Bodies: Citizens, Migrants, and States in the Postcolonial World*, edited by Thomas Blom Hansen and Finn Stepputat, 1–38. Princeton: Princeton University Press.

Harcourt, Wendy, ed. 1999. *women@internet:creating new cultures in cyberspace*. London: Zed.

Harvey, David. 1989. *The Condition of Postmodernity: An Enquiry into the Origins of Culture Change*. Oxford: Blackwell.

Harvey, Penny, and Gaby Porter. 2000. "Infocities: From Information to Conversation." In *Digital Desires: Language, Identity and New Technologies*, edited by Cutting Edge, Women's Research Group, 103–24. London: I. B. Tauris.

Haugerud, Angelique. 1995. *The Culture of Politics in Kenya*. Cambridge: Cambridge University Press.

———. 2013. *No Billionaire Left Behind: Satirical Activism in America*. Stanford: Stanford University Press.

Hepner, Tricia. 2003. "Religion, Nationalism, and Transnational Civil Society in the Eritrean Diaspora." *Identities* 10: 269–93.

———. 2005. "Transnational Tegadelti: Eritreans for Liberation in North America and the EPLF." Special Issue—Eritrea Abroad: Critical Perspectives on the Global Diaspora, edited by Tricia Hepner and Bettina Conrad. *Eritrean Studies Review* 4 (2): 37–84.

———. 2009. *Soldiers, Martyrs, Traitors, and Exiles: Political Conflict in Eritrea and the Diaspora*. Philadelphia: University of Pennsylvania Press.

Hepner, Tricia Redeker, and Bettina Conrad. 2005. "Eritrea Abroad: An Introduction." *Eritrean Studies Review* 4 (2): v–xvii.

Hirschkind, Charles. 2012. "Beyond Secular and Religious: An Intellectual Genealogy of Tahrir Square." *American Ethnologist* (39) 1: 49–53.

Holston, James. 2008. *Insurgent Citizenship: Disjunctions of Democracy and Modernity in Brazil*. Princeton: Princeton University Press.

Horton, Sarah, and Judith Barker. 2009. "'Stains' on Their Self-Discipline: Public Health, Hygiene, and the Disciplining of Undocumented Immigrant Parents in the Nation's Internal Borderlands." *American Ethnologist* 36 (4): 784–98.

Human Rights Watch. 2009. *Service for Life: State Repression and Indefinite Conscription in Eritrea.* New York: Human Rights Watch.

———. 2011. *Ten Long Years: A Briefing on Eritrea's Missing Political Prisoners.* New York: Human Rights Watch.

Ignacio, Emily. 2005. *Building Diaspora: Filipino Community Formation on the Internet.* New Brunswick: Rutgers University Press.

Iyob, Ruth. 1995. *The Eritrean Struggle for Independence: Domination, Resistance, Nationalism, 1941–1993.* Cambridge: Cambridge University Press.

———. 2000. "The Ethiopian–Eritrean Conflict: Diasporic vs. Hegemonic States in the Horn of Africa, 1991–2000." *Journal of Modern African Studies* 38 (4): 659–82.

Itzigsohn, Jose. 2012. "A 'Transnational Nation'?: Migration and the Boundaries of Belonging." In *Politics from Afar: Transnational Diasporas and Networks*, edited by Terence Lyons and Peter Mandaville, 181–96. London: Hurst and Company.

Jacobs, Michelle. 2000. "Coming Full Circle: The African-American Struggle for Full Citizenship Under Color of Law." *Transforming Anthropology* 9 (1): 44–46.

Jacquin-Berdal, Dominique and Martin Plaut, eds. 2004. *Unfinished Business: Ethiopia and Eritrea at War.* Trenton, NJ: Red Sea Press.

Jelin, E., and S. Kaufman. 2002. "Layers of Memories, Twenty Years After in Argentina." In *Genocide, Collective Violence, and Popular Memory*, edited by D. Lorey and W. Beezley, 31–52. Wilmington: Scholarly Resources.

Jordan, Gebremedhin. 1989. *Peasants and Nationalism in Eritrea: A Critique of Ethiopian Studies.* Trenton: Red Sea Press.

Joseph, Suad, ed. 2000. *Gender and Citizenship in the Middle East.* Syracuse: Syracuse University Press.

Kadende-Kaiser, Rose M. 2000. "Interpreting Language and Cultural Discourse: Internet Communication among Burundians in the Diaspora." *Africa Today* 47 (2): 121–48.

Kapteijns, Lidwien, and Annemieck Richters, eds. 2010. *Mediations of Violence in Africa.* Leiden: Brill.

Keneally, Thomas. 1990. *To Asmara: A Novel of Africa.* New York: Grand Central Publishing.

Keniston, Kenneth. 2001. "Language, Power, and Software." In *Culture, Technology, Communication*, edited by Charles Ess, 283–306. Albany: State University of New York Press.

Khleif, W., and S. Slymovics. 2008. "Palestinian Remembrance Days and Plans: Kafr Qasum, Fact and Echo." In *Modernism and the Middle East: Architecture and Politics in the Twentieth Century*, edited by S. Isenstadt and K. Rizvi, 186–220. Seattle: University of Washington Press.

Kibreab, Gaim. 1985. *African Refugees: Reflections on the African Refugee Problem.* London: Africa World Press.

———. 1987. *Refugees and Development: The Case of Eritrean Refugees.* Trenton: Red Sea Press.

———. 1995. "Eritrean Refugee Women in Khartoum." *Journal of Refugee Studies* 8 (1): 1–25.

———. 2000. "Resistance, Displacement and Identity: The Case of Eritrean Refugees in Sudan." *Canadian Journal of African Studies* 34 (2): 249–96.

———. 2009a. *Eritrea: A Dream Deferred*. Rochester: James Currey.

———. 2009b. "Forced Labour in Eritrea." *Journal of Modern African Studies* 47 (1): 41–72.

Kifleyesus, Abebe. 2006. "Cosmologies in Collision: Pentecostal Conversion and Christian Cults in Asmara." *African Studies Review* 49 (1): 75–92.

Kligman, Gail. 1998. *The Politics of Duplicity: Controlling Reproduction in Ceausescu's Romania*. Berkeley: University of California Press.

Knott, Kim, and Sean McLoughlin, eds. 2010. *Diasporas: Concepts, Intersections, Identities*. London: Zed.

Koser, Khalid. 2003. "Mobilizing New African Diasporas: An Eritrean Case Study." In *New African Diasporas*, edited by Khalid Koser, 111–23. London: Routledge.

Laguerre, Michel S. 2006. *Diaspora, Politics, and Globalization*. New York: Palgrave MacMillan.

Landzelius, Kyra. 2006a. "Introduction." In *Native on the Net: Indigenous and Diasporic Peoples in the Virtual Age*, edited by Kyra Landzelius, 1–42. London: Routledge.

———. 2006b. "Postscript: *Vox Populi* from the Margins?" In *Native on the Net: Indigenous and Diasporic Peoples in the Virtual Age*, edited by Kyra Landzelius, 202–304. London: Routledge.

Lax, Stephen. 2000. "The Internet and Democracy." In *Web.Studies: Rewiring Media Studies for the Digital Age*, edited by David Gauntlett, 159–69. New York: Oxford University Press.

Low, Setha. 2000. *On the Plaza: The Politics of Public Space and Culture*. Austin: University of Texas Press.

Lyons, Terrence. 1996. "The International Context of Internal War: Ethiopia/Eritrea." In *Africa in the New International Order: Rethinking State Sovereignty and Regional Security*, edited by Edmond Keller and Donald Rothchild, 85–99. Boulder: Lynne Rienner.

———. 2012. "Transnational Politics in Ethiopia: Diaspora Mobilization and Contentious Politics." In *Politics from Afar: Transnational Diasporas and Networks*, edited by Terrence Lyons and Peter Mandaville, 141–56. London: C. Hurst and Company.

Lyons, Terrence, and Peter Mandaville, eds. 2012. *Politics from Afar: Transnational Diasporas and Networks*. London: C. Hurst and Company.

Malkki, Liisa. 1995. *Purity and Exile: Violence, Memory and National Cosmology among Hutu Refugees in Tanzania*. Chicago: University of Chicago Press.

Mallapragada, Madhavi. 2000. "The Indian Diaspora in the USA and Around the Web." In *Rewiring Media Studies for the Digital Age*, edited by David Gauntlett, 179–85. New York: Oxford University Press.

Mani, Lata. 1998. *The Debate on Sati in Colonial India*. Berkeley: University of California Press.

Mannur, Anita. 2003 "Postscript: Cyberscapes and the Interfacing of Diasporas." In *Theorizing Diaspora*, edited by Jana Evans Braziel and Anita Mannur, 283–90. Malden: Blackwell Publishing.

Marcus, George E. 1995. "Ethnography in/of the World System: The Emergence of Multi-Sited Ethnography." *Annual Review of Anthropology* 24: 95–117.

Matsuoka, Atsuko, and John Sorenson. 2001. *Ghosts and Shadows: Construction of Identity and Community in an African Diaspora*. Toronto: University of Toronto Press.

———. 2005. "Ideas of North: The Eritrean Diaspora in Canada." *Eritrean Studies Review* 4 (2): 85–114.

Mbembe, Achille. 2002. "African Modes of Self-Writing." *Public Culture* 14 (1): 239–73.

———. 2003. "Necropolitics." *Public Culture* 15 (1): 11–40.

———. 2005. "Sovereignty as a Form of Expenditure." In *Sovereign Bodies: Citizens, Migrants, and States in the Postcolonial World*, edited by Thomas Blom Hansen and Finn Stepputat, 148–66. Princeton: Princeton University Press

McCoy, Daniel Stewart. 1995. *Nationalism and Cultural Hegemony in the Public Sphere: The Cultural Paternalism of the Eritrean People's Liberation Front in Africa's Newest Nation*. MA thesis, University of California–Los Angeles.

McLagan, Meg. 2003. "Principles, Publicity, and Politics: Notes on Human Rights Media." *American Anthropologist* 105 (3): 605–12.

McSpadden, Lucia Ann, and Helene Moussa. 1993. "I Have a Name: The Gender Dynamics in Asylum and Resettlement of Ethiopian and Eritrean Refugees in North America." *Journal of Refugee Studies* 6(3):203–25.

Miller, Daniel, and Dan Slater. 2000. *The Internet: An Ethnographic Approach*. Oxford: Berg.

Moran, Erin Joy. 2012. *Geographies of Belonging: Mapping Migrant Imaginaries in Ireland's Ailing Celtic Tiger*. PhD thesis, University of California–Irvine.

Moran, Mary. 2006. *Liberia: The Violence of Democracy*. Philadelphia: University of Pennsylvania Press.

Moussa, Helene. 1995. *Storm and Sanctuary: The Journey of Ethiopian and Eritrean Women Refugees*. Dundas, Ontario: Artemis.

Müller, Tanja. 2006. "State-making in the Horn of Africa: notes on Eritrea and Prospects for the End of Violent Conflict in the Horn." *Conflict, Security & Development* 6 (4): 503–30.

———. 2008. "Bare Life and the Developmental State: Implications of the Militarisation of Higher Education in Eritrea." *Journal of Modern African Studies* 46 (1): 111–31.

Ndangam, Lilian. 2008. "Free Lunch? Cameroon's Diaspora and Online News Publishing" *New Media and Society* 10 (4): 585–604.

Negash, Tekeste and Kjetil Tronvoll. 2000. *Brothers at War: Making Sense of the Eritrean-Ethiopian War*. Oxford: James Currey; Athens: Ohio University Press.

Negroponte, Nicholas. 1995. *Being Digital*. New York: Alfred A. Knopf.

Norris, Pippa. 2001. *Digital Divide: Civic Engagement, Information Poverty, and the Internet Worldwide*. Cambridge: Cambridge University Press.

Oiarzbal, Pedro, and Alonso Adoni, eds. 2010. *Diasporas in the New Media Age: Identity Politics, and Community*. Reno University of Nevada Press.

Ong, Aihwa. 1999. *Flexible Citizenship: The Cultural Logics of Transnationality*. Durham: Duke University Press.

———. 2006. *Neoliberalism as Exception: Mutations in Citizenship and Sovereignty*. Durham: Duke University Press.

Page, Ben, and Claire Mercer. 2012. "Why Do People Do Stuff? Reconceptualizing Remittance Behavior in Diaspora-Development Research and Policy." *Progress in Development Studies* 12 (1): 1–18.

Paley, Julia. 2004. "Accountable Democracy: Citizens' Impact on Public Decision Making in Postdictatorship Chile." *American Ethnologist* 31 (4): 497–513.

Panagakos, Anastasia, and Heather A. Horst. 2006. "Return to Cyberia: Technology and The Social Worlds of Transnational Migrants." *Global Networks: A Journal of Transnational Affairs* 6 (2): 109–24.

Pandolfi, Maria. 2006. Introductory remarks. Panel on "Radical Biopolitics and Iatrogenic Violence." Annual Meeting of the American Anthropological Association, San Jose, November 15–19.

Pateman, Carole. 1988. *The Sexual Contract*. Cambridge: Polity Press.

Pateman, Roy. 1998. *Eritrea: Even the Stones are Burning*. Trenton: Red Sea Press.

Parham, Heather. 2004. "Diaspora, Community and Communication: Internet Use in Transnational Haiti." *Global Networks* 4 (2): 199–217.

Petryna, Adriana. 2002. *Life Exposed: Biological Citizenship After Chernobyl*. Princeton: Princeton University Press.

Piot, Charles. 2010. *Nostalgia for the Future*. Chicago: University of Chicago Press.

Poole, Amanda. 2009. "The Youth Has Gone from Our Soil: Place and Politics in Refugee Resettlement and Agrarian Development." *Biopolitics, Militarism, Development: Eritrea in the 21st Century*, edited by David O'Kane and Tricia Redeker Hepner, 34–52. New York and Oxford: Berghahn Books

Poole, David. 2001. *From Guerrillas to Government: The Eritrean Peoples Liberation Front*. Oxford: James Currey.

Portes, Alejandro, Luis E. Guarnizo, and Patricia Landolt. 1999. "The Study of Transnationalism: Pitfalls and Promise of an Emergent Research Field." *Ethnic And Racial Studies* 22 (2): 217–37.

Riggan, Jennifer. 2009. "Avoiding Wastage by Making Soldiers: Technologies of the State and the Imagination of the Educated Nation. In *Biopolitics, Militarism and Development: Eritrean in the Twenty-First Century*, edited by David O'Kane and Tricia R. Hepner, 72–91. New York: Berghahn Books

Robins, Kevin. 2000. "Cyberspace and the World We Live In." In *The Cybercultures Reader*, edited by David Bell and Barbara M. Kennedy, 77–95. London: Routledge.

Rude, John. 1996. "The Birth of a Nation in Cyberspace." *Humanist* 56 (2): 17–22.

Ryang, Sonia, and John Lie, eds. 2009. *Diaspora without Homeland: Being Korean in Japan*. Berkeley: University of California Press.

Sassen, Saskia. 2005. "Electronic Markets and Activist Networks: The Weight of Social Logics." In *Digital Formations: IT and New Architectures in the Global Realm*, edited by Robert Latham and Saskia Sassen, 54–88. Princeton: Princeton University Press.

Sawyer, Suzanna. 2001. "Fictions of Sovereignty: Prosthetic Petro-Capitalism, Neoliberal States and Phantom-Like Citizens in Ecuador." *Journal of Latin American Anthropology* 6 (1): 156–97.

Scott, James. 1992. *Domination and the Arts of Resistance: Hidden Transcripts*. New Haven: Yale University Press.

Senft, Theresa. 2008. *Camgirls: Celebrity and Community in the Age of Social Networks*. New York: Peter Lang.

Shaw, Rosalind. 2007. "Displacing Violence: Making Pentecostal Memory in Postwar Sierra Leone." *Cultural Anthropology* 22 (1):65–92.

Sieder, Rachel. 2001. "Rethinking Citizenship: Reforming Law in Postwar Guatemala." In *States of Imagination: Ethnographic Explorations of the Postcolonial State*, edited by Thomas Blom Hansen and Finn Stepputat, 203–20. Durham: Duke University Press.

Silver, David, and Adrienne Massanari, eds. 2006. *Critical Cyberculture Studies*. New York: New York University Press.

Tesfagiorgis, Abeba. 1992. *A Painful Season and a Stubborn Hope: The Odyssey of an Eritrean Mother*. Trenton: Red Sea Press.

Tezare, Kisanet, Tshehay Said, Daniel Baheta, Helen Tewolde, and Amanuel Melles 2006. *The Role of the Eritrean Diaspora in Peacebuilding and Development: Challenges and Opportunities*. Toronto: Selam Peacebuilding Network.

Theidon, Kimberly. 2013. *Intimate Enemies: Violence and Reconciliation in Peru*. Philadelphia: University of Pennsylvania Press.

Tronvoll, Kjetil. 1999. "Borders of Violence—Boundaries of Identity: Demarcating the Eritrean Nation-State." *Ethnic and Racial Studies* 22 (6): 1037–60.

———. 2009. "The Lasting Struggle for Freedom in Eritrea: Human Rights and Political Development, 1991–2009." Oslo: Oslo Center of Peace and Human Rights.

Turner, Simon. 2008a. "Studying the Tensions of Transnational Engagement: From the Nuclear Family to the World-Wide Web." *Journal of Ethnic and Migration Studies* 34 (7): 1049–56.

———. 2008b. "Cyberwars of Words: Expressing the Unspeakable in Burundi's Diaspora." *Journal of Ethnic and Migration Studies* 34 (7): 1161–80.

United Nations. 1994. *Report on Eritrea*.

———. 2006. "Summary of the High-level Dialogue on International Migration and Development." UN General Assembly. Cited in Page and Mercer, but their cited URL did not work.

UNICEF. 1994. *Children and Women in Eritrea*.

Varisco, Daniel Martin. 2002. "September 11: Participant Webservation of the 'War on Terrorism.'" *American Anthropologist* 104 (3): 934–38.

Varzi, Roxanne. 2006. *Warring Souls: Youth, Media, and Martyrdom in Post-Revolution Iran*. Durham: Duke University Press.

Voice of America. 1998. Carol Pineau reporting from Asmara, June 24. http://www.voa.gov. Accessed July 24, 1998.

Wallechinsky, David. 2009. "The World's 10 Worst Dictators." *Los Angeles Times*. March 22. *Parade*, 4–8.

Warner, Michael. 2005. *Publics and Counterpublics*. Zone Books: New York.

Weber, Annette. 2011. "Women Without Arms: Gendered Fighter Constructions in Eritrea and Southern Sudan." *International Journal of Conflict and Violence* 5 (2): 357–70.

Werbner, Pnina. 1998. "Diasporic Political Imaginaries: A Sphere of Freedom or a Sphere of Illusion?" *Communal/Plural* 6 (1): 11–31.

———. 2002. *Imagined Diasporas Among Manchester Muslims*. Oxford: James Currey.

———. 2004. "Theorising Complex Diasporas: Purity and Hybridity in the South Asian Public Sphere in Britain." *Journal of Ethnic and Migration Studies* 30 (5): 895–911.

———. 2005. "The Place Which is Diaspora: Citizenship, Religion, and Gender in the Making of Chaordic Transnationalism." In *Homelands and Diasporas: Holy Lands and Other Places*, edited by Andre Levi and Alex Weingrod, 29–48. Stanford: Stanford University Press.

West, Harry G., and Todd Sanders. 2003. "Power Revealed and Concealed in the New World Order." In *Transparency and Conspiracy: Ethnographies of Suspicion in the New World Order*, edited by Harry G. West and Todd Sanders, 1–37. Durham: Duke University Press.

Wheeler, Deborah. 2001. "New Technologies, Old Culture: A Look at Women, Gender, and the Internet in Kuwait." In *Culture, Technology, Communication: Towards an Intercultural Global Village*, edited by Charles Ess, 187–212. Albany: State University of New York Press.

White, Geoffrey. 1997. "Museum/Memorial/Shrine: National Narrative in National Spaces." *Museum Anthropology* 21 (1): 8–27.

Whitaker, Mark P. 2004. "Tamilnet.com: Some Reflections on Popular Anthropology, Nationalism, and the Internet." *Anthropological Quarterly* 77 (3): 469–98.

———. 2007. *Learning Politics From Sivaram: The Life and Death of a Revolutionary Tamil Journalist in Sri Lanka*. London: Pluto Press.

Wilbur, Shawn P. 2000. "An Archaeology of Cyberspaces: Virtuality, Community, Identity." In *The Cybercultures Reader*, edited by David Bell and Barbara M. Kennedy, 45–55. London: Routledge.

Wilson, Amrit. 1991. *The Challenge Road: Women and the Eritrean Revolution*. Trenton: Red Sea Press.

Wilson, Samuel M., and Leighton C. Peterson. 2002. "The Anthropology of Online Communities." *Annual Review of Anthropology* 31: 449–67.

Winegar, Jessica. 2012. "The Privilege of Revolution: Gender, Class, Space, and Affect In Egypt." *American Ethnologist* 39 (1): 67–70.

Woldemikael, Tekle. 1991. "Political Mobilization and Nationalist Movements: the Case of the Eritrean People's Liberation Front." Special Issue—Eritrea: An Emerging New Nation in Africa's Troubled Horn? *Africa Today* 38 (2): 31–42.

———. 1993. "The Cultural Construction of Eritrean Nationalist Movements." In *The Rising Tide of Cultural Pluralism: The Nation-State at* Bay, edited by Crawford Young. Madison: University of Wisconsin Press.

———. 1996. "Ethiopians and Eritreans." *Case Studies in Diversity: Refugees in America in the 1990s*, edited by David Haines, 265–87. Westport: Praeger.

———. 1998. "Eritrean and Ethiopian Refugees in the United States." *Eritrean Studies Review* 2 (2): 89–109.

———. 2005. "Bridging the Divide: Muslim and Christian Eritreans in Orange County, California." *Eritrean Studies Review* 4 (2): 143–64.

———. 2008. "The Invention of New National Traditions in Eritrea." In *Traditions of Eritrea: Linking the Past to the* Future, edited by Tesfa G. Gebremedhin and Gebre H. Tesfagiourgis, 263–86. Trenton: Red Sea Press.

World Bank. 2006. "Migration, Remittances and Economic Development: The World Bank Program." International Symposium on International Migration and Development, Turin, June 28–30. http://www.un.org/esa/population/migration/turin/Turin_statements/WORLDBANK.pdf. Accessed May 20, 2011.

———. 2012. *Migration and Remittance Factbook 2012.* www.data.worldbank.org. Accessed March 27, 2013.

Youngs, Gillian. 2006. "Gender and Technology: The Internet in Context." In *Ideologies of the Internet*, edited by Katherine Sarikakis and Daya K. Thussu, 47–62. Cresskill: Hampton Press.

YouTube. 2009. "Vi släpper inte Isaak." Posted by TV4Play, May 25. http://www.tv4play.se/program/nyhetsmorgon?]video id=765021; accessed August 20, 2012.

Yuval-Davis, Nira. 1997. *Gender and Nation.* Los Angeles: Sage.

# INDEX